DUNCAN PHILLIPS
AND HIS
COLLECTION

DUNCAN PHILLIPS
AND HIS
COLLECTION

by Marjorie Phillips

with a foreword by
Laughlin Phillips

Revised Edition

———

W. W. NORTON & COMPANY · NEW YORK AND LONDON
in association with
THE PHILLIPS COLLECTION · WASHINGTON, D.C.

Dedicated
to the memory of
DUNCAN PHILLIPS

FOREWORD

DUNCAN PHILLIPS made an indelible impression on hundreds of people. It was the rare impression of a totally free spirit — an independent man whose great talents and enthusiasms had been developed outside the confines of any establishment. He loved good conversation and could quickly establish rapport with an astonishing variety of people.

But I also remember him as a very private man, whose qualities of reserve and dignity discouraged easy characterization and familiarity. He did not keep diaries, write informal memoirs, or grant personal interviews to the press.

Under these circumstances I think it most fortunate that my mother undertook to write this book. She alone, as Walter Lippmann suggested to her, really knew my father intimately enough to capture the essence of his life and work. She was, in fact, his partner in both.

He was the extraordinarily articulate amateur of art who believed that an artist's unique vision can and should enrich our lives. She was the practicing artist who gave form to this ideal. Their tastes and sensitivities and judgments about art were developed together, and embodied in the Phillips Collection.

My father was a strong man, almost indifferent to publicity, sure in his convictions, and confident of his estimates about art or politics. But it was not a settled or doctrinaire sort of confidence. All who knew him, whether for a lifetime or a few minutes, were astonished by his capacity for joy — the joy of discovering beauty or talent, and the joy of making others feel it, too. This passion to share his private delights had an inspirational and even spiritual impact on us all.

I hope that this book, published on the Phillips Collection's fiftieth anniversary, will give my father's radiant message a wider scope. In this age of uncertainty we badly need the tonic of a free spirit proclaiming the enchantment of art and its importance to life itself.

LAUGHLIN PHILLIPS

FOREWORD TO THE SECOND EDITION

I AM very pleased that *Duncan Phillips and His Collection* is being published in a second edition and that its appearance coincides with the sixtieth anniversary of the Phillips Collection. I want to take this opportunity to thank my son Laughlin, who has been Director of the Collection since 1972, for editing the original manuscript and Theresa Muller for her patience and understanding in preparing the typescript. My thanks, also, to Jan Lancaster and Karen Schneider, who have diligently checked copy for this new edition.

MARJORIE PHILLIPS

Washington, D. C.
December 1981

CONTENTS

ILLUSTRATIONS

Color transparencies prepared by Henry Beville

IN COLOR

IN BLACK AND WHITE

DUNCAN PHILLIPS
AND HIS
COLLECTION

Jean Baptiste Siméon Chardin (1699–1779). *Bowl of Plums*, 17¾ x 22½

1

OUR FIRST MEETING

DUNCAN PHILLIPS and I met in the most delightful way. In January 1921 he loaned a large part of his collection which he had been forming for the last dozen years to be shown in the handsome picture gallery of the Century, his club in New York. I had heard how fine the collection was and that it would soon be open to the public in Washington, D.C., where he lived. My uncle Gifford Beal, who was also a member of the Century Club, gave me a card to the exhibition.

I shared the enthusiasm for exhibition-going with other members of my family: two of my mother's brothers, Gifford and Reynolds Beal were artists. And as a student at the Art Students League I commuted each day to New York from our home at Ossining on the Hudson. Much earlier I had seen the history-making Armory show and enjoyed its vivid contrasts. And I sometimes visited the Société Anonyme, one of the early modernist collections in its first modest headquarters.

To fill in time between classes and trains I went frequently for instruction and pleasure to the Metropolitan Museum and the art galleries which were strung along Fifth Avenue in those days. Among the dealers were Macbeth, Kraushaar, Montrose, Daniel, De Zayas, Scott and Fowles. Their exhibitions, which changed each month, were, to me, like an opera season.

For several years my older sister Eleanor and I had taken turns going to the Art Students League; we alternated so that one would always be home for company and to help my mother with the younger children. My father, Charles Ernest Acker, had been very much against my studying art, because he had known some Bohemian types he did not like in Chicago, but my mother stood up stalwartly for me, and it has meant the world to me since. He was a brilliant electrochemical engineer, who contributed many original pathfinding inventions, one being a process for making caustic soda from molten salt by electrolysis. Dr. Vannevar Bush has told me that Father made important, original contributions to science at that period. He took great interest in literature, especially poetry, and he enjoyed paintings too, so he soon became reconciled to my work as an artist. Sad to say, he died at only fifty-two years of age — over a year before my marriage.

As I look back on my sporadic study at the Art Students League, I feel that the teacher from whom I gained most was Boardman Robinson, who did stunning cartoons. In his life class he talked more of essential qualities of design than my other teachers had. Kenneth Hayes Miller used to leave me pretty much to myself in his composition class, saying that I had a natural sense of composition.

I had heard much about the Phillips Memorial Gallery Exhibition and was eager to see it. The pictures at the Century charmed me from the first moment — the distinction of the choices of Twachtman, Weir, Ryder, Davies, Daumier and Chardin! I remember standing beside a rather plump member looking at an Arthur B. Davies and on his asking some question about it the collector himself appeared, doing the honors — a man with a gracious, strong, and magnetic personality. He was tall, slight, and seemed unusually interesting and sympathetic — eyes clear and blue-gray, full of spirit and high intelligence. I soon found he had a very fine "eye" for painting, that he was as enthralled with it as I; and in addition could *express* his feelings in an original and vivid way with great sincerity and emphasis. I loved the expression he used — looking at the Davies "Springtime of Delight" and the "Along the Erie Canal": "beauty touched with strangeness."

Then there were the distinguished little Ryders. One was a tiny "Macbeth and the Witches." We agreed that everything Ryder painted conveyed an extra dimension of universality and mystery, with a marvelously simplified design. Duncan admired these designs beyond words. He was lyrical about Twachtman and already had the magical "Summer" and "Winter" landscapes. He felt that there were few if any landscape painters more sensitive and subtle, and at the same time structural, than Twachtman, and that in his "translucent snow scenes he achieved something as precious as Whistler's Nocturnes." Later he delighted in what A.E., the Irish poet-painter, said of the "Summer" — "deliciously light-bewildered."

There were also the Monet, "The Road to Vétheuil," Sisley's

Arthur B. Davies (1862–1928). *Springtime of Delight*, 18 x 40

"Showers at Moret," and Whistler's "Lillian Woakes." You could see that their lyrical poetry had tremendous significance for Duncan Phillips. Monticelli's "As You Like It" had the same quality, and "The Queen's Entry," by Matthijs Maris, had both lyricism and mystery.

The first Daumier oil that he bought was there, "The Three Lawyers" — three black-gowned figures slightly arrogant in their stance and gestures. He was delighted to have it; but felt that the later, more roughly painted Daumiers were the greatest. Chardin's "Bowl of Plums" was his particular pride and delight. He spoke of its marvelous paint quality and superb design. There were two by Weir, "A Fishing Party" and "Pan and the Wolf"; Jerome Myers' "Night, Bryant Park" and "The Little Mother"; Lawson's "Summer Night" and "Autumn Hills"; one by Childe Hassam, "The Willow Pool"; George Luks' "The Dominican"; and Fantin-Latour's "The Muses" and "Dawn." It is hard to remember all of them, but what a fascinating and distinguished collection it was. We wholeheartedly agreed that we loved matte painting (not shiny). I don't know why that sticks in my mind.

In fact, we responded to paintings in so much the same way it startled us. Looking back I believe what moved me most was the great importance we both attached to art in life. Duncan Phillips expressed this vigorously and colorfully; I was delighted by his contagious enthusiasm for the exciting paintings he had already collected. To be so articulate in expressing a keen and independent understanding was rare.

Ernest Lawson (1873–1939). *Spring Night, Harlem River*, 25⅛ x 30⅛.

At home that afternoon my mother asked, "What *is* the matter with you, Marjorie? Just sitting there in a daze instead of bestirring yourself" (as I suppose I usually did). And the next day when Duncan lunched at the club he evidently took Gifford Beal to task, much to Uncle Giff's surprise, for having neglected to introduce him to his "charming niece."

Later we did meet at my uncle's studio, after Duncan asked where he could see some of my paintings and I told him I had left some canvases there recently. Sometimes in New York that winter I would take my paintings to my uncle Gifford Beal to see or comment on at his studio apartment on 59th Street. He and his wife were always wonderfully hospitable to their nieces and nephews. During the season of 1920 I remember he said of one of my canvases — "The Hudson at Ossin-

Honoré Daumier (1808–1879). *The Three Lawyers*, 16 x 30

Claude Monet (1840–1926). *The Road to Vétheuil*, 23 x 28½

ing" — "Weir would have loved that." His friend Alden Weir had died
the previous year. As it turned out, the very canvas of mine which
Uncle Giff had said Weir would have loved, appealed especially to
Duncan and he immediately bought it; which, of course, was *thrilling*
to me. Over the years I was to see him buy the work of innumerable
young painters and I knew what it meant to their morale — that someone saw qualities to enjoy in their work and cared enough to purchase it.

Then one Sunday Duncan drove from New York to my home at Ossining. I remember my eleven-year-old brother rushing upstairs to tell me:
"There is a Mr. Phillips to call on you . . . he has fierce moustachios!"
said my brother, exaggerating. They were becoming, not fierce.

Duncan also invited me several times to the theater in New York,
where we usually dined at the old Gotham and often talked of his plans

John Henry Twachtman (1853–1902). *Winter*, 21½ x 26

for the memorial gallery. He was then forming a committee on scope and plan which he thought would meet occasionally in New York to exchange ideas on how the gallery might be developed. In a pamphlet listing the names of the committee I find myself, Miss Marjorie Acker, at the head (because of the initial A!). The committee, composed of his special friends interested in art, did meet once or twice but Duncan soon found that collecting was such a personal matter that he was better on his own.

On May 14, 1921, Duncan wrote me, "I want you and the Gifford Beals to see the collection installed" (in the first two galleries of the family home in Washington), and we went for what proved to be a most friendly visit. Mrs. Phillips welcomed me warmly and I liked her at once. She was a very small woman in her mid-seventies, whose health had been worn down by anxiety and grief. But her eyes were bright and she could be very witty, even mischievously so. Perhaps Duncan got some of his sense of humor from her. We did some sightseeing, took drives, and went for walks in beautiful Rock Creek Park (where we were to walk so often in later years). One thing stands out especially in my memory — waking up in the morning to the pleasure of seeing the Arthur B. Davies painting "Children, Dogs and Pony" hanging by my bed, and the many other paintings in the room. Following that, going downstairs in the morning to a sunny cheerful house, doors and windows flung open and Alden Weir's "Woodland Rocks" hanging in the library, paintings everywhere! A gray-haired, fat, smiling colored butler Thomas Pryde, who had been with the family for forty years, was part of the welcoming atmosphere. It seemed that here on 21st Street near Dupont Circle there was a leisurely, almost southern village atmosphere, with hurdy-gurdies playing and men pushing their carts of fresh flowers or fruits, crying "Stra-a-berries" in loud melodious voices. The hurdy-gurdies and the monkeys to pick up the pennies were frequent visitors during the day.

The next thing we did together was to go up the Hudson to Newburgh, to visit my grandmother, Mrs. William R. Beal, who had a wonderful forty-acre place, just above Newburgh, where my sisters and brothers and I had spent many happy vacations. The house was on a hilltop which commanded a glorious view of the mountains and river, and you could see all the way to West Point. A great studio occupied most of the attic.

The kindly grandmother, my uncles and my aunt always had made a great impression on me and Duncan greatly enjoyed them too. Aunt Mary had a marvelous flower garden designed for her like a wheel, its spokes the paths, bordered with flowers; there was a sundial in the center, great elms and apple trees, and stone benches, a lily pool and bust of Homer, a pergola, all placed strategically around the edges. It seemed the most poetic place in the world. During that visit we became engaged.

I did not actually study with either of my artist uncles but undoubtedly absorbed a good deal through a sort of osmosis, and hearing them talk. Uncle Reynolds — we always called him Ren — the oldest, had studied first with Ranger, of the brown foliage school of landscape; and then both he and his brother Gifford worked with William Merritt Chase, a very fine teacher, who helped them freshen their palettes.

Duncan Phillips, summer 1921

Gifford was the more accomplished; two of his paintings are in the Metropolitan Museum, one in the Art Institute of Chicago and others hang in numerous museums. He was in great demand as a juror for exhibitions and for many years he was president of the Art Students League. Lloyd Goodrich, formerly director of the Whitney Museum, remarked of him once to me, "He was the most beloved artist of his period in the American art world."

In a letter written at the time of our engagement Gifford Beal ex-

John Henry Twachtman (1853–1902). *Summer*, 30 x 53

pressed rather poignantly the help which Duncan gave the artists he believed in:

July 17, 1921
Wilellyn
Newburgh, N.Y.

Dear Duncan,

I am terribly sorry that letters bearing the joyful news arrived late in Provincetown. I don't know what you must have thought. But that's all over now and so to the point. Maude and I were most excited and overjoyed at the news and my first thought was to see you both, so I put forward my trip to N.Y. hoping to catch you and was much disappointed at missing you.

Now that you are going to be a nephew I can tell you what I think of you without reservation.

You have done me more good at crucial moments in my art life than anyone I have met. Your remark at the ball game last year about exhibition pictures caused me to think about my future and

Adolphe Monticelli (1824–1886). *As You Like It*, 17 x 29

Albert Pinkham Ryder (1847–1917). *Gay Head*, 8 x 12½

come to very definite ideas as to what I wanted to do — then again it buoyed me up to realize that you were interested in my progress, because most picture collectors I have met have not been very remarkable individuals. I say it buoyed me up at a time when I was rather discouraged because I knew that you were the type of individual that I wanted to care for my work, one of keen intelligence and sensibilities; with a deep emotional side. As a picture lover you seem quite ideal. This relates not only to my own experience but to the experience of others and I can assure you that you are most beloved not only by me but by the true artists in the profession.

I must say that you have chosen a remarkably fine girl. I have known no finer character in my experience. She combines the charm of her mother with the iron-like determination of her father, whose ideals seemed almost too high. She has a remarkable talent which I know you will foster in the future. The roots of art reach very deep into her nature. I have always thought that if she married a man of ordinary vision with no art appreciation she would gradually fade away. She would stick to her duty but in so doing would dry up and starve artistically. So you can see how pleased I am at the prospect of having you for a nephew.

The combination is quite ideal and I know great happiness will result.

If I have left anything unsaid it is due to my feeble powers of expressing what I feel.

With kindest regards to your mother,

Sincerely,
Giff

Arthur B. Davies (1862–1928). *Along the Erie Canal*, 18 x 40

Duncan
in Rock Creek Park

On October 8, 1921 we were married at Ossining, New York, in my dear old home, perched high on a bluff — a large yellow, simply designed, Victorian house with a tower. There were just close friends and family, with Gus Downing, Duncan's boyhood friend, as best man and my sister Eleanor as matron of honor. On our wedding trip we went to Asheville, North Carolina, where we took marvelous drives and walks and played golf in that beautiful high mountain country. I painted from the balcony of our hotel apartment, the subject a rather romantic balustraded terrace with little figures and a peacock, the latter very popular in those days. Duncan sat and watched with delight (so he told a friend) and I know that in his mind he was planning for the collection, and how the paintings would be alternately exhibited in those first two rooms and skylight gallery, which on our return to Washington were to be opened to the public in the family home — 1600–1608 21st Street. The following year a handsome door was com-

15

pleted for 1608 so that the large library could be used as a third picture gallery then open to the public several days a week and shortly afterwards every day.

Before going to Asheville we had spent a week in New York, and had fun purchasing furniture of our own for the third floor of his parents' old house in Washington that would be our special apartment. We bought some silvery green Herter Loom furniture; and the room we used it in was hung with Prendergast paintings. There was a little orange-red tea table and flowered chintz curtains with turquoise blue, almost peacock, silk borders. We always enjoyed that room.

We returned to Washington to work, and the accelerating preparation for the gallery; also to some friendly social times. One dinner party that we gave that fall stands out especially in my mind. It was so large that we had to seat it in the north library (the gallery where the concerts are given now). The honored guests were Chief Justice and Mrs. William Howard Taft, and I remember vividly his large, benign figure seated on the right of tiny little Mother Phillips. The room was beautiful and romantic with its oak paneling, tall columns at one end, and the very long table. There must have been at least forty guests.

Meanwhile Duncan had much to supervise: the hanging of the rooms comprising the memorial gallery, which was opened to the public for the first time that fall of 1921; a separate entrance for it built further north on 21st Street; a new storeroom completed; a final selection of the pictures to be shown in the first hanging; a catalogue of all the works of art in the buildings; the mailing of announcements to museums, collectors and numerous interested people announcing the days of the week when the gallery would be open. There was no grand reception, but many art lovers came; and from then on the collection's fame was to grow steadily.

Mother Phillips was pleased that at her pleading we decided to live with her at 1600 21st Street rather than in a nearby house. She had told Duncan she would "just fade away" if we couldn't all live together, and had then taken to her bed, albeit with a mischievous light in her eyes.

We usually had lunch and dinner together, and until she was bedridden in the late twenties Mother Phillips spent the early part of the evenings with us. We took frequent walks with Larry the airedale — often in Rock Creek Park on the beautiful slopes which Duncan called his "Forest of Arden." I painted several canvases, inspired by the park,

James A. McNeill Whistler (1834–1903). *Miss Lillian Woakes*, 21 x 14

Reynolds Beal (1867–1951). *In the Rips off Montauk*, etching, 9 x 12¾

Gifford R. Beal (1879–1956). *Circus Ponies*, 20 x 36

Gifford R. Beal (1879–1956). *Hauling the Net*, 16 x 32

either on the spot or from notes. At other times I used a studio with a
north light on the fourth floor of the old house. Mother Phillips liked
to say that "Marjorie is sketching"; it seemed to her a more ladylike
way to put it.

For a month in the early winter following our marriage, Duncan's
cousin, Leila (Laughlin) Carlisle, loaned us a lovely apartment on
Park Avenue in New York City. Leila, although ten years older, had
always been close to Duncan and had a true appreciation for him all
her life. It was a happy interlude; we visited the galleries and saw old
friends. Each morning while Duncan worked on essays for two books
he had in mind, I painted city scenes from our great height — distant
rooftops and the colorful cineraria and cyclamen plants in the windows.

Among the artists whose studios we visited were Maurice Prendergast, the painter, and his brother Charles, who worked in wood and
gesso. Charles made all of Maurice's beautiful carved frames. He also
carved and painted archaic figures, chests and enchanting screens, one
of which we acquired. When Gifford Beal saw it in our home he exclaimed impetuously, "That's the most beautiful thing in American
art!"

Maurice, who was stone deaf when we knew him, lunched with us
one day at the apartment. He was then about sixty-one (he died two
years later) and shaggy haired, with a kindly face and keen eyes. We
communicated by passing around slips of paper with our written
thoughts or observations. His were largely about his utter pleasure in

Maurice Prendergast (1859–1924). *Autumn Festival*, 21½ x 32⅛

the flowers of our centerpiece, from which he could not take his eyes.

However, when we were at the Prendergasts' studio, his brother Charles shouted loud enough so that somehow Maurice could understand; and they were great pals. As they got older, they were so absorbed in their work that they hardly took care to eat enough — mostly shredded wheat and coffee, we heard. One small room was filled to the ceiling with empty shredded wheat boxes! I believe Miss Lillie Bliss, the great collector, finally succeeded in sending Maurice to a sanitarium to build him up.

When younger, Maurice went for a while to Paris and some of the art experimentation that was in the air rubbed off on him. On his return he developed a very personal style — an all over pattern, mostly of figures in landscape, with fine color, form and paint quality. Over the years the Phillips Collection has acquired eight or nine of his works. Duncan wrote this appreciation of him in *A Collection in the Making:*

A delightful decorator, one of the most sincere and original artists of our time. . . . Prendergast was a purist in regard to the decorative function

Maurice Prendergast (1859–1924). *Ponte della Paglia*, 28 x 23

Duncan and Marjorie Phillips, at home in Washington, 1922

of painting and persisted in reducing his well trained observation of nature to a simple yet thoroughly organized pictorial pattern which required from the spectator a wholehearted acceptance of his arbitrary aesthetic conventions. He was not consciously or deliberately quaint, capricious and fantastic. Instinct ruled him and gave crispness to the contours with which he defined form and unity to the arrangement of the many colors with which he made his entrancing music.

I remember a fascinating lunch at the time with Edward Root (a son of Elihu Root, a professor of art at Hamilton College, New York), at which the lively and talkative George Luks was present. At that time Edward Root, the distinguished connoisseur collector, was studying painting with him and Duncan had commissioned Luks to do a portrait of Otis Skinner, whom he knew at the Century Club. Luks painted him as Colonel Bridau in "The Honor of the Family," and the portrait is highly prized in the Phillips Collection. Much to our delight, whenever Otis Skinner was acting in a play in Washington, he would come to the gallery to see it. And so would his daughter Cornelia Otis Skinner.

Duncan, as I have said, was working on introductions for the first two Phillips publications. Each was to be a collection of essays, the first dedicated to Julian Alden Weir; written by eight of his artist and critic friends, Duncan included; and authorized by the Century Club as a memorial to their distinguished member. It was published in 1921 and reprinted a year later by E. P. Dutton for the Phillips Memorial Gallery.

The second book, also published in 1922 by Dutton, was a monograph of four essays on Honoré Daumier, with a preface outlining plans for the Phillips Gallery. There were four contributors: Frank Jewett Mather Jr., Guy Pène du Bois, Mahonri Young, and Duncan. I thought my husband's essay was especially inspired. Although his paintings were little known in America then, Daumier was one of Duncan's passions. His first Daumier purchase was the now famous "Les Avocats," which I had seen at the Century Club; and he had recently acquired a second, "On a Bridge at Night." One passage in Duncan's essay summed up his feeling for Daumier's genius:

Today we rank him with the greatest of the great. Is it only on the quality of his few paintings executed between 1850 and 1854 while taking a vacation from Charivari, that we are to estimate his place in history?

Honoré Daumier (1808–1879). *On a Bridge at Night*, 10½ x 8½

Honoré Daumier (1808–1879). *Le Ventre Legislatif*, lithograph, 11 x 17

Emphatically, no. The fallacy of our pathos is that the lithographs were not hack-work at all, but full of genius, not handicaps to his success but stepping stones to his complete self-realization.

The lithographs of Daumier not only constitute the bulk of his life work but express him more fully and freely than a lifetime entirely devoted to painting would have done. If like Millet heedless of failure and reconciled to poverty and neglect, he had celebrated all his life long the heroic aspects of the lowly, or if like Delacroix he had been absorbed in technical experiments, and in romantic dreams, or if like Courbet and Manet he had been a "chef d'école" of realism, at war with the academies; if he had painted in any one such way or in each of them by turns . . . there is doubt whether he would have achieved a more distinguished place in the history of art than we now accord to him for his life work as a satirical draftsman of the "bourgeoisie" who permitted himself one *splendid digression* into painting with results gloriously distinguished in style and all the more precious to us because limited in quantity. All the lithographs are inherently important. We delight in their unfailing observation of physical and mental absurdities, their amazing insight and intuition. Here are evidences enough of consummate genius, not only for satire and for philosophical realism, but also for a pictorial style upon which the best contemporary art has been

Honoré Daumier (1808–1879). *Two Sculptors*, 11 x 14

modeled. Daumier spoke, in his drawings as in his paintings, with the unmistakable accent of greatness, a sonorous language of balanced light and shade, line and mass. The art of the painter may be sensed in the lithographs with their rich velvety blacks and delicately modulated half tones. His forte was the silhouette. What an affluence of these in the prints. And what a preparation for the paintings he received with his long practice of drawing from intensive observation and memory of only the essential and expressive lines. At no art school could he have learned so well what to eliminate, how to abbreviate, how to reduce a theme to its simplest terms.

Duncan's early appreciation of Daumier grew steadily stronger. He kept on improving the gallery's group and eventually narrowed it down to seven oils and several fine drawings, as well as the lithographs. The culmination for him was "The Uprising," acquired in the mid-twenties. The painting moved him deeply and he felt it to be one of the highest peaks in the collection.

James Laughlin, Duncan's grandfather

Eliza Irwin Laughlin, Duncan's mother

Mrs. James Laughlin, maternal grandmother

2

BOYHOOD AND COLLEGE

I LOVED to hear Duncan reminisce about his youth. He was born in
Pittsburgh, Pennsylvania, in 1886; and lived there with his parents
and his brother James Laughlin Phillips, who was two years older, for
most of his childhood at the home of his grandmother, Mrs. James
Laughlin. Grandfather Laughlin had died just a year before his
daughter, Eliza Irwin Laughlin, the boys' mother, was married to
Major Duncan Clinch Phillips, a veteran of the Civil War.

The grandfather, James Laughlin, fascinating-looking and full of
character, was of Scotch-Irish descent and had come to this country in
1833 at the age of twenty-one. A slender, wiry man, he had great initia-
tive and enterprise in business; and eventually became a co-founder of
the Jones and Laughlin Steel Co., and one of the colorful empire
builders of his period. He was a leading spirit in his company for
twenty-seven years; president, until his death, of the First National
Bank of Pittsburgh; president of the board of trustees of the Western
Theological Seminary of Allegheny; founder of the first college for
women in Allegheny; and a liberal contributor to worthy Pittsburgh
projects and philanthropies. At the height of his career he was offered
the post of Secretary of the Treasury, but declined.

His widow, Ann Irwin Laughlin, intellectual and kindly, was bedridden in her late years, so her only daughter Eliza and her husband
and their two little boys kept her company in the handsome old family
home at 428 Duquesne Way. The four Laughlin sons had all married
and moved into homes of their own.

Duncan's father, Major Phillips, was a son of Captain Elias Phillips
and Mary Mahon Ormsby. He graduated from Brown University in

Duncan Clinch Phillips, Duncan's father

the class of 1861; served as a cavalry officer in the Army of the Potomac, and after the war engaged in the manufacture of window glass.
He married Eliza Irwin Laughlin in 1883, and as is so often true with
those who marry late in life they were utterly devoted to their two boys.
Jim and Duncan, as shown in their very early photographs wore long
curls, Jim's being deep red and Duncan's with a tinge of gold. It remained "old gold" all his life. Duncan inherited the patrician nose of
his grandfather Laughlin, together with the shaggy eyebrows and keen
blue eyes. The two boys were inseparable; it was as if they were the
same age.

The old mansion of his grandparents where Duncan was born and
lived until his seventh year made a deep impression on him: He felt the
dignity of the great, high-ceilinged rooms — especially the drawing
room with its gilded, arched mirrors from floor to ceiling. The large
paintings with huge shadow box frames did not appeal to him at all —
they were of the dark school of Fontainebleau. But he was attracted to
the stables behind the garden and fascinated by the smell of flowers

and horses, and the delicious odor of fresh baked bread emanating from the kitchen. Smells played a great part in his early fascination with life. He remembered being wheeled in his perambulator by his nurse through a long covered bridge and a lovely, distant park. His nurse would stop at an open market, always at the cheese stall, where, according to the memories of baby Duncan, she was carrying on an affair with the man in charge. The smell of cheese always brought back those trips.

The house on Duquesne Way faced the river, the Monongahela, where there was a constant going and coming of tugs and barges carrying iron, coal, and steel. His greatest excitement was when the river flooded its banks and small boys could step out of the first floor windows into rowboats. And in the autumn there were political parades — dramatic torchlight processions which made a strong impression on the children peering through the windows of the old house. Democratic party headquarters was on the same block two doors down the street; and the strongly Republican family conveyed to the children a feeling that it was somehow rather wicked to be a Democrat.

When Duncan was taken on a family trip to Europe at age four, he returned with a frightening memory of a circus in Paris. There was a clown who seemed to be tossing babies around — dummies, of course. He plucked one from the audience, tossed it high in the air, and let it fall to the ground, face down. As the clown came toward the Phillips family Duncan let out a yell feeling sure he would be the next to be tossed, and screamed until he was taken home. Back in the hotel sitting

Duncan and Jim Phillips as little boys

Jim and Duncan at Ebensburg

room, he was comforted by a bunch of flowers — little red poppies, blue bachelor buttons, and buttercups. He later remembered how he could not let the bouquet out of his sight and always thought that was his first real aesthetic experience of color.

The parents brought home with them an excellent Swiss-French governess for the children and before long the boys were conversing as freely in French as in English. But their fluency came to them by ear and Duncan later regretted that his family had never thought it necessary for him to study French grammar. The result was that although throughout his life he read a great deal in French, he became increasingly shy about conversation, for fear of stumbling over a verb.

Duncan spent his summers in a country home built by his parents on the edge of a small town, Ebensburg, about eighty miles east of Pittsburgh. High in the Alleghenies and situated so as to get every breeze that stirred, it was an ideal place for the boys to engage in "the strenuous life." Mrs. Phillips worried incessantly about their health; but she had been an intrepid horsewoman herself, and now she delighted in the riding exploits of her sons. They rode spirited ponies over the lawns and even up the steps of the long porch. Later they graduated to thoroughbreds, Hermes and Henry of Navarre, which they would race in the very early mornings on the racetrack of the nearby county fair grounds or ride for miles through the wooded, hilly countryside. But just as strong as his delight in strenuous exercise was Duncan's love of books: he read avidly during the summers and would dream dreams "swinging in the great rope hammock on the porch at Ebensburg."

After Mrs. James Laughlin's death in 1895, Major Phillips and his wife looked around for a milder climate than Pittsburgh in which to settle permanently. The major had retired from business, and at this period was having a good deal of throat trouble. Friends in the Capitol persuaded him to try Washington for a season; and when the winter of 1896 turned out to be as balmy a one as Washington had ever known (people were still sitting out on their front porches in December), they promptly bought the property at 21st and Q streets, Northwest, and started building the residence which eventually was to house the Phillips Collection. There was a large brick stable for the boys' riding horses and their parents' team.

Jim and Duncan, at ten and eight years old, were sent for their first formal schooling to a Mr. Preston's. Each morning the pupils were expected to say: "Good morning, Mr. Preston," and when Duncan, who had been reading *Robin Hood* and was bored with the routine, substituted "Good morning, Varlet!" the humor was not appreciated and he was kept after school for the rest of the term and his classmates would take turns sitting with him. The brothers went on to prepare for

Duncan, his cousin John Phillips, a friend and Jim riding at Ebensburg

college at the Washington School for Boys, a fine country day school on Wisconsin Avenue. The teachers were of almost college-professor caliber, stimulating and companionable, and there was one for every seven boys.

The boys were in the same class, a natural outgrowth of their being taught so long at home on an even footing, and they acted together in annual school plays. One year Duncan was called on to take the part of an Irish maid. Jim reported in a letter to their mother that Duncan was "a little mad" at being assigned a woman's part. However with his remarkable capacity to mimic an Irish brogue (derived from a family maid), he made a smash hit in the part.

The school had tennis courts and a nine-hole golf course, and it was in golf that Duncan really excelled. He had a natural swing and even as a schoolboy was capable of breaking 80. On one occasion, when his school played a match with the Chevy Chase Club, Duncan won a cup much to his delight.

There is a charming letter written by Duncan to his mother when he was about fourteen and she was recovering from a dangerous operation at Johns Hopkins Hospital in Baltimore. The boys wrote to her regularly with much concern and this one of Duncan's shows the beginning of his literary bent:

Wed. 29th Jan. 1901

My dear Mamma,

I am looking forward with great pleasure to Saturday for on that day, papa has promised that I shall see you in Baltimore. Meanwhile this little note must suffice, to tell you a few of the things which I am doing and to express to you my love, and my hope, wishes and prayers for your more speedy recovery and health. We have been away from each other for so long a time that to me it will be bliss when we can live and eat in the same house again. I am getting very tired of my studies, and it is so desolate here in the winter that I am already longing for spring.

The one study in which my interest, enthusiasm, and ambition is kept alive is English. And as for composition writing, I cannot find out the reason for my passionate fondness for this occupation . . . Jamie and I are very well. He joins me in sending much love to you, my dear little mother. Good by till Saturday

Duncan

There were two boys in particular with whom Duncan formed friendships that were lifelong, Gus Downing, who lived only a few doors away and with whom he and Jim often went riding on the paths in Rock Creek Park, and Arthur Hellen, a boy of intellect and independence whom Duncan never ceased to admire.

When the brothers arrived at New Haven in the fall of 1904, they both came down with severe and prolonged attacks of whooping cough — a debilitating illness in those days. Although they had to return to Washington to recuperate and had double work to do on their return to college they managed to keep up with their class and gradually to enjoy college life.

Of the two Jim was more executive; Duncan more imaginative. English was his favorite subject and at that time he planned to make writing his career. Three of his professors saw his promise and spurred him on. The first was Professor John Milton Berdan, a brilliant, influential college personality and discerning teacher who in his course demanded a daily theme. The freshmen worked under him with respect, and Duncan with real affection, as I could well understand when I met Professor Berdan and his wife some years later.

As an upperclassman Duncan was inspired by one of Yale's greatest teachers, Chauncey Brewster Tinker, "that shy and diffident man beloved of all who came close to him." Tinker and William Lyons Phelps were the leading spirits in the English department, and it was Tinker whom Duncan talked about in later years as having given him indispensable encouragement.

Duncan began to contribute articles and stories to *The Courant* and in 1907 he was elected an editor of *The Yale Literary Magazine* (the "Lit"), which was perhaps the best college monthly of its day and there was prestige as well as fun in being on its staff. The essays he wrote for it brought him to the attention of William Lyons Phelps, who made him a member of the Pundits, a conversation club of ten juniors — men of independence and distinction who had not been tapped for a senior society. Duncan was among the first five (these were always chosen by the professor); and they in turn would elect the second five. The Pundits met regularly at Morey's and, according to Duncan, "Billy Phelps" did most of the talking which was delightful and stimulating. Billy Phelps was a prodigious reader whose enthusiasm prompted many a young man to approach with gusto books he might otherwise have missed or just plowed through.

Duncan had developed a special enthusiasm for Robert Browning and it was fanned by Professor Phelps. According to Mr. Edward Weeks, former editor of *The Atlantic* and a Harvard man, "Something of Browning's high spirits infected the entire Editorial Staff of the "Lit," prompting those of us on *The Harvard Advocate* to refer somewhat enviously to 'The Browning or Bust school at New Haven.' "

Duncan, who delighted in all phases of Browning, including his *most* obscure passages, wrote this delightful parody of a Browning poem:

> Across the gorse where the west winds blow
> In an offish sort of a place we think
> Our heaven opened up just to chink
> But we were too near to know.
>
> One reckons when ricks are up lambs bleat
> As fools — (you mark me) their hunger will glut
> But we — in the world's eyes — We are but what?
> Whatever you wish my sweet.
>
> Yet if I could match that hair on your sleeve
> With this hair on my head. Just hear the wind!
> They would think it was only I that had sinned
> So I'll take a nap — by your leave.

When Duncan later read these verses aloud to Frances Noyes, a special student of Browning's work, she toyed with the possibility that it *might* indeed be Browning; and then, when Duncan told her he had written it, one can imagine her reaction.

The June 1907 issue of the "Lit" contains an article written by Duncan (then twenty) which proved to be an omen of his future career, though he did not know it at the time. The article is entitled "The Need of Art at Yale" and in it he severely criticizes the university's policy of offering practically no courses in art history or appreciation, and ardently urges his fellow students to pay more attention to lectures on art in light of the fact that the one and *only* such course had just been *withdrawn* because of lack of interest. He speaks of the wonderful work done at Yale, and in all colleges of high standard, in *literature* — but "A thing that strikes the outsider as strange in our college curriculum here," he wrote, "is that so many splendid courses with celebrated instructors should be offered to the dilettante in literature — while the sister art of painting now receives no attention save in technical instruction to the art students.

". . . yet deplorable ignorance and indifference prevails among the majority, and many graduate without a smattering of art-history. . . . It was, I believe, a college graduate who once at dinner ventured the opinion that Botticelli is a wine, a good deal like chianti only lighter. After dinner however, he was rudely awakened by a sensitive friend to the fact that Botticelli is not a wine but a cheese.

"To know the great pictures and the great sculpture of the ages not only adds to the pleasures of travel but is invaluable to the formation of a respectable standard of public taste. . . . The fault lies then with us, when we show a disposition to learn, by attending art lectures, drawing out art books from the library and visiting as many galleries as we can, both at home and abroad, until we are sincerely interested. Then perhaps if courses are offered in the college catalogue they may be properly attended . . . yet I have specifically in mind the dilettante — the man who needs art in his life to make it more exhilarating."

(What a change we all were to see in just over half a century! How different all this is now; interest in art has snowballed to such a degree that no American city counts itself important without its museum, and of course the same is true of universities. Many of Duncan's colleagues young and old speak of his unique contribution and influence through his independent writing and collecting; his constructive criticism; and his warmhearted authoritative encouragement of individual artists over almost sixty years.)

Jim and Duncan roomed together throughout their four years at New Haven and shared many friends. Duncan was particularly drawn to classmates on the board of the "Lit": C. Law Watkins (chairman), Joseph Howland Auchincloss, George Soule, and Lester W. Perrin. Auchincloss was also a member of the Pundits and he and Duncan and Jim were members of *Chi Delta Theta*. The brothers enjoyed taking long walks with George Soule, talking every step of the way (Soule later became editor of the *New York Post* and an influential economist in the New Deal); Law Watkins, so warmhearted, popular and talented, was to join Duncan twenty years later as an associate director of the Phillips Collection and head of its art school; and in particular there was Gus Downing, their oldest and dearest friend in Washington. They had known him since childhood and found him the salt of the earth, not scholarly but keenly intelligent — a great horseback rider and a lovable companion. The man they most admired at Yale was

Walter Davis, who was a Pundit and class secretary. As a senior Walter was voted the man most likely to succeed and the member of the class who had done most for Yale.

More mature than the others was Charles Seymour, who had already spent a year at Oxford; most of the class looked up to him with awe. Charlie very early showed promise of distinction. He edited the papers of Colonel House, then became provost, and eventually president of Yale University, from 1937 to 1950. During his presidency, he and Duncan were drawn together. There was an increasing appreciation of the fine arts at New Haven, as well as throughout the nation.

Some might think of Duncan as primarily interested in art, but a concern for people was always at the center of his thought. His humanist outlook was at the base of his deep interest in politics, in enlightened government, and in ways of preventing war. He always felt that extreme nationalism was at the root of much evil. When he submitted a magazine article along that line shortly after graduation, the editor wrote back advising him to put it away for the time being; it was twenty years ahead of its time.

3

ABROAD AND HOME

IN the immediate years after college the brothers lived at home with their parents in Washington. Jim went to work for an investment banking firm, N. W. Halsey and Co., but later left to take part in the Republican presidential campaign of 1912. Duncan was intent on writing and lecturing on art, and made frequent trips to New York. He published poems in the *Forum;* articles of appreciation and criticism in *Art and Progress* and *Scribner's;* and an essay on Giorgione, the Italian artist he especially revered, in the *Yale Review.* He was thinking about his first books and collecting material for them.

In a letter to his class of 1908 secretary, he reported:

My life since graduation has been devoted to self-development and careful preparations for self-expression. During the winters I have lived in my home in Washington enjoying the interesting social life of this city and devoting much study to the technique of painting and the history of art. During the spring and summer months I have traveled extensively over this continent and abroad. At Madrid, London and Paris as well as New York and other American cities, I have met and talked with many artists in their studios and gone the round of exhibitions. In my forthcoming books of art appreciation entitled "Impressionists' Viewpoint" and "The Decorative Imagination" I have attempted to act as interpreter and navigator between the public and the pictures and to emphasize the function of the arts as means for enhancing and enriching living.

When in Washington Duncan enjoyed meetings of the Reading Club, most of whose members were friends and contemporaries. Among the young women were Martha Bowers (later Mrs. Robert

Taft), Sophie Johnson (Mrs. Randolph Mason), and Helen Taft (later Mrs. Frederick Manning), whose father was then President of the United States. At the club's meetings, which were frequently held in the White House, the members read aloud parts from Shakespeare or good contemporary plays. Martha Bowers and Duncan were frequently given leading roles because their voices were "more expressive"! Several of the colorful bachelors in the Reading Club were members of the House of Truth — men like Edward H. Hart and Louis Bissel, Lord Eustace Percy of the British Embassy, Harvey Bundy, who was then secretary to Mr. Justice Holmes, and Felix Frankfurter, special assistant to Secretary Stimson. Living together in a rented residence, their chief requisite for membership was that they had to tell the truth to each other down to the last detail.

Duncan's high spirits were irrepressible and from time to time overflowed into pranks which contrasted sharply with his usual rather serious and thoughtful bearing. There was, for example, the time that Jim and Duncan were invited to a house party at Ellen Shipman's, at her family's country place near Cornish, New Hampshire. One morning when the party walked down to the post office to get the mail, Duncan remarked that he had been expecting a large package, but its arrival seemed to be delayed. When asked what he was expecting, he said, "a bird — a curlew." No one believed him and they laughed incredulously.

But on his return to New York, Duncan followed up on his inspiration. He managed to find a rather bedraggled, molting curlew in a pet shop and had it boxed and shipped to Miss Shipman with the instruction, "Feed fish." Poor Ellen! She told me later that it was the one time she was a little cross at Duncan because she hated fish.

In a more serious vein Duncan early formed the habit of making notes of his travels. His journal entries written in Europe during the summer of 1911 show his keenly sensitive reactions:

Paris, August 22nd, 1911

I spent the morning in the Louvre — studying the landscape backgrounds of the Primitives and tracing the growing interest in nature and deepening conceptions of its significance through the Florentine and Umbrian Schools to the beautiful landscapes of Titian and Giorgione. I noted with interest the charming vistas of Italian scenery by Andrea Solaris and Cima de Conegliano and many other lesser men of that great epoch. The cool diffused sunlight in both the out of doors and indoors scenes of Guardi and other 18th century Venetians, interested me with its anticipation of modern effects. The colour of Tiepolo and his followers certainly influenced such dissimilar masters as Chardin, Claude, Watteau and Goya and served as a connecting link between the great Venetians and the disciples of colour for its own sake in modern painting. A small canvas by Chardin delighted me. It is the portrait of a youthful musician but the interest is less psychological than aesthetic. Against a coat of exquisite grayish green velvet a rich toned flame tinted violin sounds a delicate colour chord. Titian is superb in the Louvre, especially in the Holy Families and their landscape settings, the Mars and Venus — Jupiter and Antiope and the Man with the Glove. The exquisite harmony of black-white-pink-gray and gold in the little Velasquez portrait of the royal child Margarita — casts its usual spell. The Mona Lisa was away being photographed as the attendants were busy telling the outraged tourists in the Salon Carrée.

I have not yet seen the Thoney Thierry Collection and the other collections on the second floor. The Cabinets of little Dutchmen also had to wait for another day. In the afternoon about three o'clock I drove to the apartment of M. Durand-Ruel in the Rue de Rome and presented my card of introduction. Immediately I was ushered into the midst of many Americans — for one can only see the pictures on Tuesdays between 2 and 4 P.M. The American tourist does not miss a trick. The walls seemed to shout at me — rather loudly at first but gradually with growing effectiveness of appeal. Here are to be found the best canvasses that the Independents of 1860–90 have to show. An amazing uniformity of clever craftsmanship. The harder the problem, the more insolently easy the mastery. Renoir, Monet and Degas are especially convincing, and Renoir most of all. There is an infectious good humour about his work — a thrilling vitality in his vivacious raptures over modern life. Pretty girls in a box at the Opera or dining on a terrace — children playing on an opal beach — a group of Parisians lunching up the river on a hot holiday — anything — everything gives him inspiration for the production of rich shimmering colours and honest appreciation of the pleasures of the day and the hour. And Monet — the man we had suspected of being important chiefly as being the precursor and progenitor of naturalistic landscape painters who have become greater than he — Monet is here supreme in his own audacious way. Such versatility is amazing. On one wall a frosty mist veils the snow covered hay-rick which the pale morning sun faintly flushes. On another it is late afternoon, the river is glassy in the glare and the red roofs of the village on the farther shore glitter and glow. Across the room the wind has made the whitecaps leap all over the green sea, flecked with violet lights, in the sky white, white clouds are moving rapidly. Degas delights in freaks of Japanese composition and drawing, made interesting by the artist's mastery of line and ironical temper. Then of course there are Manet and Sisley and Pissarro and Boudin. Pictures even in the bedrooms and actually in the bathrooms through which the crowd passes with as much interest in the toilet articles as the paintings. In one bedroom nude girls on the wall — and a crucifix over the bed. Altogether a most diverting experience. Afterwards I drove to the Latin Quarter and bought Riviere prints from a very pretty girl with eyes worth remembering. Received a telephone call from Jim at Fontainebleau urging us to join him there for lunch tomorrow and return in the automobile.

Paris, August 23rd.

I went to the Musée du Luxembourg to continue my studies of modern French painting. First I went to the Impressionist room to get another look at Monet and Renoir. Renoir's Moulin de la Galette is fascinating — has an open air café-Chantant where les ouvriers s'amusent. Refreshments are being served at small tables and some people are dancing with rollicking awkwardness. There is much animation of look and movement. But one notices no attempts at story telling — interest being centered at once in the general impression which is one of gayety and colour — a blur of sapphires and emeralds and opalescent pinks. Monet's La Gare St. Lazare has caught the moment when a locomotive has just entered the vault of a train shed. The smoke from its engine rises blue in the enclosed foreground, and drifts away pink in the open sunlight beyond. The tracks in the station yard are checkered with the sunlight filtered through the glazed dome. There is a moonrise over many fields and red roofed farms by Alfred Lebourg which is charming. . . .

Cazin's austere Paysage de Nage and René Ménard's winter evening in the homely provincial town are attractive by reason of their poetry and colour, in spite of subjects — meanly prosaic.

Stanislaus Lepine and René Billorte paint much like Cazin. There is a trick picture by Devambez representing a packed peanut gallery under the roof with the glare of the amphitheatre below. . . . Whistler's "Mother" is really a bit disappointing. Not enough color in the curtain and the wall is too greenish a gray. But the face and hands and the whole beautiful design — make it far and away the finest picture in the gallery.

The sculpture of the Luxembourg is its most distinctive feature. Rodin's *The Kiss* is a work of inspiration. The relaxed and passionate yielding of the woman — the man's desire held under firm control — his strength and ugliness — her weakness and grace — to express these elemental things directly yet without offense — such is an art symbolical yet vital. Van Bresbroeck's *The Tears of the People* might well be Rodin's lovers grown older and sadder with the world's experience. Again the woman leans on the man who again strains to express his overmastering emotion.

The Mona Lisa at the Louvre has not gone to the photographer's as the guides announced, with strange faces, as I think it over on Monday morning. The masterpiece of Leonardo — the inscrutable Gioconda has been abducted — probably by a maniac who will hide or destroy it, or let us rather hope — by a practical joker who wishes to make an object lesson of the lax guardianship of the gallery — and will in time return it to its place with facetious remarks. All Paris is wrought up about it.

During college vacations and sometimes in later years Duncan and Jim went together to dude ranches in the Far West. Sometimes their old friend Gus Downing would join them or their zestful, older cousin John Phillips. They had wonderful times and Duncan told many entertaining stories of their adventures and the personalities who made the most impression on them.

But no account of their early years would be complete without the August snowstorm episode — a dangerous adventure which Duncan recounted so well in later years. Jim, Duncan, Gus Downing and a guide started from Eaton's ranch on a packsaddle trip toward the Canadian border, on a trail between Idaho and Montana. The August weather was so perfect that at nightfall they decided not to put up their tents but to camp out in their sleeping bags under the stars.

About midnight it began to snow hard, increasing rapidly. It quickly became such a blizzard that they abandoned the idea of pitching their tents. Their guide urged them to head for a lean-to that he thought he remembered and felt they could reach by late afternoon the next day. That meant riding the rest of the night as well as the following day. So they hastily packed their gear on the horses' backs and started for the shelter they hoped to find. All that night and the following day they rode, freezing cold, searching for the shelter, with icy snow pelting down on them relentlessly, but found no sign of the lean-to. When someone called for some whiskey to offset the extreme chill, it turned out that Duncan, who had been assigned as keeper of the emergency canteen had in the hurry of breaking camp left it hanging on a limb of a tree. Poor Duncan was for the time being the most unpopular man imaginable! All he had himself for nourishment that day was the cold juice of a can of pears. When Gus Downing looked back and found Duncan looking "positively green around the gills," he dove down into his pack for spirits of ammonia. As a doctor told them later it was really much better for them in their predicament than whiskey, which would have made them sleepy at a time when they needed all their wits about them on the slippery narrow trails. One pack horse did slip and fall over a precipice-like bank. Duncan started to go after it but the guide yelled "Don't be a tenderfoot, do you care more for that hoss's life than your own?"

Finally late at night they came to the lean-to, open all along one side, which the guide had been looking for, the snow blowing in and still falling heavily. They were all chilled to the bone. The guide made a great fire and Duncan thought he should strip off some of his wet clothes and dry them before the fire; but the guide said, "Are you crazy, you just stand close to the fire and let them dry on you." The guide cooked for them the rest of the night, serving up repeated supplies of rice pudding and prunes, and quantities of hot coffee. They all ended up with awful indigestion but at least more fit to continue the next morning in the blinding snow. The guide said, "Now you have something to tell your grandchildren!"

The second day, by late afternoon they finally came to a small cabin or ranch house in which the owner had just one large bed to spare. They all plumped onto it and tried to rest, though they soon found it was full of bedbugs! The next morning they left the horses with the guide and took a train from a little town nearby to their planned destination. Duncan said the plush seats of that old-fashioned train looked like luxury personified.

As noted above, Jim took an active part in the presidential campaign of 1912. During the preconvention fights he represented President Taft and Charles Hillis in the states of Massachusetts, New Hampshire, and New Jersey; at the Chicago convention he acted as secretary of the Reception Committee; and during the campaign proper he was assistant treasurer of the Republican National Committee and chairman of the committee in charge of organizing Republican campaign clubs throughout the country. How passionately Jim felt about his losing cause can be seen in this letter to Duncan:

> 1600 Twenty-first St.
> Washington, D.C.
> Wed. May 29th, 1912

My dear Duncan —

On my return here Sunday morning after three weeks in New Jersey I enjoyed immensely reading your extremely interesting letters from Spain, also Leila's. I am so glad you are having such an enjoyable trip.

I had three weeks of hard work, long hours, often from 7:00 A.M. taking a train until midnight, when an evening meeting would be over. The morning papers show that T.R. swept the state yesterday and will get the great majority if not the entire delegation of the state. Unlimited amount of money, and the corrupt use of it, the prestige of victory, especially in the President's home state of Ohio, great superiority over President Taft in his ability to inflame the passions of the mob, in the use of lies and personal abuse of his opponent with the methods of the circus. And the language of the gutter or the prize ring, and finally unquestionably better political generalship, physical endurance and personal magnetism, all these things far more than overbalance the academic arguments that Roosevelt doctrines and still more himself, spell the complete overturn of our institutions, revolution and the establishment of a one-man autocracy for life.

The sickening side of a pitiable national situation is that many conservatives the country over hate Roosevelt, are very lukewarm about Taft, on account of his Trust prosecutions, etc., and are staying away from the primaries, expecting blindly to vote for a Democrat whom they can control in November. They little realize T.R. power. Never have the unreasoning, imaginative masses of the people the country over believed more implicitly in their God, than they do now. And politicians in both parties with bated breath admit to their best friends that Napoleon of the 20th Century, whether running as the Candidate of the Republican party or of a party of his own which he has given warning he will run on "if the will of the people does not control the Chicago convention" will break all party lines, will even break the solid south, and sweep irresistibly to complete control of the nation. Only yesterday he defied the National Republican committee by announcing he would not accept their choice of Temporary Chairman of the Convention his own Ex. Sec. of State Elihu Root, and insists that Senator Clapp be named instead.

President Taft has now on paper enough votes to nominate him. But whether he can hold the Southern delegates from either being bought by T.R. money, or flocking over to him to get on the band wagon and be on the winning side is extremely doubtful. Perkins, McCormick — Flinn — Dan Hanna — etc. etc. are spending fortunes to put T.R. in the White House. The Chicago convention will be the most exciting in the history of the country. If Taft controls it, T.R. will lead a riot and it will end in another convention which will name him. If Roosevelt controls the convention the Republican Party ceases to exist.

When I reached New Jersey I found that practically nothing had been done. A little work had been started in the North, nothing in the South. I went at once to the Southern part of the State, and spent 10 days in the seven counties there. Finding out the situation, putting plans and action into the leaders. Arranging meetings, getting the delegates to travel around and see the leading citizens in all the towns and villages. Flattering, cajoling, bullying as it seemed best. Coming directly from the President you always had the prestige to impress and get an attentive audience. I also arranged and put through a large number of big noon day meetings at big mills and factories — like for instance the New York Ship Yards in Camden with 6,000 employees. With a strong speaker to address them, this is the best way to reach the labor vote. I then went North and arranged a lot of similar meetings the last week around Newark etc. The work is trying but extremely interesting. You meet the queerest kind of types of all sorts. And have to be ready for the unexpected at any time.

The family have no plans, but they will have to leave here soon, as great heat might begin now any day. We hope to hear from you from Italy any day now. With ever so much love to you and Leila, in which Mother and Father join.

Devotedly,
Jim

When the campaign was over and Taft and T.R. had been defeated by Woodrow Wilson, Jim made this summary: "We succeeded in placing in the field a party standing for a representative constitutional republic along sanely progressive lines and headed by a big-hearted, true statesman. We also succeeded in making the Democrats nominate their very best man — a man who, however radically one may differ with him on certain issues, is personally worthy of the great office he fills."

In 1910, with their parents and their cousin Leila Laughlin, the brothers made a memorable trip to Japan and China. In Tokyo they all stayed at the American Embassy, as guests of our ambassador, Mr. Thomas O'Brien, and his wife, whose daughter Kitty, was a good friend and schoolmate of Leila's. From there, they chartered a yacht and sailed into the Inland Sea, very seldom visited by Westerners in those days, and stopped off at remote little towns along the coast. There would always be some Japanese who had never seen a Westerner before and were amazed at their white skin, strange speech, and clothes. The kimonoed women would bow deeply, making little hissing sounds, and feel the dresses of the women of the party to see what the material was like.

On their return to Honshu they climbed Mt. Fujiyama, stopping for tea at attractive little tea houses to renew their energy. In Tokyo they were introduced to the elaborate tea ceremony. Seated on the floor, they learned its special ritual and grace and drank a greenish tea which Duncan found unpleasantly tart.

Accepting an invitation to the Emperor's garden party, they were dismayed to find the Emperor dressed in clothes that simply hung on him, the baggy trouser legs sweeping the ground. His person was regarded as so sacred that no tailor was allowed to touch him but was limited to standing behind a screen peering at his sacred person and guessing at his measurements. No fittings ever took place.

The journey continued to China, where the high point was a horseback ride to the Great Wall. Duncan's mother was so impressed that she picked out a fairly large stone from the wall for her curio cabinet in the Washington drawing room. For their part Jim and Duncan acquired Japanese prints — Hokusai, Hiroshige, Harunobu. Duncan became absorbed in tracing the influence of Oriental art, through the Japanese wood-block prints, on Western artists such as Whistler, Degas, and later Bonnard, who in admiration simplified their own designs to broader, flatter areas of color and tone.

A real adventure occurred one night in Peking when the travelers were returning from the theater by rickshaw. Back at the hotel they suddenly discovered that Major Phillips was missing. His rickshaw boy had not returned him with the others; but had run in a different direction. The hotel manager said, "This is bad, very bad. Major Phillips may be in great danger!" and immediately a search party was sent out. Indeed the boy *had* taken him to a bad section of the city; but when Major Phillips realized what was happening, he beat the boy around the shoulders with his cane (weighted as was the custom at that time) and compelled him to turn around; and so the major arrived safely back before the searching party.

In 1914 Jim and Duncan took an apartment at 104 East 40th Street in New York City, where they were to spend some of their happiest years together. It became a gathering place for their friends and classmates — Walter Davis was already living in the same building — and here they began to pursue their careers in earnest. The Japanese prints were hung on the walls and the brothers continued, as they had from the time they left college, to collect American paintings, which fascinated them both. Duncan put together and read proofs of his first book, *The Enchantment of Art*, published by John Lane in 1914. It is a collection of essays about some of his favorite writers and artists, with such titles as: "Velasquez: The Enchanter of Realism," "Nationality in Pictures," "Impressionism in Prose," "Impressionism in Poetry," "Spirit of Romantic Comedy," "Giorgione," "Tintoretto," "Shakespearean Beauty," "Watteau and His Influence on Modern Poetry."

The book was exhilaratingly youthful in spirit and yet full of wisdom, too. He sent it to me soon after we met in 1921, along with books of his favorite poets. He wrote in answer to my letter of appreciation: "I am so happy that you liked my book *The Enchantment of Art*. No praise for that early work has ever pleased me so much as you saying that it stimulated and refreshed you and spoke to you in terms of your own joy in living." Later in the same letter he added, "Reading over some of the earlier chapters today, the ones written shortly after I left college, I am embarrassed by my emphatic expression of opinions which I would now repudiate or at least modify . . . just the same I am a bit envious of the facility, the freshness and the gusto of the style in such essays as the Decorative Imagination, The Spirit of Romantic Comedy, The Giorgione and the Tintoretto."

In a history of the Yale class of 1908 covering that period Duncan wrote, "My book, *The Enchantment of Art*, was published and received excellent reviews. As I felt that I had been delivered of most of my accumulated wisdom on that subject, I decided that before writing another book I would turn to some other field and broaden my mind and experience. For several years, therefore, while writing articles and book reviews, I studied sociology and problems in education."

Duncan's interest in sociology led him to become a member of the Big Brother movement and he worked individually with one especially incorrigible boy who had been in and out of reformatories several times. The boy had come from a farm in Hungary; his father was dead and his mother a prostitute. He never could hold a job for even a week, and Duncan after getting one for him as a printer's devil managed to en-

J. Alden Weir (1852–1919). *The Fishing Party*, 28 x 23

HOMER 1890

Winslow Homer (1836–1910). *Rowing Home*, 13½ x 19½

courage him to remain in it for most of a season. But when spring came the boy disappeared from town telling a neighbor he did not like to be "pushed from behint." The neighbor thought he would hitchhike to an uncle's farm in the midwest. So all Duncan could do was to telegraph the Big Brothers in the Ohio town to keep an eye on the youngster.

In 1915 Duncan was elected a member of the Century Club in New York. He was, I believe, the youngest member to be elected up to that time. He found much pleasure in lunching there and relished friendships he made with older members already distinguished in the field of art. He developed a special affection for Professor Frank Jewett Mather, the critic, who was head of Princeton's art department and director of its art gallery. They remained good friends throughout Mather's life and Duncan welcomed his views on the collection during its formative period, as Mather did those of the younger critic. Herbert Brownell was another member whom Duncan especially admired. I remember how impressed I was with Brownell's statement that you can tell the style of a work of art from any isolated square inch of its surface. Then there were the artists — my uncle Gifford Beal, Augustus Vincent Tack, and J. Alden Weir — all good friends whose work Duncan was collecting.

With his discriminating eye Weir had been making a small but choice collection of his own. One day he mentioned that he had to sell something from it to help finance his Connecticut farm. Duncan who had seen the paintings, instantly said he would love to purchase one. So off they went to Weir's home where Duncan immediately spotted a Twachtman landscape and suggested that that was the painting he would prefer. To his surprise Weir bristled with temperament, showed unexpected spirit and exclaimed, "I would sooner lose my right arm than sell one of Johnnie Twachtman's paintings!" Duncan understood and settled for a watercolor by Winslow Homer, "Rowing Home," broad and simplified to a few essentials, almost Marin-like, modern forever. He already had an exquisite snow scene of Twachtman's and

Augustus Vincent Tack (1870–1949). *Storm*, 37 x 48

later was able to acquire several others. He always regretted that he never knew Twachtman personally.

Duncan seldom missed a new exhibition and on one of his rounds he encountered the artist William Merritt Chase. Although strangers, they were soon exchanging comments about the pictures they had come to see. Later Duncan ran into Chase on Fifth Avenue, walking with his dandified air and bristling mustachios. As if dimly remembering their chance meeting Chase stopped Duncan and asked, "Sir, are you a painter?" When Duncan said no, Chase retorted, "Well you ought to be: You talk like one, you act like one, you *should* be one. Good day!"

With his first book winning favor, Duncan was in a blithe and expansive mood, and when Frank Crowninshield asked him to take a job with *Vanity Fair*, which was just starting, Duncan accepted and became managing editor for some months until Crowninshield could free himself from other work. He enjoyed being an "idea man," suggesting articles for future issues, interviewing notable people in the art world, planning the layout of articles, etc., etc. During this period, Duncan was elected to the Coffee House, a congenial lunch club, and also began writing a novel which he later told me was a flop since he simply could not handle dialogue.

There was a glorious streak of absurdity in Duncan and no one, not even Jim, could anticipate when it would take over. Arthur Hellen, one of Jim and Duncan's boyhood friends in Washington, loves to tell a story of the time in 1916 when Jim, still deeply involved in Republican politics, was a delegate to the convention at which Charles Evans Hughes was eventually nominated. Arthur, Jim and Duncan had all gone to Chicago but Duncan had neglected to get hotel reservations for Arthur and himself, and as it turned out they had to put up at a small, dingy hotel. To make things worse it rained constantly, the skies gloomy and dark, dousing the city the whole time they were there. One afternoon Duncan was seated morosely in the shabby lobby. It was raining pitchforks outside and even the lobby walls were damp. Duncan for fun had put up an umbrella and sat beneath it gloomily reading the convention bulletins. In the crowded lobby a group of rather tough-looking politicians delegated one of their number to go over and talk to the stranger. The man approached and said, "Pretty wet in here, isn't it?" "Yes," said Duncan, feeling the wall back of him, "it's a plain case of saturation." With that he got up and, still holding his umbrella, said politely, "Now if you will excuse me, I'll make a run for the elevator."

John Sloan (1871–1951). *The Wake of the Ferry II*, 26 x 32

Arthur remembers many such instances of Duncan's impetuous nonsense and how he personally would get self-conscious at these times and try to disappear. But he added, "Thank *goodness* for them, what fun they were, how they *added* to *life!*" And of the close tie between the two brothers he said, "It was a love and appreciation for each other that ran very deep, never mawkish."

From the time the brothers left college they had been spending their own money on contemporary Amerian paintings, which could be bought quite reasonably at that time, and they spurred on their parents, who already had the habit, to augment the family collection. In the letter that follows Jim speaks for them both.

> January 6th, 1916
> 104 East Fortieth St.
> New York

Dear Father —

This letter is a joint one to you and mother. Since my return to N.Y. I have had it brought home to me forcibly what a very unusual winter in the Art world we are facing. So I feel it is timely to take up with you both what Duncan and I feel our policy should be toward picture buying.

It is perfectly apparent that if the number of pictures we are to own is to be limited by our present wall space on the first floor of 1600–21st Street — then roughly speaking we have bought our last picture. We both however feel very strongly that this could be awfully unfortunate and deprive us all of a lot of pleasure. We would all of us cease to get the great enjoyment and enrichment in living which good art with something to say brings into life, and in addition Duncan and I would no longer have the opportunity of seeing so many interesting pictures — at the various galleries — which to a degree at least are only shown to at least possible buyers.

Our suggestions are neither impractical nor extravagant — they are along the same line as scores of the most successful and conservative business men — except in two respects. 1. Our suggestions are far more conservative. 2. The average picture collector has not nearly the knowledge, experience and appreciation of Art that Duncan and I possess.

For instance J. Pierpont Morgan the greatest financial genius America has produced had over half of his fortune as finally assessed in works of Art. Frick, one of the industrial kings, and Altman, New York's greatest merchant, both have a good percentage of their wealth in such investments.

Among men of more moderate wealth the art dealers here tell me that no one has any idea of the number of fairly important collectors that there are in this country. Collections which have been made (are often) unknown to the general public — except when from time to time some such collection is either left to a museum or else perhaps comes before the public for dispersal at an auction

1600 21st Street, built in 1897, showing to right the wing added in 1907

sale on the death of the owner. Now our suggested plan is that a very small percentage of your annual income and mother's should be regularly laid aside for buying pictures. . . .

He then suggests ten thousand dollars a year and adds that it

. . . would in a short time build up an Art collection of distinction and charm. . . . When I go back to Washington a week from next Sunday for the National Civic Federation meeting the next day I shall bring you a catalogue (of an important auction coming up) and I hope to return two days later with your authorization to bid on some of the pictures.

With ever so much love to both in which Duncan would join if he was not out.

Devotedly your son
JLP

Their father thought from a business standpoint, but he always tried to cooperate with his sons' enthusiasms, and in this case there was an immediate response to Jim's letter. The fund for new acquisitions was

The wing built in 1907. Above it is the second-floor gallery, added in 1920. The entrance at left was built when the whole wing became a public gallery in 1921.

agreed to and the need for space clearly recognized. In 1907, when the sons were in college, the parents had built the first addition to their home on 21st Street, a large mahogany-paneled library; now in 1916–17 the whole family participated in planning for a skylight gallery and storeroom above the library which was built by McKim, Meade and White.

With the additional fund at their disposal here are some of the paintings the two brothers bought for the family collection:

1915	*Interior of a Turkish Cafe*	Decamps
	A Corner of the Hague	Maris
	The Queen's Entry	Maris and Monticelli
1916	*Visions of Glory*	Davies
	Twilight in Spain	Lawson
	Under the Bridge	Lawson
	As You Like It	Monticelli
	Band Concert Night	Myers
	Little Mother	Myers
	End of the Day	Spencer
	Pan and the Wolf	Weir
	Classic Landscape	Wilson
1917	*Eve's Garden*	Davies
	Bailey's Beach	Hassam
	Gray Day, Goochland, Virginia	Inness
	A Windstorm	Inness
	Spring Morning, Washington Bridge	Lawson
	Warmth in Winter	Lawson
	Allegro Giocoso	Tack
	Visiting Neighbors	Weir

57

J. Alden Weir (1852–1919). *Pan and the Wolf,* 34 x 24

Childe Hassam (1859–1935). *Washington Arch in Spring*, 26 x 21½

I believe that the only painting now listed in the collection which the parents had acquired on their own is "Moonlight Tarpon Springs," by George Inness.

In 1917 when the United States entered the First World War, both brothers volunteered, but each was turned down for physical disabilities. As Duncan later wrote for his class history:

I made many unsuccessful efforts to get into the Army or Navy — always thirty or forty pounds under the proper weight for my height. Finally I became associated with the Division of Pictorial Publicity and worked independently inspiring and organizing American artists for war work and making use of war pictures to drive home the issues of the war to the American People. Hundreds of slides were made and captions written, and lectures were prepared for camps and civilian centers. Later I assembled the Allied War Salon (a great exhibition of pictures in every conceivable medium relating to the war) at the American Art Galleries on Madison Square, New York, but failed in an effort to persuade the government to purchase the entire collection as a nucleus for a War Museum.

This was a year of both happiness and tragedy. Jim fell in love with Alice Conyngham Gifford of New York and their engagement was announced. They were married at Nantucket in June with Duncan as best man. But Major Phillips had developed a dangerously high blood pressure, a fact which the doctor had confided to Duncan alone. Each day for many years the old gentleman would walk down to the Metropolitan Club to lunch with his Civil War cronies and talk over the old campaigns. But he was not thought well enough to attend Jim's wedding, and in fact the Major died suddenly in Washington on the very day of the ceremony. The New York apartment was given up; Duncan came back to live with his widowed mother; and Jim with his pretty, piquant wife settled into a home in Chevy Chase, Maryland.

Jim became associate director of the Bureau of Personnel of the American Red Cross, in charge of all applications for foreign service; and as was true of so many on the home front in 1918, he contracted the Spanish flu. Having twice suffered from pneumonia before this, he did not have enough strength to throw off the disease, and he died at the family home fifteen months after his father. Duncan and his mother were inconsolable. So much light went out of Mrs. Phillips' life that she was a semi-invalid thereafter.

Duncan himself was slow to recover from shock and what pulled him back was the thought of creating a memorial to the two men he loved

Major Phillips and General Young

best. The means were at his disposal; his mother shared in the ideal, and they founded it together. He summed up his feelings years later in this passage from his book *A Collection in the Making*, published in 1926:

So in 1918 I incorporated the Phillips Memorial Gallery, first to occupy my mind with a large constructive social purpose and then to create a Memorial worthy of the virile spirits of my lost leaders — my Father, Major D. Clinch Phillips — an upright, high-minded, high-spirited soldier, manufacturer, and citizen, and my Brother, James Laughlin Phillips, who was on his way to the heights when death overtook him — an idealist in politics and business — a keen student of men and social conditions — a broad-minded, warm hearted, lovable and very noble American. Both of them had liked good pictures and my brother would have been an enthusiastic and wise collector. No mortuary monument, remindful of the accident of death would adequately commemorate two such men. Something of even greater practical helpfulness than art might have been more appropriate. But I needed to put my own best powers to a coordinated purpose. And I saw a chance to create a beneficent force in the community where I live — a joy-giving, life-enhancing influence, assisting people to see beautifully as true artists see. This aim of trying to understand and then to communicate the artist's point of view is made easier now through the life partner-

James Laughlin Phillips

ship I have formed with a painter. My wife helps me to build the Collection in the spirit of seeing beautifully with which she builds her own pictures out of the substance and romance of life.

We all give according to our gifts. In founding and developing the Memorial Gallery, Duncan was not simply fulfilling a wish to create a fitting memorial, but also and equally putting to high purpose his eminent natural gift for collecting art and interpreting it creatively

61

and independently. One cannot paint, write poetry, or be a scientist without some flair or bent for it to begin with.

So he used his original endowment and developed his great flair, passionately acquiring the art he loved and building a great collection, as an architect would build a house — and as great collectors have done from time immemorial. He also had a fine literary gift which made him an eloquent critic, both in speaking and writing. Before the fall of 1921 when the gallery was first opened to the public in a few rooms of 21st Street, Duncan had already acquired a good-sized collection of the works of living painters, along with some very fine older paintings. He continued to build on this foundation over the years, eliminating here and there, and always combining contemporary paintings with those works of previous periods which he felt would be forever modern, with a quality of innate life and necessary balance. In 1921, although small compared with the large and great museums, the Phillips Memorial Gallery was large enough to become the first real museum of modern art in this country; that is, a public gallery with its main stress on living painters.

Pierre Auguste Renoir (1841–1919). *Luncheon of the Boating Party*, 51 x 68

4

PARIS AND THE RENOIR

In June of 1923 Duncan and I went to Paris, taking along our eleven-month-old baby and her nurse. At first we stayed at a very French hotel, Le Gallia, in a noisy spot just off the Champs-Elysées and I remember painting a small canvas in palette knife of the Rue de la Boetie from our balcony. Then we moved to the Trianon Palace Hotel at Versailles, where the baby could be outdoors more. From there we often went into town and it was during that period that we first saw Renoir's great "Déjeuner des Canotiers."

It happened when we were invited to lunch at the home of the Joseph Durand-Ruels — a home filled with fascinating paintings of the Impressionist period. Much to our delight, we were seated opposite that fabulous, incredibly entrancing, utterly alive and beguiling Renoir masterpiece.

Duncan knew that the sons were beginning to sell the collection made by their father, the great connoisseur dealer Paul Durand-Ruel, founder of the firm, and we found we would be able to purchase the great Renoir for the Memorial Gallery and that it could be sent to the United States early the following year. In later years if any one was curious as to what its price was at that period, Duncan would always tell them directly that it was exactly $125,000. It did not seem outlandishly high to us at that time, since we had few institutional expenses, knew the greatness of the painting, and realized that it would be a great cornerstone to the collection. We have never bought anything since quite to equal it in price, but then the days of the devastating, ever increasing income tax had not yet arrived. Probably M. Durand-Ruel (père) paid Renoir around two thousand dollars for it!

It would be interesting to know. Later, when Lord Duveen desperately wanted to buy it to give to the National Gallery of London, he waved a blank check before my husband's eyes and said, "Fill in any amount and I will pay it." Naturally with our great feeling for the painting there was not a chance for Duveen.

The Joseph Durand-Ruels lived in a very nice town house, none of the furnishing of which I remember in particular because Duncan and I were so interested in looking at the paintings — Pissarro, Monet, Renoir, etc. — which lined the walls everywhere, living rooms, bedrooms and baths! Of the pictures in the dining room, the only one I remember is Renoir's "Boating Party." Mr. Joseph Durand-Ruel was definitely a businessman, and I do not recall anything of particular interest he said about art. His wife was gracious, fine-featured, and quite aristocratic-looking.

Renoir had done portraits of all the family, painted in his rather late period when he was seeing almost too much red in flesh tones and making all his women very ample and plump. According to his son, Renoir admired his own wife's stoutness, and was proud that she looked so well nourished. However, one felt that he had changed Mme. Durand-Ruel too much. In her portrait he had painted her in a generalized way with plump red arms, reminding one of the proverbial washerwoman.

I remember with pleasure that an attractive daughter of Durand-Ruel wanted to buy a little painting by me, a landscape with imaginary figures on a cardboard panel which must have been in my paint box when they lunched with us at the Trianon Palace. Duncan, however, was anxious for me not to let it go. I also painted one of these small panels at St. Cyr, when Duncan played golf at the club there with Mr. Mesmore of the firm of Knoedler and Co. Earlier on that same visit he had purchased from them a small Daumier, of Sancho Panza lumbering along on a donkey with Don Quixote dashing off in the distance. I was sorry that it later had to be included in a trade for a painting even more desirable for the collection.

In his book *Renoir, My Father*, Jean Renoir writes of the painting we bought, the "Déjeuner des Canotiers":

Just as Montmartre had served as an artistic inspiration for Renoir, the Banks of the Seine between Chatou and Bougival stimulated him to the same degree . . . The large "Boatmen's Luncheon" in the Phillips Collection in Washington was the crowning achievement of a long series of

pictures, studies and sketches at the Grenouillière Restaurant at Chatou.
. . . One day in 1881 Renoir told Baron Barbier . . . that he was plan-
ning a large picture of boatmen lunching with friends on the terrace of the
Fournaise's restaurant.

His son continues:

I am not certain of the identity of all the people in the picture. Lhote is
there, in the background, wearing a top hat; Lestringuez is to be seen
leaning over a friend, who is perhaps Rivière or Caillebotte. The young
woman with her elbows on the railing is Alphonsine Fournaise, "the lovely
Alphonsine," as the habitués of her parents' restaurant called her. The
young person drinking is "little Henriot," and the woman looking at
Lestringuez must be Ellen André. The figure in the foreground, patting a
little dog, is my mother.

In the light of time it does not matter much who the figures are. They
are every man, all people.
 Duncan wrote of Renoir and of the "Déjeuner" in his book *A Collection in the Making*, published in 1926.

His genius of course was that of the colorist who cannot rest from color
because it is his natural expression. His light gaiety resembles that of the
French decorators of the eighteenth century. But the grim Revolution lay
between Fragonard and Renoir and Renoir's art is of the people and for
the people. Like Titian and Rubens he employed form and color to express
joy in the abundance of light and life rather than to analyze or dramatize.
He was in love with youth and sunshine and shadows dappled with color-
reflexions. His art of laying on pure color made fluid with medium, allow-
ing one hue to pass into another with rapturous evanescence, even as our
unforeseen pleasures mingle and merge, enabled him to express his epicurean joyousness and at the same time to model in diffused radiance, the
soft and rounded forms he loved. The High Renaissance reaches a belated
culmination in the ripe perfection and the marvelous modeling of the
Déjeuner des Canotiers, undoubtedly one of the great pictures of the world.
It has apparently no repression and yet it is a well pondered composition.
Every inch of the canvas is alive and worth framing for itself, yet an in-
tegral part also of the complex pattern in which we note an interesting use
of inverted perspective. In spite of all the people, the landscape, the spar-
kling, sumptuous "still life" there is no division of interest and no crowding
nor confusion. We feel that to the grand manner of Titian and Rubens is
added the Impressionists' art of expressing the passing moment in the softness of a woman's dancing glance, the flapping of the striped awning in a

fitful breeze, the unity and vivacity of the caressing enveloping light. After this triumph Renoir studied Ingres for sculpturesque line and rhythmic pattern and cared more and more for abstract qualities. His later years at the villa at Cagnes were burdened with illness and infirmity, yet they did not change him. Nor did success. He experimented and improvised with his failing powers up to his last day.

One incident from our visit to Paris amused us both to think of afterwards. To be outdoors and to keep my hand in at painting we decided it would be fun if I could paint in the Tuileries Gardens. So I took a rather small canvas and set up my easel at the edge of a wide path across the gardens from the Pantheon. Duncan sat alone on a nearby park bench "getting the air" and watching me work, as did a handful of children and their parents. Duncan sat leaning forward, his hands on top of the cane which he always carried at that period. Suddenly a couple of young men, Latin Quarter types in black cloaks, saw our little group and, as they passed, called back, "Son Britannic Majesty!" Duncan was indeed a most distinguished, confident, independent-looking person (with his rather colorful tweeds) and they spotted it instantly. But with all this confidence of Duncan's, there also was a shyness, along with great friendliness.

Duncan enjoyed taking me to Parisian restaurants he had enjoyed on his earlier visits. I think in particular of the Tour d'Argent, on the Left Bank and very much of the old world, with its famous roast duck, cooked before your eyes, and its chocolate soufflés. Actually Duncan was nothing of a gourmet. He always said that his digestion had been ruined in his freshman year at college when he too often frequented the hot dog stands. He was satisfied with the simplest food and would shock the waiters often in these restaurants by ordering two plain poached eggs and a small portion of bread pudding. We went to Lapérouse with its little separate dining rooms, like box stalls, and very special "specialités de la maison," and to Voisin and Lavenue and a beautiful restaurant in the Bois, and one on Montmartre. We had delightful times!

On our return in August we went as usual to the Phillips country place, Ormsby Lodge in Ebensburg, Pa. Built in 1888, when Duncan was two years old, it was an ideal place for him to do uninterrupted writing and for me to paint the beautiful countryside of farms and hills against distant mountain ranges. Duncan's enjoyment of the country around this summer home in the Alleghenies amounted to ecstasy. Here was another great bond and it was really thrilling to see and listen to his delight! We would drive out to farm roads and walk together. Usually I would paint or make notes for paintings part of the time. One always found sweeping mountain ranges in the distance, with dipping farmlands and patches of woods and cultivated fields making fascinating natural patterns in the foreground. While I was painting Duncan would take wonderful, adventurous walks or sit in the car and write.

I remember in those early days asking him a silly question: "Who would you have liked to be if you were not yourself?" (thinking he would name a literary figure). Instantly and gaily he shot back, "You, because you're a landscape painter."

But it did not occur to him to paint until about 1928. That summer he did some subjects that showed a natural sense of simplified design with feeling, organization and originality. He also experimented tentatively with abstractions (which he later destroyed). In the mid-thirties he again took up painting for several summers, but he destroyed too many of them. He painted very fast; but if he carried a promising canvas too far he would suddenly cross it out with black paint an inch wide, making it impossible to recover what was underneath, no matter how charming. As a critic he was tantalized and tormented when he did not do well — even more than a person like me, painting more continuously, though I could suffer, too.

A dozen or so delightful canvases of Duncan's remain, which he did not destroy. I remember once in the thirties Sandy Calder went through the gallery with us, and then came to the house afterwards. When he saw a painting by Duncan hanging in his study, a still life of a bowl of plums, he said, "I enjoy that more than anything I have seen today." And I know what he meant; It was *unique*, felt, unsophisticated, refreshingly direct and simplified, yet subtle in color.

Duncan was playing a lot of golf during this period — especially in the summer. I played with him at times and he had some very fine competition from several men living near Ebensburg. One was his close friend Law Watkins, a classmate at Yale and colleague on the "Lit," who was managing some of his father's nearby coal mines. Duncan and Law had a standing invitation to play whenever they wanted to on Charles M. Schwab's private course at Loretto, but they really preferred to play on a challenging nine-hole, uphill and down-dale course, the Summit Club at Cresson, which Law Watkins had himself designed.

Then there was Ralph Moore, also a coal operator. He and his wife were true friends of ours, both great readers. A note to Duncan from Ralph written on a Christmas card in 1931 is delightful: "My dear Duncan: Twice this week I wrote you Christmas notes and tore them up. Funny, isn't it? But the truth is, that I'm such a 'nut' when I get a fountain pen in hand, that I felt that my two former jumps into letters did not display the proper degree of respect to a man who could successfully drive number one green four times in a row — or was it six?" Duncan consistently drove well over two hundred yards, with great accuracy.

In the fall of 1927, on a trip to New York we went to Arthur B. Davies' studio. My husband, as I have said, published a book on Arthur Davies as a Phillips Publication in 1924 and the collection already had several of his paintings.

Davies lived on East 52nd Street over a veterinary hospital, and we climbed rather narrow steep stairs to get to his studio. It was a nice big front room with tall windows, absolutely *packed* with objects, his small wood carvings, his cloisonné work, books, papers, lithographs, drawings, etc. No cleaning woman or *anyone* was allowed to move anything by a hair's breadth. There were some lovely new paintings to see for the first time!

While we were looking at them Davies spotted my short gazelle skin coat and when I explained we had bought it on our recent trip to Paris, he smiled and said he also had a new *suit* from Paris. "I'll show it to you." He disappeared to emerge shortly wearing the new suit (rather a skimpy cut), pirouetted slowly in it for us to see, and announced it had only cost him thirty-five dollars. He reminded me somewhat of my uncle Ren and it turned out he especially liked Reynolds Beal's work.

This was the period when Davies was interested in the Greek theory of inhalation, and was painting all his figures with lifted thorax and chest to give them a more vital appearance. Leafing through his great deluxe books of Raphael's drawings, he pointed out that Raphael also was well aware of the inhalation principle.

The collection now has about twenty examples of Davies' work, but I find it difficult to remember exactly which ones we bought that day. Among those in the collection's unit are "Tissue Parnassian," "The Hesitation of Orestes," "The Flood," "Horses of Attica," and the "Along the Erie Canal."

Davies was an intellectual, charming-looking man and a splendid

Arthur B. Davies (1862–1928). *The Flood*, 18 x 30

critic and organizer. He had had much to do (indeed it was his idea) with the history-making 1913 Armory show; along with Walter Pach and Walt Kuhn, when Americans first saw on a large scale the innovations that were going on in Europe hung together with their own artists' work.

Davies, who was given to consulting astrologers, told us in a matter of fact way that one woman astrologer had predicted that he would die on his contemplated trip to Europe the next summer. Luckily for our peace of mind, we took no stock in it, no more than we did in astrologers. But, incredibly, that rare and distinguished man did die on that trip in a little Italian hill town. He had been doing exquisite, poetic watercolors as he traveled.

Although the Metropolitan Museum held a large retrospective exhibit of his paintings soon after his death, Davies received little acclaim for some years. But he has emerged from this temporary eclipse and the Phillips Collection now receives frequent requests to lend Davies' paintings — especially the very early "Along the Erie Canal" — to exhibitions.

About 1925, Duncan and I saw in New York the unique and remark-

Arthur B. Davies (1862–1928). *Horses of Attica*, 8¼ x 15¼

Arthur B. Davies (1862–1928). *Tissue Parnassian*, 26 x 40

able music room that Arthur Davies and Charles Prendergast created together in the home of Miss Lillie Bliss, one of Davies' great patrons. I wonder what became of that room. Davies of course did the mural panels.

The beautiful book on Arthur Davies which came out in 1924 as Phillips Publication No. 3 contained essays on the man and his art by Duncan Phillips, Dwight Williams (Mr. Davies' first teacher), Royal Cortissoz, Frank Jewett Mather Jr., Edward W. Root, and Gustavus Eisen. In a keen passage from Duncan's essay he notes: "It is significant that Davies' art . . . has been inspired . . . by the Greece of Pompeian frescoes . . . terra cotta statuettes from Tanagra . . . the painted or incised vases and indeed all the exquisite luxuries created for the homes of art patrons by craftsmen who were also poets in their various plastic ways and who no doubt more truly resembled our modern artists than the great architects and sculptors of the time of Phidias."

For me one of the many inspiriting things about Duncan was the extreme interest and enjoyment he had in my painting (and which he maintained to the end of his life). I remember that at first I could hardly believe the interest he took, it was so remarkable and stimulating. He always had something by me hanging in the gallery and held at least eight one-man shows of my work there between 1927–1965. Also he was genuinely pleased when I had exhibitions in New York or other cities. He was so forthright and sincere — he never could dissemble for long! — that all this interest genuinely did me good and was exceedingly constructive.

Duncan himself painted in the summers for some years from the late twenties through the early forties. It was irresistible and inevitable that he should, and wise besides. The results were some delightful canvases, deeply personal and full of feeling, with an innate sense of color and design. In the process of painting we both tried to criticize or comment on each other's work only if *asked*, agreeing that it was all important that each make his or her own decisions; and we came to be able to take or leave criticism or praise as we saw fit.

I was lucky that Duncan enjoyed having a painter perpetually around. He especially enjoyed my landscapes and though we both were strongly enthusiastic about the many good things (often great) being done in abstract or semi-abstract painting, he never suggested that I change to the more fashionable approach of the period. Actually he regretted (as I did) that there was not more realistic painting of style and distinction being done. We both had a longing that art throughout the world should carry on all sorts of realism, along with the many kinds of abstraction; and of course all good realism that is art has inherent in it the abstract qualities: measure, interval, rhythm, order, balance, etc., and then some.

Also I feel about my work what Bonnard expressed when he was asked why he did not become a cubist. He said that he often sat in on their councils and greatly admired what many were doing; adding however, "It is not for me."

MAIN GALLERY, PHILLIPS MEMORIAL GALLERY

5

PIERRE BONNARD

In the early twenties Duncan was a decade ahead of other museums and collectors in this country in his appreciation of Pierre Bonnard. America took a long time to catch up with the vast importance of Bonnard, because it was so enamored and influenced by Picasso and Matisse and their "strong" and more obvious followers. In comparison Bonnard was thought to be a little "soft" or "a leftover impressionist." Actually he was one of the strongest, most original and inventive of all the post-impressionists and his works are now among the most sought after paintings of this period. America has at last recognized his great importance as a draughtsman, especially in such rare and delightful works as his beautiful illustrations of *Daphnis and Chloe* and *Histoires Naturelles.* As one indication, Bonnard's canvases now sell for as much or more than those of the painters who were supposed to overshadow him. It is dramatic to realize that a large Bonnard which we acquired for the gallery in the twenties for eleven thousand dollars was recently loaned to an exhibition at an insurance value of five hundred thousand dollars.

Bonnard's avid, unremitting study of nature and his use of it in his highly organized, almost mural designs, his movement in space, his unexpected color juxtapositions and delectable dissonances, his very unpretentiousness — all are the marks of a master. I remember when my husband spotted the first Bonnard he bought, at the Carnegie International Exhibition at Pittsburgh in 1924. It was the painting "Woman with Dog" and it stood out like a jewel in that vast exhibition. After that we developed a passion for his work and acquired at least nine others for the gallery during the nineteen twenties. Still others followed in later

Pierre Bonnard (1867–1947). *Early Spring*, 34½ x 52

years. If you have a Bonnard it is *impossible* to trade or sell it. It keeps unfolding and has a quality of life that is entrancing.

We did not meet Bonnard personally until 1926, when our friend Homer Saint-Gaudens persuaded him to be a juror for the International of that year at the Carnegie Institute Museum in Pittsburgh. As director, Saint-Gaudens always took the foreign members of his juries to Washington and New York. I remember that on their visit to the Phillips Collection there were usually one or two show-off members, but Bonnard struck us as having absolute artistic integrity.

I must say, though, that much to our consternation he wanted to change a whole area in one of his paintings "Early Spring" (done back in 1911), and asked if I could let him have some paint and brushes. We had come from our country place in Pennsylvania to meet him, so I had a good alibi — that all my paints were either locked up or in the country! Fortunately, he never got around to the repainting.

At the time we met him, Bonnard was slim, of medium height, with dark hair and eyes. We thought his eyes were the brightest (except perhaps Brancusi's) and keenest we had ever seen. He wore a dark, almost black suit with a very French cut. With his rather shy dignity and quiet self-assurance, it would not have mattered to him if he had received no attention whatsoever. But Duncan and he took to each other almost immediately and talked with great interest while touring the collection. Bonnard was a bit limited in the scope of his appreciation and like many artists stuck especially to canvases close to his own way of seeing. Among the collection's American paintings hanging at that time, Twachtman's "Summer" and "Emerald Pool" were his main enthusiasms — especially the latter, which he really loved.

When Duncan asked him to look at half a dozen of my paintings, which we stood around the floor in a small gallery, he seemed to enjoy the work and kindly gave a few Bonnardian suggestions. "Draw more," he said. "Get the *character*." "Do you *love* flowers?" He liked best a picnic scene I had done in Ebensburg, with imaginary figures in the foreground and an imagined river in the distance.

Pierre Bonnard (1867–1947). *Circus Rider*, 10¾ x 13¾

Pierre Bonnard (1867–1947). *Narrow Street in Paris*, 15⅛ x 8⅜

Pierre Bonnard (1867–1947). *Woman with Dog*, 27 x 15½

Pierre Bonnard (1867–1947). *The Open Window,* 46½ x 37½

Pierre Bonnard (1867–1947). *The Palm*, 44 x 57½

Duncan and I treasured the experience of having him at the gallery and afterwards at lunch with Homer Saint-Gaudens. There was so much good talk. Bonnard spoke of Van Gogh as a "grand maître"; Rouault he thought "trop fort." He said that Monet was the artist to whom he owed most: he had learned a vast amount from Monet's intellectual approach, his innovations, and his subtle sensibility.

We were charmed when he ordered dessert and said it was important to him to try the great American "ah-pul" pie. Like most Frenchmen he appreciated food, and Saint-Gaudens told us that in the dining car coming from Pittsburgh he was so intrigued with our American club sandwiches that he made a little outline drawing or chart of their structure.

That evening Duncan attended a stag dinner in honor of the Carnegie jury at the Chevy Chase Club. After dinner Bonnard and Duncan had a delightful hour talking together. Duncan asked him if he admired Debussy and if the composer had had some influence on his work. Ah yes! Bonnard considered him a very good friend and agreed that his work well might show Debussy's influence. Bonnard always said that people would be blind, deaf and dumb if they showed no influences. He was witty and charming to be with, and Duncan was elated with pleasure when he returned that evening. During his short stay in America Bonnard was quoted as saying that he particularly liked American men. I am sure Duncan Phillips was one of them.

The Phillips Collection and the family eventually came to own sixteen Bonnard oils and four drawings, as well as lithographs. Of all these I believe the painting "The Riviera" was Duncan's favorite. He never tired of delighting in it visually, or of singing its praises. Next perhaps came "The Open Window," rare and wonderful indeed in color; and I like to quote Yehudi Menuhin's remark before it: "It has such marvelous, perfect *intervals*." Also Duncan's first purchase "Woman with Dog" always remained very high in his estimation. Of "The Palm" (1926), a masterpiece, he wrote:

This is one of Pierre Bonnard's most important canvases. . . . It goes beyond Monet into lyrical Expressionism. Such Enchantment of Vision as he possessed cannot be charted, can only be enjoyed if one has any part of his sensitivity and love of life. Note the violet figure standing in shadow against the full orchestra of light and color. He needed the cool violet as a foil to the orange and green and wanted the spectator to be in the picture

August 1931

Dear Mr. Phillips:

Today I received your book through the kind attention of Mr. de Hauke who personally brought it to me, in which you describe and characterize your collection. In it I see again with great pleasure reproductions of many of the paintings which I had admired so much in your gallery. I am touched by the interest you take in my painting despite the many great faults that I myself find in them. I always work with the hope of correcting my style or way of painting, and I am not at all indifferent to the knowledge that certain (kindred) souls follow me in this effort.

I keep happy memories of my visit to your gallery and often think of the enjoyable painting of your charming wife, who, it seems to me, should continue to cultivate her gift.

With kind regards,
P. Bonnard

Later, during the Second World War, we sent Bonnard photographs of a special exhibition of his paintings which we hung in our upper main gallery. During that long and trying period the collection gave untold pleasure to countless people involved in war work; many of them told us at the time and long after that the gallery, with its domestic setting, became a home to them, which they visited often for a renewal of spirit. Bonnard seemed very pleased at the way the exhibition looked in the photographs and he wrote to thank us (reproduced opposite):

September 28, 1942

Dear Mr. and Mrs. Duncan Phillips

Today Mr. de Hauke brought me your very kind letter. I am extremely grateful for your generous remembrance and as for me I too, often think of my delightful time with you in Washington. Today I also received the photographs of the special exhibition you have put on at this time, of paintings by me in your collection. I thank you for your kind consideration. — I still work despite my age. I imagine Mrs. Duncan Phillips continues to paint as sensitively as in the paintings I saw on my American trip.

With kindest remembrances,
Bonnard

Duncan and I treasured the experience of having him at the gallery and afterwards at lunch with Homer Saint-Gaudens. There was so much good talk. Bonnard spoke of Van Gogh as a "grand maître"; Rouault he thought "trop fort." He said that Monet was the artist to whom he owed most: he had learned a vast amount from Monet's intellectual approach, his innovations, and his subtle sensibility.

We were charmed when he ordered dessert and said it was important to him to try the great American "ah-pul" pie. Like most Frenchmen he appreciated food, and Saint-Gaudens told us that in the dining car coming from Pittsburgh he was so intrigued with our American club sandwiches that he made a little outline drawing or chart of their structure.

That evening Duncan attended a stag dinner in honor of the Carnegie jury at the Chevy Chase Club. After dinner Bonnard and Duncan had a delightful hour talking together. Duncan asked him if he admired Debussy and if the composer had had some influence on his work. Ah yes! Bonnard considered him a very good friend and agreed that his work well might show Debussy's influence. Bonnard always said that people would be blind, deaf and dumb if they showed no influences. He was witty and charming to be with, and Duncan was elated with pleasure when he returned that evening. During his short stay in America Bonnard was quoted as saying that he particularly liked American men. I am sure Duncan Phillips was one of them.

The Phillips Collection and the family eventually came to own sixteen Bonnard oils and four drawings, as well as lithographs. Of all these I believe the painting "The Riviera" was Duncan's favorite. He never tired of delighting in it visually, or of singing its praises. Next perhaps came "The Open Window," rare and wonderful indeed in color; and I like to quote Yehudi Menuhin's remark before it: "It has such marvelous, perfect *intervals*." Also Duncan's first purchase "Woman with Dog" always remained very high in his estimation. Of "The Palm" (1926), a masterpiece, he wrote:

This is one of Pierre Bonnard's most important canvases. . . . It goes beyond Monet into lyrical Expressionism. Such Enchantment of Vision as he possessed cannot be charted, can only be enjoyed if one has any part of his sensitivity and love of life. Note the violet figure standing in shadow against the full orchestra of light and color. He needed the cool violet as a foil to the orange and green and wanted the spectator to be in the picture and to pass around and look over the shoulder of this incidental attractively arresting person, to the red roofs, the over arching palm — the distant sea. Bonnard's mastery of color has never been surpassed. His feeling for time passing and for the abundance of nature carries us back to Giorgione.

There were two practices of Bonnard's which became well known: his "continuous constant observation" and his way of attaching perhaps a whole roll of canvas to his *wall* where he was painting. On it he would often start several pictures and fix their boundaries later. We sometimes wondered if this technique might not be one reason why even the smallest Bonnard painting has a mural quality and keeps its plane on a wall so well. In his youth Bonnard often painted before nature, but he later worked more and more indoors from notes and "remembered" observation.

As a member of the Carnegie jury Bonnard had fought hard for the first prize to go to his friend Roussel, for a small painting called "Faun and Nymphs under a Tree." However, it only received the second prize, whereas a large academic nonentity of a painting received the first prize. My uncle Gifford Beal who was also on the jury, voted as Bonnard did, for Roussel.

When the exhibition opened in October, Duncan purchased the Roussel, a little beauty. I remember we ran into an artist friend, Robert Spencer, at that show who was walking on air because Bonnard had admired the beautiful handling of grays in his street scene in the exhibition. Our collection has a large unit of Spencer's work and already had several at that time.

For years Bonnard would not hold exhibitions at his Paris dealers unless Roussel *and* Vuillard were included. Vuillard's work was marvelous in that early period when he lived at home with his fat, little dressmaker mother. He would paint interiors — usually with her in them among her stuffs and materials — which had great style and a rather austere originality. Intricately patterned wallpaper fascinated him and sometimes a figure would seem to merge into the whole pattern of the wall. The Phillips Collection has two splendid Vuillards of that period, "The Newspaper" and "Woman Sweeping."

When Duncan's book *The Artist Sees Differently* was published in 1931, he sent a copy to Bonnard and received a note of thanks (reproduced opposite). The following is a translation:

Monsieur

J'ai eu par les soins de M.
de Hauke que me la affecte
un mon votre lettre qui
décrit votre collection. J'ai
beaucoup de plaisir à m'expliquer
et beaucoup de la valeur que
j'avais toujours donné aux
gravures de m. Touche. De
l'intérêt que vous pour a
ma peinture malgré que grands
efforts que M. Bonnard j'ai
toujours été à faire
de comprendre ma manière
et il ne m'est pas indifférent
de savoir que certains estiment
me suivent dans cet effort

J'ai gardé un bon
souvenir de ma visite
à votre atelier et j'eus
vu mieux a l'avenir
pourtant de votre charmant
femme que a du couteaux
à cultiver les vous

Veuillez lui mon
respectueux souvenir et
croyez à mes meilleurs
sentiments

Vuillard

Bonnard
16 bis rue Caulaincourt Paris

13

Dear Mr. Phillips:

Today I received your book through the kind attention of Mr. de Hauke who personally brought it to me, in which you describe and characterize your collection. In it I see again with great pleasure reproductions of many of the paintings which I had admired so much in your gallery. I am touched by the interest you take in my painting despite the many great faults that I myself find in them. I always work with the hope of correcting my style or way of painting, and I am not at all indifferent to the knowledge that certain (kindred) souls follow me in this effort.

I keep happy memories of my visit to your gallery and often think of the enjoyable painting of your charming wife, who, it seems to me, should continue to cultivate her gift.

With kind regards,
P. Bonnard

Later, during the Second World War, we sent Bonnard photographs of a special exhibition of his paintings which we hung in our upper main gallery. During that long and trying period the collection gave untold pleasure to countless people involved in war work; many of them told us at the time and long after that the gallery, with its domestic setting, became a home to them, which they visited often for a renewal of spirit. Bonnard seemed very pleased at the way the exhibition looked in the photographs and he wrote to thank us (reproduced opposite):

September 28, 1942

Dear Mr. and Mrs. Duncan Phillips

Today Mr. de Hauke brought me your very kind letter. I am extremely grateful for your generous remembrance and as for me I too, often think of my delightful time with you in Washington. Today I also received the photographs of the special exhibition you have put on at this time, of paintings by me in your collection. I thank you for your kind consideration. — I still work despite my age. I imagine Mrs. Duncan Phillips continues to paint as sensitively as in the paintings I saw on my American trip.

With kindest remembrances,
Bonnard

28 Septembre

Monsieur et Madame Duncan Philipps

J'ai reçu par l'entremise de Mr de Hauke une
lettre très amicale de vous — Je suis
bien sensible à votre bon souvenir et moi
je pense souvent à votre aimable accueil
à Wasington — Il vient de m'arriver
aujourd'hui des photographies d'une
exposition de mes tableaux faite
par vos soins Je vous remercie de
votre délicate attention — Je travaille
encore malgré mon age — Je pense que
Madame Duncan Philipps continue
à faire sa peinture si délicate comme
je l'ai vue ie mon voyage d'Amérique
    Croyez a mon bon souvenir

        P Bonnard

Pierre Bonnard
Villa du Bosquet
le Cannet
    A M

Pierre Bonnard (1867–1947). *Movement of the Street*, 14 x 19

When we later asked Bonnard to write the dates of his paintings on the backs of a group of photographs we sent him, he kept them for a very long time. He finally returned the photographs but often with double dates written on the back; e.g., "1915–1925," which meant that he had worked on a painting from time to time, often putting on a few last touches ten years after it was started. What captivated us was that he had even spent time making experiments and corrections on the photographs. On many he had put accents or stronger lines here and there. On the photograph of "The Riviera" (Duncan's favorite) Bonnard had drawn stronger contours in pen and ink on the distant mountain edges, perhaps to bring them up to the picture plane.

I remember Bonnard saying that his dealer Bernheim–Jeune had an exhibition of his work every two years, and that about a dozen new canvases were always required from him. It made us happy to know that at last Bonnard had come into his own. We were fascinated by one story about him told to us at the war's end. During the Occupation the French artists had a hard time keeping aloof from the Pétain government and German connoisseurs; and some did not succeed. We heard that during that trying period Bonnard was asked to do a portrait of Marshal Pétain. He hedged and hedged but they kept after him so that finally he thought of a way out. He said they must understand that he always reserved the right in any portrait he did (even after it was paid for) of recalling it at any time to work it over as he desired. The Pétain officials tired of these discussions and Bonnard was freed of the commission they were trying to force on him.

Another amusing anecdote concerned a French actress who stopped at Le Cannet to see Bonnard's work, having just come from seeing Rouault and his work. She reported to Bonnard that Rouault had said, "In my recent painting I find that 'Je me Bonnardise.'" Bonnard looked surprised, thought a minute and answered, "Il faut que je me Rouaultise."

His final picture was of a blossoming almond tree done in brushwork very like one of the peach trees from John Marin's orchards, and revealing a close kinship to Marin's inspired improvisation.

I remember Duncan reading with delight a passage from Claude Anet on Bonnard: "While it would seem that I should have become accustomed to his enchanting talent, this amazing man manages each time to surprise and move me. . . . If we reflect on the matter, it is really a surprising thing, and it indicates a rare power of renewal in Pierre Bonnard. This is the most precious of all gifts."

In the foreword for a small loan exhibition we had in 1958 of paintings by Bonnard, Duncan wrote:

The death in 1947 of Pierre Bonnard (still painting at top peak) has at last established for him recognition as one of the greatest painters of the twentieth century. His indifference to publicity and his independence from the more conspicuous trends of his contemporaries had retarded his acceptance by a self-conscious period which in spite of its many-mindedness, is nevertheless inattentive to the lone individual in its attraction to group movements. Bonnard's free spirit has now been revealed as one of the greatest sources of inspiration to freedom from formula. It is no less clear that all through his life he had been pointing the way of liberation from all extra pictorial irrelevance. He was in a very real sense a pure painter. Yet he was also a prophet of much that we call modern. . . .

Born in 1867, the son of a government official, he studied law to please his father and it was not until after he had sold an advertising poster which Lautrec admired that he was permitted to enter the Ecole des Beaux-Arts. Later at the Académie Julian he met Denis, Vuillard and Roussel.

Attracted to Japanese prints in the little shops of Paris, he decided to adapt their lively patterns of line and their harmonious patches of color to depictions of Parisian boulevards, cafés and circuses. The low toned street scenes and interiors which Bonnard and Vuillard painted in the 1890's were enlivened by a few bright notes of accented color. There was an inner resistance in both the young Intimists to the theories of Denis and Sérusier and to the exotic appeal of Gauguin. They persisted in looking around them indoors and out. They limited their observation to their homes and families and to the neighbors they knew best in city and country. All his life Bonnard was to be consistent in one aim, to preserve through many revisions and elaborations the first mental image and the first ardent, spontaneously expressive urge. His was an art of immediate impressions and then of long and loving recollections and refinements which kept the freshness of the first conceptual sketch.

In later years there was one painting which Duncan especially wanted for the collection — a painting which spoke to him with a poignant message of reality and strange beauty. It was Bonnard's "Circus Horse," and he tried very hard to purchase it; but it belonged to Bonnard's nephew, Charles Terrasse. Bonnard had given it to his nephew because he had liked and understood it so well when it was painted in 1946. Understandably Terrasse could not part with it and probably he also wanted to keep it in France. But he and his wife did a wonderfully kind thing. While lunching with us at our home in 1964 and knowing of my husband's touching appreciation of the painting, Terrasse said he would lend it to hang in the gallery for a season, or in our home. Duncan decided to share it with others and it created in many hearts an affection close to that which he felt for it. In an article on Pierre Bonnard published in the *Kenyon Review* of Autumn 1949, Duncan wrote of this painting:

. . . Bonnard's art in essence continued to the end very much as it began. Yet his genius developed in his latest phase into an ecstatic Expressionism, attaining during the twenty years 1927–1947 to an indisputable greatness.

Pierre Bonnard (1867–1947). *The Riviera*, 31 x 30

One of his last works was a unique masterpiece, unique for so blithe an artist, tinged as it is with a melancholy of introspection and compassionate tenderness. It portrays a wise, white circus horse, his long nose and neck a pyramidal shape, his searching eyes a symbol of the little more than animal that is still a little less than human. The background of burnt orange, red, blue and brown, reveals a sunlit stable truly sublimated by the artist's tribute.

6

DOVE, STIEGLITZ AND MARIN

WHEN Duncan and I were in New York, we often visited An American Place, the midtown gallery established by Alfred Stieglitz after he gave up the famous 291, opened in 1905, where he had been one of the very first in the United States to exhibit Picasso, Matisse, and other European modernists. In his high-up, bare, office-building showrooms (flooded with light and containing just one metal chair!) Stieglitz held alternating exhibitions of Arthur Dove, John Marin and Georgia O'Keeffe — the three artists he had narrowed down to when he decided to show only American paintings. A few of his own magnificent, pioneering photographs were also on the walls.

ARTHUR DOVE, 1880–1946

Arthur Dove's work appealed to Duncan from his first exposure to it in 1922. There was a tang and originality, a simplification and large feeling about his painting which Duncan responded to wholeheartedly. Dove had very few patrons in those days when he was experimenting with his highly personalized abstractions.

After graduating from Cornell, Dove had won immediate success illustrating fiction for magazines. But after a chance encounter with Stieglitz in New York and the famous gallery at 291, about 1910, following his own discovery in Paris in 1908 of Picasso, Braque and Gris (and especially of their collages), he decided to devote himself to painting and went to work on a farm far from gallery distractions, close to nature and the elements. But success as a painter was slow to come, and Duncan, because of his sincere admiration for and understanding of what Dove was trying so independently and bravely to achieve, subsidized him to quite an extent for a number of years, and had first choice of one or two of Dove's paintings each year.

Duncan wrote of Dove:

His work life was changed when, in Paris, he discovered that the potentialities of abstract pattern would enable him to create plastic equivalents to "various conditions of light" and to the interesting variety of shapes and textures to be found anywhere. The intrinsic character of each object challenged him to a typical metamorphosis in which its essence persisted. And he would find a rural environment which would be his research laboratory and his haven of creative independence. All his inspiration as an artist would be drawn from his simple life close to the soil and the stars. This design for living was undertaken and sustained against stern parental antagonism and persistent public indifference. The liberating sponsorship of Stieglitz, with the chance to show his progress once a year for a few who understood and cared and purchased, was all that he needed.

In the catalogue for a Dove exhibition at our gallery in 1937, Duncan made this early and perceptive comment on Dove:

Isolated on his farm, far from the city's art movements and art politics, he is intimate with the sun and the soil and with the rough-hewn objects of his daily use. In his creations the form and the substance are one. All his inspiration as an artist is drawn from his simple life and his surprising thoughts as a man. It is his stubborn plan to achieve a unity, a synthesis of his own material and spiritual resources in complete independence from the mass minded collectivist world. Consequently he is a lonely person and both his serious vision and his humorous caprice seem strange to those accustomed to a more urban, cosmopolitan and worldly point of view. What he wants for himself is an intimate understanding of the rural environment.

Many an artist wrote or spoke to Duncan in the confiding tone of these early letters from Arthur Dove:

Halesite, N.Y.
November 1927

Dear Mr. Phillips:

Your interest in my paintings leaves me free to tell you that I think a vital step has been taken in modern expression in the later ones.

Yesterday on seeing the new paintings hung together for the

Arthur G. Dove (1880–1946). *Cows in Pasture*, 20 x 28

first time I felt that there was beauty there that had gone much farther toward a new reality of my own.

I feel that you should and will go to see them

Yours truly,
Arthur G. Dove

Halesite, N.Y.
February 1928

Dear Mr. Phillips:

Thank you for your letter. Of course I am delighted by the way both you and Mrs. Phillips have shown your generosity of spirit in coming again to room 303. It was fine of you to do it just the way you did.

Apropos of mediums mentioned in your letter — both you and Georgia O'Keeffe have shown a delightful tendency recently which amuses me very much. She has often spoken of wanting to see more of my work in pastel while your preference seems to be oil.

However she is the owner of "Rain" and "The Sewing Machine" and now you have "The Sail Boat." All three of them being composed wholly or partially of actual substances [collages, all].

Of course that does not preclude doing the finest thing yet in either medium but the fact did interest me. . . .

Arthur G. Dove

[undated, probably 1932–33]

Dear Mr. Phillips:

This is in the nature of an S.O.S. as I have just attempted to draw a very small check on the estate in Geneva [his parents'] and it comes back marked no funds, which happens to be a good portrait of me just now.

There is a man there willing to give a small mortgage on the home, but at present I am unable to get there as my brother has drawn everything from the bank. As soon as I can get there some different arrangement will have to be made.

Knowing your vital interest in the development of the whole idea, I am anxious to know when the work can go forward. Time makes a march on us while we are marking time and I have the dread of losing any moments.

Perhaps you are in Chicago (at the Century of Progress Exposition) with the paintings and did not receive the last letter?

Would love to see the things there, especially some few. They tell me you have the finest Renoir in existence. I hope so.

Mrs. Dove and I send our best thoughts to you and Mrs. Phillips. My address will be Halesite, N.Y., until I can raise enough funds to drive to Geneva, after that Geneva, N.Y. is sufficient.

Thanking you again for your generous offer, I am

Sincerely,
Arthur G. Dove

Duncan was really excited about Dove's work and loved having it around at home or in the gallery:

May 3, 1933

Dear Arthur Dove:

I am having a grand time enjoying the paintings from your last exhibition which Stieglitz was good enough to send down so that I could study them at leisure. I want to write an article about your work, for which I have the greatest sympathy and admiration. There is an elemental something in your abstractions, they start from nature and personal experience and they are free from the fashionable mannerisms of the hyper aesthetic and cerebral preciosity of Paris. Your color thrills me and your craftsmanship in the making of sumptuous surfaces and edges. It is a sharp distress to me that I cannot get three or four of the pictures that were sent down. Unless I succeed in selling a valuable painting which is now under consideration at a museum, I may find it impossible to get more than one and would even have to ask your indulgence in paying for that. The Sun Drawing Water seems to us all to have the largest number of fine qualities, but the best passage of painting you have ever done is contained in the painting entitled "The Bessie of New York" * . . .

Sincerely,
Duncan Phillips

Again Dove writes:

1934

Dear Mr. Phillips:

Fortunately we sold a small piece of ground next us and out of that paid the taxes on this place as we had to. So here we are free for a year at least.

I might add that your letter gave me so much encouragement that the paintings are developing at a much swifter pace. I can hardly tell you the situation here. It is most difficult. But the light you throw on from the outside, I really mean the inside is unusually fine and I know will make everything possible. Some day I may be able to tell you what you have done. In the mean time I am thanking you and Mrs. Phillips tremendously.

Truly,
Arthur G. Dove

* Unfortunately the "Bessie of New York" was traded in later for an Arthur Dove Duncan liked even more!

Arthur G. Dove (1880–1946). *Rain or Snow*, 35 x 25

Arthur G. Dove (1880–1946). *Flour Mill II*, 1938, 26 x 16

Although we only met Dove once (in 1936), he sent Duncan many touching letters of appreciation. He had a vigorous, charming personality. When Stieglitz brought us together at An American Place, Dove said he felt he had to celebrate the occasion, so he was wearing the suit in which he had been married some years back, even though it was too tight. I remember he talked about his use of musical principle — rhythms, measures and intervals — in his paintings.

Perhaps Duncan's favorite of the Dove paintings purchased for the collection, one which is always hanging, is the "Flour Mill II." I very much like what he wrote about it for *The Arts* magazine:

In his *Flour Mill* Arthur Dove made a Chinese "character" out of square, modulated brush strokes of pure color, yellow, deep blue, brown and black on an ivory white. It is chromatic calligraphy of vibrant and dynamic power which symbolizes a condition of intense light at an exciting moment of time. It communicates the exhilaration of sunshine at high noon, of gleaming chimneys with smoke and sun-drenched factory walls with cast shadows. The source of the technique might be traced back to a memory of Kandinsky of 1912, when his improvisations were in colored shapes of dark and light brush strokes, the sum of which was a high powered landscape abstraction. Dove had grown beyond explosive pyrotechnics. This arabesque has not only movement but a certain majesty. This is a return of the abstract symbol into the original impression until the two are one.

Other canvases in the collection by Dove which Duncan particularly admired through the years were "Rise of the Full Moon," a collage entitled "Goin' Fishin'," "Waterfall," "Huntington Harbor I," "Golden Storm," "Rain or Snow," and "Cows in Pasture." This last is a beauty. Duncan reveled in its rich, rare color and pattern, and treasured it greatly. He liked to point out that it had the very essence of a cow's world about it, "with nothing but pasture on the cow's brain, and rich lush grass to lie in."

Duncan's discovery of Arthur G. Dove in 1922 was important to his evolution as a critic and collector. "At that time," as he wrote, "I still had the writer's attraction to painters whose special qualities could be interpreted and perhaps even recreated in words. Fascinated from the first by Dove's unique vision, I found that I was being drawn to an artist because his appeal was exclusively visual, because his whimsically imaginative images were inseparable from his resourceful craftsmanship. He was so unstandardized that in his own period he embarrassed

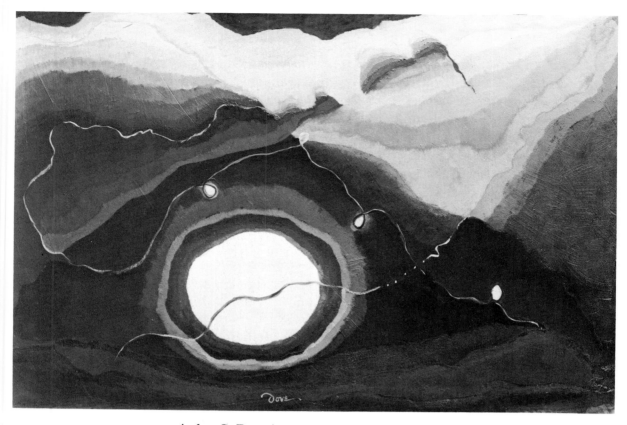

Arthur G. Dove (1880–1946). *Rise of the Full Moon*, 18 x 26

the literary critics, and even the painters and teachers of painting who deal in theories and group movements."

The best of Dove's paintings hold up superbly with the years. Many collectors have now bought his work and exhibitions of it are held steadily and with pride by museums and university galleries. We seem to be constantly lending his paintings for exhibitions throughout the United States.

In 1958 a large Arthur G. Dove Retrospective Exhibition was organized by the art galleries of the University of California at Los Angeles. It was shown by seven participating museums, of which the Phillips Gallery (as it was then called) was second on the list. Duncan wrote the foreword for the catalogue and Frederick S. Wight the text.

Duncan's short essay on Arthur Dove was included in *New Directions* annual, Number Eleven, in 1949, published by his cousin James Laughlin. A quotation from it follows:

Arthur G. Dove was one of the few lyrical individualists among the many contemporary painters of abstraction. His paintings are visual poetry,

Arthur G. Dove (1880–1946). *Huntington Harbor I*, collage, 12 x 9½

or more accurately visual music. It is difficult to communicate in words a sense of their distinction and delight. One cannot analyze Dove as one can the cerebral theorists and the diagrammatic designers. His art is as different from the spacially geometrical cubists and from the precisely proportioned Purists as it is from the complicated literary painters of Surrealism. He was never theoretical, never literary, never anything but painterly and sincere.

ALFRED STIEGLITZ, 1864–1946

Alfred Stieglitz, in whose galleries we first saw Dove's work about 1926, was a force in art in America. Duncan admired greatly his single-minded dedication toward his goal of making better known the three American artists whose work he liked best. Also he shared his faith in American art; and felt that Stieglitz was a true artist in photography. After his death in 1946 Duncan wrote this appreciation:

He challenged the misconception that a photograph must remain mechanical and he affirmed that by a camera's mechanism an artist can produce miracles of sensitized individual perception and interpretation while remaining true to the medium's sharpened focus and its concern with objective truth. His own creations — especially the clouds with moon, are proof of his claim.

Stieglitz believed that John Marin's watercolors were the best ever painted. He priced them accordingly, refusing to wait for time to confirm his opinion. He denied that a watercolor is less important than an oil, also that the size of a work of art is a measure of its value.

He affirmed that a place is the habitation of a pervading spirit. A few bare rooms of an office building in midtown Manhattan could be vibrant with the personalities of great people of our own period — great painters whose works he could hang on the walls — whose lives he had liberated from commercial compromise by this constant support and selfless sponsorship. The power of works of art to expand the lives of those who are made ready to enjoy them, this he proved every day and in so doing he affirmed the inviolable integrity and the human fellowship of art as an ideal.

I will miss Stieglitz poignantly at An American Place where I trust that somehow his work can be carried on. Even though he will never come out again from his little office to greet the old friend or the fellow worker or to fight the never-ending fight against the cynic or the Philistine — yet his challenging and affirming spirit and his crusading zeal cannot be forgotten or forsaken. What he did for Marin will live on in the immortality of Marin. Such work is never finished. There is always the inspiration afforded for another conceivable collaboration of two artists who trust and supplement each other.

My wife and I could go to see the annual Marins, and O'Keeffes and Doves, and we knew that the exhibitions would be like no others anywhere since there, in the midst of the pictures, an ancient prophet with white hair and dark, burning, searching eyes would stand guard over the latest creations of his friends to defend them from deprecation as if to protect them from defilement. Magnetic, hypnotic, fanatic if you will, aggressive if necessary, Stieglitz was also and essentially mellow, serene and kind. I think that he knew we were allies in the same Cause; that we also had an "experiment station" as well as an intimate gallery where art can be at home. We became very fond of him and grateful for his appreciation of what we did which was manifested in many ways we will long remember. When we were together in his gallery there was little time for exchange of thoughts for we were all eyes and so was he and we understood and respected our separate purposes and functions. The challenging idealism and technical distinction of the grand old man, the selective and mystical magic of his camera, the tonic vitality of the paintings by the three artists of his choice, each a master of his particular instrument, made an ever deepening impression on us. We knew An American Place as a source of inspiration.

JOHN MARIN, 1870–1953

Another American artist in whose work Duncan took endless delight was John Marin. The collection has twenty-one of his paintings, acquired gradually from the mid-twenties to the mid-fifties.

As in the case of Dove, Duncan met Marin at An American Place, and their friendship steadily grew. Duncan's first estimate of Marin's work appeared in *A Collection in the Making*, published in 1926:

An epigrammatic poet painter who flashes images of swift suggestion with an inspirational "wash" of watercolors on white paper. He sings of vibrant skies and moving earth forms and luminous, veiled or sharply defined distances. The color accents are intuitive. What seems to be accident or casual caprice proves on close study to be constructive intention. As Paul Rosenfeld has expressed it, Marin has implicit confidence in his senses and in his own swiftness of decision and execution. The medium of which he is a supreme master precludes hesitations. And yet this Marin who speaks emotionally or not at all, whose works are "immediate realizations," is more than an improvising wizard. With his amazing intuition he hints at strange truths freshly apprehended. He puts down a world out of focus as it seems in a suddenly leveled glance into distance — the centre of vision alone

John Marin (1870–1953). *Fifth Avenue at Forty-second Street*, 28 x 36½

clear — the rest, blotches and indefinite masses of color. He gave us, more-over, the quickened sense of our intense modern life in the midst of en-circling and bewildering elements. He is a modernist in his emotional tempo even more truly than in his technique, which is akin to the consummate calligraphy of the great Chinese designers. Sooner or later one cannot evade the thought, "Is this Marin one of the far-sought, important men?" When-ever he misses his aim his effects seem slight or incoherent. He is not afraid to fail, since he is frankly experimenting on the frontiers of visual consciousness. When he succeeds he is an impressive master of space and light, and of the dynamics of color. Watery sunshine seeps through silver-edged clouds with a magical spread of radiance. Far-away islands make a clear call to our romancing imagination from the blur of the near and from the world that cannot hold us. There are whimsical notions about the agitation of objects as we look beyond them or rush by them in our headlong way. Webs that are almost diaphanous alternate with "electric moments of vision." Downtown New York is sensed as a world rocking with the throbs of energy.

Whether or not we like this staccato expressionism we must concede that it grows out of our age. French descent — Yankee birth and independence — training as an architect — the influence of Whistler — then of the Chinese — then of Cézanne and Stieglitz — that is the story. "Grey Sea" is as weighty and as powerful as a Homer, — as rare in its reserve of tone as a Whistler — and more intense, more shaggy and elemental than either. The method, however, is so brusque that we are kept at a distance. Marin is one of the most provoking, challenging innovators since Cézanne.

Duncan and I delighted in John Marin's visits to Washington. For some years he came frequently to see his elderly stepmother, of whom he was very fond, and his stepbrother Commander Bittinger. He would either stay with them or with us; sometimes he came alone, and sometimes with his wife.

Everything that Marin said had a touch of the unusual about it. His appearance was equally distinctive — long dark bangs, straight long hair, and Burgundian features. When he was pleased with something, his voice had a melodious depth and timbre, a mellow vital blend of wit and enthusiasm. But if he were in a critical mood, it could have quite a sting. Marin was a law unto himself; but he lived for his art, which was the central meaning, joy and excitement of his life. He enjoyed looking at other artists' paintings of any period, *if* they spoke to him in terms of his own work (an attitude close to Bonnard's). Every year when he would come to our gallery or house, Marin would focus his attention on a special painting that spoke to him at that time and not disperse his energy over many. One year it was Constable's "On the River Stour," which he thought magnificent in its dynamics. Another year it was Degas' "Dancers at the Practice Bar," the action of which Duncan described so well as "split second motion and balance." This visit to the Phillips household happened to coincide with V-J day in 1945 — a day when Duncan and I were eager to hear every scrap of war news, since our son Laughlin was in the Philippines — and we asked Marin to join us in listening to the radio. But as he sat in our living room, his eyes became fixed on the "Dancers at the Practice Bar," a painting which had the kind of dynamic movement that he loved and wanted to savor. He could not listen to the array of "generals and politicians" who might

John Marin (1870–1953). *Bryant Square*, 21½ x 26½

talk on the radio that day. He said he would listen to one general only and that was Eisenhower.

I must tell one really funny story about Marin because I am sure he thought of it himself with inner glee. In 1941 on the great occasion of the grand opening reception of Washington's National Gallery, Duncan, as a trustee, volunteered to give one of the dinners before the opening and one of our guests was John Marin. Since it was a large party, our guests left for the reception in several cars. Marin, who was riding with Law Watkins, our associate director, discovered on the way to the museum that he had forgotten his ticket! He had left it at his home in

Francisco Goya (1746–1828). *The Repentant Peter*, 29 x 25½

Cliffside, New Jersey. Law thought quickly and said, "Put on this long raincoat of mine, pull your hair forward and we'll say you're Mrs. Watkins, as my invitation reads Mr. and Mrs." Marin must have looked like an eccentric bluestocking of a woman! The guard did give a peculiarly sharp look, but there was the ticket. He let them pass.

As I look back I think of another painting, Goya's "Repentant Peter" — with Peter portrayed as a stocky peasant-like figure, intense and moving in his attitude of prayer — which Marin singled out for special admiration. After reveling in and studying the painting silently for some time, Marin said, "I wish I could tell that old son of a gun what I think of him for painting that picture! It's like an old tree: it's so nice and rotten ripe."

One time when we were in New York, we invited Oskar Kokoschka to lunch and afterwards went to An American Place to see an exhibition of John Marin's work. Marin was there and so we were present when Marin and the great Austrian painter met for the first time, although they already knew and admired each other's work. We witnessed a charming scene when Marin presented a book, his biography, to Kokoschka and Kokoschka his biography to Marin (both books having come out that year). They gave each other bear hugs in mutual admiration and thanks!

Marin once gave an illuminating talk at the Phillips Gallery on how he approached his work. Using only a few notes, he spoke about his underlying dynamics — how important that the elements of a painting work as the human frame; limbs must be in their sockets, a thrust in one direction begets another to balance it, etc. At our table he loved to illustrate smaller points: "Take these white cuffs at my wrists; how much better they make a man look than if he didn't wear them. So some touch of white — some meaningful, salient accents with style — will enhance a canvas." He would illustrate his concept of dynamics with matches stuck in the edge of a matchbox.

Probably the most exciting time we had with Marin was when we prevailed on him to paint a picture of the view from our terrace. He and his wife, Duncan and I, had just taken an energetic walk in the woods and were sitting resting on our porch looking out over the distant Potomac River when we said we wished we could watch him paint a watercolor.

"Oh," said Marin, "if I start, I'll have to finish it." But all of a sudden he got up, placed his easel beside a small table, asked for a big pail of water, and got his paint box out of the car. Facing southward to the wooded knolls, hills and river, he began to paint. Much to our surprise he worked part of the time with a brush in each hand. One was a fat shaving brush, which he used to soak parts of the wonderful Whatman paper (he always used it for his watercolors) with a good wash of some general color, or with plain water. Gradually he would define things, in keeping with his principles of dynamic structure — force lines, supports, balance, etc.

He did not mind our standing behind him, watching; in fact, he performed with great gusto, like a symphony conductor, and maintained the warmth and dash to the finish, even in the last bits of pencil drawing. He painted rapidly throughout this particular work, using an up-and-down stroke. When we thought an area complete and beautiful, he would add some ravishing stroke of color to enforce, enrich, accent, or subdue it — only he knew. It was an upright watercolor which he gave to us when it was finished.

During the thirties, when Duncan had gotten quite engrossed in his own painting, he showed one of his canvases to John Marin. Marin passed his hand over quite an area of the picture and said he liked it. "You are one of us," he said. As any one can imagine, that was one of Duncan's high spots. Marin seemed to be impressed with the amount we both accomplished, and said once with some surprise, "Why, you two are workers!"

November 8, 1946

Dear Duncan and Marjorie

So you see I am still up here in Maine. So wonderful here. So hard to get away . . .

Well fourteen canvases have received their daubings and of course watercolors. I would like to have a room one hundred feet long with canvases up there on the hundred foot wall, pots of paint and brushes and go to it handling one subject matter throughout, a stepping along from one canvas to the other with different versions and plannings.

Yes I miss dreadfully our Stieglitz. The yearly letters I wrote to him up at Lake George. Then too the bringing back and showing to him the season's output and as to how he looked at them, how he really responded — that even if I could never quite fathom nevertheless there was that something he gave me that was for him to give alone.

As the room is financially taken care of for another year I suppose that I'll have an exhibition maybe beginning some time in the latter part of this month — if so of course I'd let you know — but somehow I don't much care — only for a few including yourselves.

.   .   .   .

Howsome ever, there's your very kind invitation to visit you the which I cherish and will make all effort to accede to — and as you speak of a visit to Cliffside would make me happy — of course if I do have an exhibition the labor connected with that will have to be taken care of — after which — I'll be at your warm disposal.

John Jr. asked me to give to you both his greeting

affectionately
John

Duncan writes again:

March 11, 1947

Mr. John Marin
        243 Clark Terrace
            Cliffside, New Jersey

Dear John:

We enjoyed every moment of your visit and hope it did you as much good as it did us.

Since you left I have been simply swept off my feet by the power and loveliness of the oil entitled "Marin 1945," the one we moved around until we found it beautifully presented as an over-mantel in Gallery D. We were enchanted by it when we visited that exhibition from which we purchased the oil of Tunk Mountain and the watercolor "Blue Sea," and if those two pictures had not been so expensive I would have been tempted to acquire it for the Collection. As I remember Stieglitz had a big price on it and we had to choose between it and Tunk Mountain. For several days I have been trying to decide whether I dare to propose giving up the oil entitled "Cape Split" 1939, for which we paid seven thousand dollars, in an even exchange for this "Marin 1945." I find that it is marked N.F.S. and it may well be that you do not wish to part with it, at least for the present, but it will do no harm for me to ask you whether my idea had any appeal to you since I know how much you are interested in our Gallery and its magnificent Marin Unit. There is nothing among all our Marins quite like its opal-

John Marin (1870–1953). *Grey Sea*, watercolor, 16½ x 20½

escent light and inspired calligraphy. Since it is not clear in my mind who is in charge of the sales of this present exhibition and since I believe you have not yet decided who is to be your dealer, I am writing to you and I know that if you do not wish to attend to business transactions yourself you will refer it to the right person, either Mrs. Halpert, or Georgia O'Keeffe, or perhaps in this case the initiator of the exhibition Mr. Plaut. Of course you will not hesitate to give me a positive no if you do not wish to sell the picture. And if you consider the trade uneven and there would be additional funds needed for the exchange I am afraid that I would have to wait until another year since during the past season we have been so extravagant in getting those two great pictures, the Cézanne and the Rouault. I hate to trouble you for an answer at a time when you are busy with your New York exhibition which, by the way, we fully intend to see. I remember that you said that some of your latest paintings are somewhat in the same style and perhaps we will find a Marin with that same intense and dynamic lyricism and so I will not expect an immediate answer. But when you have a moment please send me a line either suggesting that I write to someone else about the proposed exchange or telling me that you will speak about it to whoever is in charge of the sales. If the picture is definitely not for sale nor to be exchanged for any other I will perfectly understand and count myself fortunate to have enjoyed it so much during these privileged weeks of the exhibition.

I do hope that you and your son enjoyed your visit in Washington and that you got home feeling as well as the morning you left. You have given to us and to many of your friends a lot of pleasure. You and your paintings are one and communicate the same life giving exhilaration.

Affectionately,
Duncan Phillips

The "Marin 1945" remained not for sale and the collection still has the oil "Cape Split" ('39) which luckily has stood the test of time magnificently. In the end Duncan was very glad he had not traded it.

In 1955 Duncan wrote the foreword for the John Marin Memorial Exhibition catalogue published by the Art Galleries, University of California, Los Angeles. He said in his foreword:

John Marin has passed into history. He now takes his place in the story of American painting with Whistler and Homer and Ryder. To each of them he had some affinity: to Whistler in his ability to vignette the pictorial essence of a moment of vision; to Homer in his passion for and knowledge of the sea off the coast of Maine and in his special mastery of watercolor as a medium; and to Ryder in his self reliant invention and his integrity. Marin's telegraphic speed and fresh, exuberant expression may seem at art's opposite pole from Ryder's long cherished dream and labored alchemy — yet for me their basic kinship is very real. They were yankees both and ancient Mariners both — the lonely voyager over the perils of enameled pigments and untraveled, profoundly imaginative designs and the bold adventurer of the moment's intuition who knew all the ways of the sea

Gaston Lachaise (1882–1935). *Head of John Marin*, bronze, 12¼″ high

and who dared to be the intimate, the on-the-spot reporter of the flashing lights, the thrashing waves, the thrusts and tensions for which he knew the axis and the resolving balance. Marin had no equal as a wizard of equilibrium within a space construction of precariously active lines. His dynamism and his spontaneity are, we like to think, American qualities, yet surely no more so than the persistent inner vision of Ryder, whose imagery was less of the adventuring eye and hand than of the withdrawn, contemplative mind. Ryder and Marin were nature poets whose complete absorption with their own intimate sources of inspiration resulted in works of art so different that their only underlying resemblances to each other were their single-minded independence and their regional American expression transcended by intimation of the universal.

We are witnessing a period in art of private symbols and of subconscious calligraphy. It is really a survival of romanticism whether the romance has to do with the exploration of space at the expense of the picture plane or the discovery of drama in design itself. This new manifestation of art for art's sake is called abstract expressionism and becomes fanatical when it is merely automatic writing by a more or less uncontrolled hand. It may be claimed that John Marin, especially in his latest canvases, when he opened up his compositions from their former enclosures extending the rhythms and cross currents around and beyond the frames, anticipated such improvisations, just as the cubists could claim him because of his superimposed planes and the geometrical shapes which he used arbitrarily. Yet whatever he did was independent of all isms and his impetuosity was that of a poet painter who used abbreviations and formal idioms either as means to convey his visual sensations or of extending the painter's expressive freedoms. His genius for explosions of line and color, especially in the Manhattan street scenes was dedicated to the theme of energy. Marin regarded himself as a lyrical realist, which of course he was, although an expressionist rather than an impressionist by temperament. His triangle for a pine or his zigzag for a wave was crisply, almost colloquially descriptive and the rectangles and the handsome hieroglyphics with which he played were frankly decorative and never abstract or automatic. Mere illusion was seldom, if ever, his aim even in the representative landscapes of Maine, New Hampshire and New Mexico. He wished to paint "after nature's example" and with an intensified economy of means appropriate to the tempo of his period. It is true that he aspired to the abstract condition of music, that he wished to make his art as structural and sequential as Bach. "That is the kind of music my piano likes to have played on it," he remarked to MacKinley Helm when his visitor, who later became his biographer, found him practising his favorite composer in the glassed-in veranda of his cottage by the sea. "Did you note how the little tunes struck at each other? Balance and Force." Just as his piano

John Marin (1870–1953). *Spring No. 1*, 1953, 22 x 28. How often the
last pictures by older artists are of blossoming trees! This was painted
during Marin's last year — an exquisite work!

liked that kind of music so his paper had its own enjoyment. "You just put
down a color that the paper will like." This reveals that Marin was not only
an expressionist but a virtuoso in love with watercolor, his favorite instrument. Later in such oils as the musically organized Tunk Mountain in Autumn he was equally solicitous for the special needs of the canvas and the
colors. For a half century of research and urgency he experimented on the
frontiers of visual consciousness and his ardours amounted to a joyous dynamic pantheism. Far from escaping from our tragic world into abstraction
he seemed to challenge fate with an ever brave and debonair philosophy of
design.

John Marin (1870–1953). *Maine Islands*, 16¾ x 20

7

THE MUSEUM DEVELOPS

THE nineteen twenties with their optimism and outward prosperity were an inventive, creative period, with a wide appreciation of the arts. After its opening in 1921 in part of the family home, the Phillips Memorial Gallery had come alive almost overnight (as the Museum of Modern Art in New York was to do in 1929 in a few rooms of the Heckscher building).

Duncan worked as museum director with tremendous zest; he wrote and lectured with astuteness and feeling about the artists he most admired in the collection and searched constantly for new acquisitions that appealed to him personally. He always wanted me to accompany him on his scouting trips and from the first made me feel a partner in the enterprise, with the title associate director. Although the small museum opened with only a few galleries, it already had a wealth of distinguished paintings which Duncan hung in alternating exhibitions. And when he so early (1923) added Renoir's "Luncheon of the Boating Party," he was thrilled to see what a magnet it instantly became in the Memorial Gallery.

Among the great paintings our gallery already owned in those earliest years were Courbet's "The Mediterranean," Delacroix's "Paganini," two Daumiers, Greco's "Repentant Peter," Chardin's "Bowl of Plums" and Odilon Redon's "Mystery," as well as works by outstanding Americans, many of whom I have already mentioned, such as Twachtman, Inness, Ryder and Prendergast.

Among the friends to whom Duncan confided his "plans and aspirations" at this time was Frank Jewett Mather Jr., professor of art history and director of the Princeton University art gallery. Mather was eighteen years older than Duncan, but they had been drawn to each other by kindred tastes. Duncan admired Mather's erudition, enjoyed his gusty, friendly personality, and was happy to lend him pictures for exhibition at Princeton. He wrote him in December of 1924 about the rising interest in a proposal for a greatly enlarged national gallery in Washington. A committee had been formed and Duncan was delegated to enlist Mather's help in organizing a loan exhibition of superb masterpieces which would attract national attention, including that of the great billionaire collectors, and impress upon Congress the need for a substantial appropriation. This was the beginning of the National Gallery, which was eventually completed in 1941, thanks in great part to the generosity of Andrew Mellon, who gave the building and placed in it his own superb collection as an encouragement for other donors.

Duncan's part in the groundwork for the new National Gallery was to result in his becoming a charter trustee and a good friend of its first director, David E. Finley. But at this early stage the planning for the great undertaking also clarified his own museum objectives. He did not believe that a national gallery would necessarily displace his more individual collection. When Mather reassured him on this point, Duncan wrote back:

> It cleared my mind considerably to have a brief talk with you on the problem of our Collection in relation to the plans for the new National Gallery. After all there is no imperative need that I should abandon my plan. If as time goes on I can demonstrate the educational value of my ideals for Exhibition Units and if the National Gallery should have an enlightened director with full authority and no Boards to baffle him there might be an opportunity to carry out my dream and at the same time help in the great project of enlarging the National Gallery. Meanwhile I shall continue to develop my plans and to build up the Collection with its Units of favorite artists and I have several alternative ideas for enlarging our exhibition space, dependent, however, upon whether or not people will sell their real estate.

Duncan said from the first that he wanted the collection to be shown in a *home*. So on our walks or drives we often looked at houses for sale that might eventually suit the purpose and give more ample space. However, as he wrote in his first prospectus, the eventual museum should not be large, "no matter to what size the Collection may grow."

In the midst of all his numerous activities during the gallery's first five years Duncan was writing his book *A Collection in the Making*. It was Phillips Publication No. 5, published in 1926 by E. Weyhe of New York, a unique, beautifully illustrated volume in which he "confides" to the world at large his ideas and hopes for the future of the collection and tells of its exciting progress and growth in the few years since its founding. Among those who wrote about the book, Virgil Barker, European editor of *The Arts*, expressed "pleasure in the thought that all these handsome reproductions mean that their originals . . . are safe in the hands of one who knows their meaning and their value."

In the text of *A Collection in the Making* Duncan demonstrated his extraordinary gift for short critical appreciations of an artist's work, written almost as if he had spoken them to a friend in the gallery. Alfred Barr, who became director of the Museum of Modern Art in 1929, spoke of them when he reviewed Duncan's book in the *Saturday Review of Literature* in 1927: "The brief estimates are sensitive, personal,

Lower gallery, formerly the North Library, opened to the public in late 1921. This is where the gallery's concerts are held.

Gustave Courbet (1819–1877). *The Mediterranean*, 23 x 33

and often possessed of extraordinary charm of language — a collection of charming and discerning critical vignettes."

Mather also mentioned them in a letter to Duncan:

Many thanks for the inscribed copy of *A Collection in the Making* and congratulations upon the successful accomplishment of a difficult task. I envy you your facility in brief characterization. My own habits were formed in the days of the three-decker essay, with the result that I can do little that meets modern tastes and needs. A copy of my *Modern Painting* will be coming to you as soon as the publisher finds a paper that will receive the half tones. I am glad to see that your plans include such great objective painters as Monet and Eakins. At present you are long on the subjective and romantic. If I were you, I should pick a good Eakins from those in the *widow's hands* before the supply vanishes and the price rises.

Odilon Redon (1850–1916). *Mystery*, 29 x 21½

El Greco (Domenikos Theotokopoulos) (1541–1614). *The Repentant Peter*, 37 x 30

To which Duncan replied:

Thank you so much for your good letter about the book and especially for the sentence in which you praise the condensed characterizations of the artists. Naturally they are not all good but there are a few which satisfy me as having said everything in a small space through suggesting more than is told. I am interested in what you say about Eakins. I admire the man immensely and very soon I hope to have just the right example. Thank you for the suggestion about the pictures in his *widow's possession*. This year, however, I can buy no more! I have just come back from the Alphonse Kahn Auction Sale the proud possessor of the Egyptian Stone Head of the 18th Dynasty, a sensitive, subtle, marvellous thing when seen in a proper light. . . . Joseph Brummer [the dealer] is sending me his own ideas about the Egyptian piece and what he can gather about it after conference with Egyptologists. I understand this piece could have gone for much more in Paris and that it was valued by Mr. Kahn upward of twenty thousand. I got it for eight. I can hardly wait for your book on Modern Painting. Again thank you for your letter.

One of the most significant passages in *A Collection in the Making* is that in which Duncan defines his aim as the director of a small museum with a large collection; it shows not only the spirit and breadth of his judgment but especially what he was doing in building up his "units" of Daumier, Bonnard, Braque, Marin, and the others that were to follow:

The Phillips Collection is based on a policy of supporting many methods of seeing and painting. There are excellent reasons why collectors of taste limit themselves to one chosen school (or style). They feel that its tenets express their personal preferences and convictions and fear that the admission of alien influences might distract them. . . . For a small collection there is validity in such reasons for limiting the choices to artists of closely related method and purpose. When however a large collection is formed we are dealing not with a family but with a world. . . . It should be the best of many different kinds which the museum [or] large collector should delight to honor. Differences are not irreconcilable and impossible to fuse. The really good things of all periods can be brought together and thus the universality and the continuities of art's many traditions and families of artists — and the recurring affinities of artists down the ages.

The bane of impassioned preference and conviction among artists, crit-

117

Albert Pinkham Ryder (1847–1917). *Moonlit Cove*, 14 x 17

ics and collectors is the issue of tolerance. Even among the most tolerant modernists — who are not ready to destroy the museums on behalf of progress and change — there is a persistent refusal to acknowledge that as the great artists of the past felt about nature so our contemporaries are still entitled to feel.

The policy of the Phillips Collection is to choose the best representative as well as the best creative and abstract design and to do reverence to both.

With his catholicity of taste Duncan put on a stimulating series of temporary loan exhibitions in the Memorial Gallery, showing painters of many different styles. In December 1925, Bernard Karfiol had a one-man exhibition. This was followed in January 1926 with "Nine American Artists" which included works by Preston Dickinson, Charles

Sheeler, Vincent Canadé, Niles Spencer, Stefan Hirsch, Maurice Sterne, William Zorach, Charles Demuth and Fiske Boyd. In late 1926, George Luks and Jerome Myers were each given one-man exhibitions. In 1927 there was a group show of Matisse, Braque, Marsden Hartley, Man Ray, Walt Kuhn, Georgia O'Keeffe, Karl Knaths and others. In 1927–28 we had "Leaders of French Art Today" (Matisse, Braque, de Segonzac, Bonnard, Derain, Maillol and Picasso), followed by a Tri-Unit Exhibition of "American Old Masters to Contemporary American Painting." In 1928 the gallery showed an invited exhibition of "Paintings

John Henry Twachtman (1853–1902). *The Emerald Pool*, 25 x 25

George Luks (1867–1933). *Blue Devils on Fifth Avenue*, 38 x 44

in Water Color" by seventeen American artists, including Arthur B. Davies, Edward Hopper, Charles Burchfield, Gifford Beal, Reynolds Beal, John Marin, Rockwell Kent, and Charles Demuth.

We were to hear for years to come of the vital and unique contribution made by the gallery in the nineteen twenties and thirties. During all that time it was the only museum in Washington that owned and showed the work of contemporary Europeans along with living American artists. For example, John Ulric Neff, formerly professor at the University of Chicago, told me recently that in 1925 and '26, when he and his wife were living in Washington, they "must have visited the collection forty times." What a wonderful thing to know! Friends from Baltimore have told us that whenever they were "upset by anything"

Paul Cézanne (1839–1906). *Mont Sainte-Victoire*, 23½ x 28½

Vincent Van Gogh (1853–1890). *Entrance to the Public Gardens at Arles*, 28½ x 35⅝

during this period they would come over to visit the gallery, enjoy its inspiration, and take note of all the new acquisitions and loan exhibitions, as well as Duncan's stimulating gallery publications.

Among the major acquisitions of this period were two landscapes: Cézanne's "Mont Sainte-Victoire" 1925 (painted in 1886–1887), a classic in its beauty and style, and, a little later, Van Gogh's "Entrance to the Public Gardens at Arles" (painted in 1888). Duncan was thrilled with them both; and the comparison of the two which he later published shows it:

Compare Van Gogh's "Public Gardens at Arles" with Cézanne's "Mt. Ste. Victoire," both supremely important landscapes by great artists at the culminating point of their careers, when each of them had found what he was born to do, what no one else had ever done better. Van Gogh's Garden was painted in 1888, not long after he was settled at Arles. He was sane, well, happy, yes and exultant and ecstatic over the sunlight of the south and his own powers coming into their fulfillment. He was developing new and inspired devices, a new control of line and colors. It is an outcry of the soul that canvas, a shout of triumph, of joy in the sun, of thanks to God for a brush and some good pigments wherewith to surpass the light of life itself in intensity.

How to catch that pulse of nature, the repetition, the wave-like ripples of the heat, the saturated glaze of the soil along the garden walk, the pungent aromatic fragrance, the scintillant opulent colors, blues and greens, yellows and oranges in full cry under the sun, the trees of many shapes and textures, at the depths of which one could plunge and find shelter in the inner recesses of dark cool shadow. How blue black the men and women look in the hot light silhouetted in grotesque contours, like the peasants of Hokusai against sunlit spaces.

The Cézanne "Mt. Ste. Victoire" is a world in itself. The lines lead into deep space by Roman roads in long diagonals. The foreground trees tell us how far they are from the little houses of the valley and the houses keep their places on the way back to the old Roman aqueduct which in its turn reveals the remaining distance to the base of the mountain. The air is equable and refreshing, the saffron tones advance to the eye and the grey blues and violets recede. Perfect equilibrium is established, a beneficent harmony. Nature seems to breathe easily, rhythmically. No touch of the painter's brush fails to function in the sparing application of a few colors, while the canvas is left bare with wonderful knowledge of the properties of stress and interval, of warm and cool. A symmetry like the Parthenon and a strange solidity are achieved with the simplest means — a mere slipping of the brush from one color-plane imperceptibly to a warmer or cooler one. And so there is life and there is movement, and all within a great cosmic

Georgia O'Keeffe (1887–   ). *Pattern of Leaves*, 22 x 18

Georgia O'Keeffe (1887–   ). *Large Dark Red Leaves on White*, 32 x 21

vastness. Abstract art can only make a chart of what is there bewitchingly, profoundly and naturally revealed.

Two great masterpieces of landscape. Why must we choose one or the other and not have and hold them both? The artists themselves made the choice for their own creative purposes. But we are the inheritors of the classic and the romantic in art and life and we would be fools indeed not to rejoice in both, in the wisdom and serenity of the classic, in the depth and intensity of the romantic.

In 1928 Duncan had the good fortune to purchase Édouard Manet's "Ballet Espagnol" (painted in 1862). He delighted in the painting — we both did! — and I especially like the brief commentary which he wrote about it:

Without the bold step toward abstraction which Manet took in the Ballet Espagnol, Matisse might never have found the Twentieth Century Idiom. Flatten the modeling of those little figures into two dimensions and spread the silhouette into an arabesque which curves all over the canvas, and with the flat patches of sharply contrasting colors enlivening the dance of line, you have a typical Matisse, a master more doctrinaire but also more decorative. The names of Velasquez and Goya come lightly to our lips as we note the poise and elegance of these costumed dancers in a sensuously enchanting color scheme dominated by salmon pink and black, but Manet in this Ballet is the link between the two great Spaniards and the two modern Frenchmen who imported exotic influences from the East, Gauguin and Matisse.

Duncan loved to hang paintings by his favorite contemporary artists alongside works by great painters of the past or present, if in so doing he could create a satisfactory hanging of a whole gallery. He had a special talent for these juxtapositions, and took infinite pains and pleasure in planning them, knowing that they would encourage the contemporaries.

Among the American artists whose work Duncan was especially drawn to from the early twenties on was Karl Knaths. Duncan first saw Knaths' work at the Daniel Gallery in New York, later engaged in a considerable correspondence with him and soon came to regard Karl as a great friend.

In 1926 Duncan bought his first Karl Knaths painting, "Geranium in Night Window," and continued to buy his work with such relish and use it in exhibitions that at last (in 1929) he decided to write directly to the artist:

Édouard Manet (1832–1883). *Ballet Espagnol*, 24 x 36

Mr. Karl Knaths
Provincetown
Massachusetts

Dear Mr. Knaths:

For a long time I have meant to write to you. I admire your handling of oil paint and the sensitiveness and rare distinction of your color. You are gifted with a knowledge of when to stop, of how to suggest the character of an object without imitating it and without too much stylistic distortion. Your compositions in still life have dignity of line even when they have humor in the point of view. Best of all, your pictures decorate with a style of decoration absolutely of our own time. As I have now four examples of still life from your gifted brush I would like very much to add to our Knaths Unit fanciful and imaginative pictures which I know you must have painted or which perhaps have not yet been consummated to your satisfaction. Some time ago at Daniel's I saw two large landscapes and liked them immensely. Like all your work, they are broadly painted and suggestive rather than precise in statement. I asked to have them sent down to Washington on approval. One especially had delighted me; it represented a lane of a fishing village with a fisherman lighting his pipe at the door of his own little house. The scene was eloquent of twilight and one felt the ocean, although it was not in view. There may have been faults in this picture but the essential truth and beauty have been poignantly rendered. To my great disappointment I received a note from Mr. Daniel saying that he considered both pictures unsuccessful and had sent them back to you for revision. Whenever I am in New York I go to the Daniel Galleries and my first question is what is new from Knaths. There is hardly ever anything new and I am made to believe that you only produce one good picture out of a dozen efforts. Whatever is exhibited is always still life. The breadth and subtlety of your work seems all the more distinguished because of the hard edgy, almost mechanical, quality which predominates in the usual Daniel exhibition. I am in constant fear that you will lose some of your precious fluidity and power to evoke mood by suggestion through too much contact with this new kind of American modernism which delights in mechanical efficiency and labors long and hard on problems of linear achievement. The reason that you are a favorite artist of the Phillips Memorial Gallery and that I can hang you with Pierre Bonnard in our present exhibition with pride in the way your picture holds its own is the fact that you are a painter rather than a draftsman, that yours is newer language and that your color is never commonplace, always the essence of beauty.

You will wonder what I am driving at. Simply this. I had to tell you how much pleasure your pictures were giving me and to express the hope that you would tell me about that picture of the fisherman going home in the dusk and about any other landscapes, with or without figures, which you have been doing. If they are not good enough for Daniel, they are certainly good enough for me and I would like to see them on approval. Unfortunately this year we are getting established on a permanent basis and building a home outside the city. The old house will be the Gallery from now on and the museum will function on a larger plan. But our funds for purchase of pictures are next to nothing. All I have to spend is what I can make from the sale of a few pictures I have decided to sacrifice. This year therefore is not the best time for me to take up with you the question of purchasing more of your work. However, I have a little left over from the sale of a picture and if you have one canvas which you think I might especially like and if you are under no obligations to show everything to Daniel, please send it to us direct, Phillips Memorial Gallery, 1608 21st Street. Hoping to meet you some day and to show you all our treasures,

Sincerely yours,
Duncan Phillips

Provincetown, Mass.
February 20, 1929

Dear Mr. Phillips:

Your letter about my painting has made me very happy. I value your appreciation. It has been very encouraging to me. Also in pointing out the characteristics and merits of the painting which have given you pleasure. It is a pleasure to hear that four of my canvasses are in the Phillips Memorial Gallery. I did not know of your interest in the "Fisherman" or the other composition. Mr. Daniel never says much. He considered them unsuccessful and wished me to revise them. But I do not see why they could not

Karl Knaths (1891–1971). *Clam Diggers*, 50 x 30

Karl Knaths (1891–1971). *Cock and Glove*, 36 x 26

have been sent when you wanted them. I certainly desire that he show you all my canvasses. I cannot always judge the merit of a picture when I send it. I expect him to edit them for exhibition. But surely he can show them to you.

This winter I did do one canvas that is not a Still Life which Mr. Daniel considered a success. It is a Rooster on a grocery box, looking down at a glove that has fallen by the way, with that peculiar uncomprehending curiosity that has something of alarm in it. The play of color is between the yellow green that cheap leather gloves from Sears Roebuck have, and the deep orange tones of the Rooster. These are harmonized with the background colors that may be brushes.

In the "Fisherman" picture that you liked I have countered the yellow and orange tones with the blue twilight and this I think all right. In the other composition, the "Deer" picture, I have been wondering if it might not have been better to merely have harmonized the deer to the surrounding pine brush without bringing in the rising moon element.

I hope you see this latest "Rooster" picture, as I think you would like it. That could be sent down to you. I have no imaginative paintings here except some early ones. Did not Mr. Daniel show any water colors?

I am working on an imaginative figure composition and will send it on to you when it is finished on approval if you like. Your appreciation has given me the courage to take up some others that I have in mind.

I have no contract with Mr. Daniel but he has always had my work.

I am looking forward to seeing the Phillips Memorial Collection and also to meeting you some time.

Sincerely yours,
Karl Knaths

March 12, 1929

Dear Mr. Knaths:

The "Cock" and "The Fisherman" arrived from Daniel's and I have given them each a good deal of thought and study. We have very little left of our purchase fund, in fact only enough to buy one of these pictures at the prices asked. The choice is difficult. The "Cock" is a perfect success, subtle and exquisite in its delicate color relations. It is nevertheless a slight thing both in subject and style and I would like to see you paint serious and important pictures giving them greater weight and majesty for you have it in you to be a great decorator. Your patterns carry superbly at a great distance and your juxtapositions of color are entrancing and very strong when you wish them to be strong. The "Fisherman" picture seems to me in its present state to fall between two conceptions. As a whimsical, almost farcical impression of the funny shapes of the rubber boots and the sprawl and spread of the hound it is diverting but of no great consequence, and this mood of flippancy, which it insists upon, jars on one's sense of the grandeur of the composition and the extraordinary beauty of the color. Here, if ever, was a chance to paint a masterpiece with human interest added to your usual aesthetic preconception in the arrangement of colors and forms. This moment of twilight has always appealed to me and you have given it an added significance with your Fishermen returning to their humble shingled cottage at the end of toil . . . Mrs. Phillips and I admire your work so much we have always wanted to know you and we feel confident that you would be repaid not only in working out a solution of the Fishermen picture so that we can acquire it, but in seeing a great Collection in which you are one of the favorite contemporary artists. . . .

Sincerely yours,
Duncan Phillips

April 9, 1929

Dear Mr. Knaths:

I was glad to hear that you had decided on another version of the Fisherman subject. I hope you follow the same color scheme which I especially admire in the earlier version. Another of the features which I hope you will repeat is the shingled building to the left, its lines repeated to the right by another smaller building. The more I see of your work the more I feel that you would do beautiful things in pure landscape. . . .

Early in May I hope you will come down with the new picture finished and then we can consider together the proposed exhibition for next year.

Sincerely yours,
Duncan Phillips

November 11, 1929

Dear Mr. Knaths:

The pictures arrived safely and in good condition and I am delighted with them. There were more than I needed to cover every available wall space, and after listening to the comments of a few of our visitors from the general public I decided to show fewer pictures and perhaps to change them from time to time. The room is very small and when the pictures are hung close together a visitor unaccustomed to the new idioms is apt to be confused. He can learn the language better by concentrating on a few, spaced far enough apart so that he can master each one separately before enjoying the group as a whole. . . .

I am sending you our new magazine with the article about your work and feel sure you will be delighted with the excellent reproductions. Perhaps before the exhibition is over, the end of January, you will have had time to run down to see it and to see the whole Collection.

Sincerely yours,
Duncan Phillips

The magazine mentioned in this letter is *Art and Understanding*, which Duncan began to edit and publish in November 1929 as a museum publication. In the foreword to the first issue he wrote that he planned "a magazine devoted to the encouragement of tolerance and openmindedness in art and life and the cultivation of intelligent enjoyment of the intentions of artists and the varied qualities of their work." The few issues which appeared have recently been reprinted by the Arno Press in a series of what they feel to have been outstanding critical and stimulating art magazines of their period.

In Knaths' acknowledgment he writes:

There has been no disinterested American Art Magazine and the critics are more at ease in discussing conditions about art than in any competent estimation of art itself. If I were to express an opinion on your magazine, it would be of what you are highly conscious of yourself and have stated so clearly and delightfully in your magazine. I am very glad about the article on my painting and have taken to heart my poor batting average, which I hope to improve. We have had some lively discussion on your article The

Many Mindedness of Modern Painting, also in interpreting the Six Points. I enjoyed the Symposium. Altogether it would be too bad not to continue your magazine. You would fill a much needed position, a sort of Moderator in a needed dissemination of "Art and Understanding."

For various reasons, including worry caused by the stock market crash of 1929, Duncan discontinued *Art and Understanding* after a few issues, to the regret of numerous subscribers. He continued, however, to work on a multitude of other projects. Among these was his book *The Artist Sees Differently*, which was published in 1931 by E. Weyhe as Phillips Publication No. 6. He was also building a house, adding to the staff and program of the gallery, and continuing to add to its collection.

Many people had been eager to see the paintings in the residence part of the building on 21st Street in addition to the gallery part of it, and we found it increasingly difficult to take them all on private tours. In addition, we wanted more privacy and thought it would be good for the children to move away from the downtown area. Our daughter Mary Marjorie was then seven years old and our son Laughlin was five. The little girl had contracted encephalitis when she was a year and a half — a great tragedy for all.

Duncan and I had been redecorating several of the rooms in the old house — the dining room, the little library (where the Daumiers are now hung), and the drawing room. The walls had been repainted and "stippled" in a soft gray or gray-green which we liked as a background for paintings; in the drawing room antique French furniture replaced the Victorian; and perhaps it was to some degree this transformation that gave Duncan the idea of giving over to the gallery the entire house on 21st Street and to build a new home for Mrs. Phillips, ourselves, and the children on the outskirts of town. Unfortunately, Mother Phillips was never to occupy the rooms which we had planned for her: her health had been declining and her death at eighty-two in the late fall of 1929 was a gentle one.

A year later we moved into our new home which the architect Nathan Wyeth had designed for us and which we loved. Maryland colonial in style, it was built of warm red handmade brick from ancient kilns. The house faces the Potomac River and the distant Virginia hills and the lawn slopes down to a valley, with tall trees and woods be-

Karl Knaths (1891–1971). *Cin–Zin*, 24 x 30

yond. It was then real country on Foxhall Road, and only a ten minute drive from the museum.

I was happy to see Duncan turn with renewed zest and delight to the exciting prospect of converting nine additional rooms of the old house into galleries for his treasured works of art. He was engrossed in the challenge of rehanging the collection, feeling as he did that in a museum the composition of the walls and the juxtapositions of paintings were almost as important as the pictures themselves. Sometimes he would welcome my suggestions or those of other members of the staff.

Now for the first time our whole former residence would be open to the public as a homelike museum, a quality which has appealed to people as unique and creative. Since the gallery was never publicized to the extent that museums are nowadays, when people of discernment found it, they had a delicious sense of discovery, as if something warm, simple and informal, yet magnificent, had unexpectedly come into their lives.

Duncan loved to take people around the gallery, talking about the paintings with a constantly rekindled glow of delight in them — an élan which made one think of the phrase written about Bonnard's approach to his painting, "born fresh daily." Duncan was born fresh daily in his explanations and new discoveries. He shared the paintings with such exhilarating, quiet and intelligent ardor, and so informally, that many found it an unforgettable experience. He always cast light on unsuspected but important aspects of each work and enjoyed hearing others' opinions, comparing notes and sharing observations with intense interest and pleasure.

As he approached the tenth anniversary of the opening of the Memorial Gallery, with its expanded quarters and new facilities, Duncan decided he would now need more help in the museum's contacts with the public as well as in its educational work to "reenforce the gallery's original purpose and philosophy."

In the summer at Ebensburg he had been seeing and frequently golfing with his old friend and Yale classmate C. Law Watkins, who was living in a nearby town and serving as vice-president and manager of his father's coal mines. When the coal business dropped to an all-time low in 1929 and Law was about ready to quit and start some other endeavor, Duncan had the inspiration to suggest that he become an associate director of the gallery. He had always thought of Law as "an artist at heart," and it was an inspiration and a gamble that paid off. Although Law had not majored in the field of the arts he had done a

The entrance hall at
1600 21st Street

The little library and drawing room beyond.

1600 21st Street. Manet's *Ballet Espagnol* (25 x 36) over little library
mantel. Bonnard's *Early Spring* (34½ x 52) on wall in the drawing room.

John Constable (1776–1837). *On the River Stour*, 24 x 31

good deal of drawing and cartooning, was a good writer, and had done fine work in organizing local orchestras in the coal mining towns.

We always took about thirty paintings each summer to be hung in our house at Ebensburg, and it wasn't long before Duncan and Law were talking about these pictures, the gallery, and art in general. Law studied hard in preparation for his new career. With his gift of going to the heart of a subject and his warm interest in the thoughts and problems of gallery visitors, he was soon sharing with Duncan in an enlarged program of lectures and informal talks to the public about the work of the gallery.

Law was especially dedicated to working and talking with young artists. And with Duncan's encouragement he prepared to open an art

Charles Despiau (1874–1946). *Head of Mme. Derain*, plaster, 13″ high

school in the spacious rooms on the top floor of the gallery. He began by teaching a group of amateurs, Y.W.C.A. girls, but he learned so fast through his teaching that in a short time he was attracting to the school young painters and even artists of some experience. Each year we had an exhibition of the students' work in the print rooms, and Duncan often purchased some of these paintings for what he called "the encouragement collection," as well as work by other young artists, as he had done from the time the museum first opened its doors.

Three of the great paintings in the collection were added in 1928. They were Bonnard's "The Riviera" and "The Palm" and Cézanne's "Self-Portrait." Another, John Constable's landscape, "On the River Stour," had been added in 1925. This is one of the freer, sketchier examples of Constable's work — the type so prized today — and Duncan used to say he could "almost hear Constable's shout of exuberance while he was painting it!" To Duncan he was "the best of all British painters, the acknowledged discoverer of naturalistic landscape and the first to sense the *freshness and immediate impact of nature*. In the earliest years of the nineteenth century such a canvas as this was considered, possibly even by himself, as a sketch but the vigor and directness was the essence of Constable the pioneer, and his important place in history. Without such a lead we can scarcely imagine Delacroix, the later Monticelli, the later Monet, Van Gogh. This landscape sparkles with the highlights of sun after rain and scintillates with jewelled pigments."

8

OUR GIORGIONE TRIPS

Duncan's trip to Europe back in 1912 had led to the publication in the *Yale Review* of his first essay on Giorgione, in July 1913, entitled "Giorgione, the First Modern Master," and from then on his interest in the master and his work mounted steadily. In 1932 he and Bernard Berenson, whom he had never met, began comparing notes about Giorgione, and following our Italian trip of that year he set to work on a monograph which eventually grew into a book published in 1937, *The Leadership of Giorgione.*

In 1932 we were freer to travel, as we no longer had the constant anxiety about Duncan's mother, whose last illness had lasted for several years, or of our daughter's immediate welfare. We chose Sicily for our first overseas voyage since the purchase of the Renoir, in order to see the great mosaics, as well as the wonderfully romantic countryside. Duncan as usual took his golf clubs along just on the chance of some games. And his luck was good: he met a fellow enthusiast on shipboard and they played their first game the day we landed in Palermo — on a course which was kept cropped by a flock of sheep.

On this journey we took Laughlin, who was then seven years old, and it was a trip of amazement and enthusiasm for us all, starting with Palermo. We particularly enjoyed the church of the Martyrama, in which are some of the earliest and most beautiful of eleventh- and twelfth-century mosaics, with their restrained color against a prevailing blue background. Also, the great and ancient cathedral of Monreale, with the romantic cloisters and more fine mosaics. To us they were superb, their great simplification approaching modern painting. We agreed that one of the most significant mosaics was the large mag-

Duncan Phillips

nificent twelfth-century head of Christ at Cefalu in the cathedral not far from Palermo — a haunting and beautiful head peculiarly unforgettable in its dignity, warmth, and strength.

I remember that when we stopped for a picnic lunch at the golden-tan ruins of the temple near Segesta, a native boy and his shepherd dog closed in on us, at a respectful distance but looking hungry and eager. The patient gaze of the pair and their sad eyes were too much for us and gradually about a third of the food became theirs.

We also stopped at the marvelous temples at Agrigento and Syracusa, along the way to Taormina at the end of the great island. Our driver, James Tiburzi, entertained us en route with colorful stories of bandits and the dangers we might run into. Traveling in Sicily, even in the days of Mussolini, was considered a hazardous adventure. When we got out of the car at the hotel in Taormina, our hearts were in our mouths, for a pack of six big black police dogs rushed towards us across the hotel terrace! We were concerned that Laughlin might be scared and the dogs would know it. But no, he put out his little hand and patted them one by one with great pleasure. It turned out they were fully grown puppies about a year old, and we saw them every day after that. Unfortunately, we did not see the whole of Mt. Etna. There was a perpendicular veil of mist halfway across the mountain all the time we were there.

After proceeding to Naples by train, we had a few bad days. Duncan, whose digestion was always delicate, became deathly sick, apparently from spoiled meat on the train. And the English doctor recommended by the hotel made matters worse by prescribing overly strong medicine. He had spent years in India treating cholera cases!

After Duncan's recovery we made repeated visits to the Naples museum. It was unheated and my fingers would turn blue with the cold, but despite this we reveled in the wonderful large Bellini of Christ and the disciples. I remember Duncan poring over that superb painting with utter joy and admiration.

From Naples we went to Venice for the joy of seeing the great Giorgione painting "The Tempesta" (or "Thunderstorm at Castelfranco"). I remember that Laughlin spent a morning fishing in the Grand Canal and managed to catch a small *moule*, which was elaborately served to us at lunch that day at the Grand Hotel, though considerably shrunken.

We later drove to Florence, where Duncan became absorbed in Giorgione — in particular, "The Fire Ordeal of Moses," the Giorgionesque "Three Ages" in the Pitti Palace, with the boy possibly by the master, and the "Knight of Malta" in the Uffizi, which has at times been attributed to Giorgione.

Duncan was in seventh heaven when we got to that enchanting spot, Ravello. Following one of our walks in Ravello he wrote in his travel notes:

Not even after Taormina did I have any reservations to my unbounded joy in the superlatively lovely Ravello. Our return to the hotel was a lingering saunter — exclamations of delight bursting from us every now and then in spite of the fact that we had long since used up all our adjectives. The clear narrow streets are utterly charming in themselves in their medieval atmosphere and architecture, so that the marvelous backgrounds of mountains and Mediterranean are rather overwhelming. After a delicious luncheon, Marjorie and I painted in our room. My effort with oils on paper was a mess and I lamented the loss of the golden afternoon out of doors. But at least I was concentrating on a bit of natural magic and learning the old lesson of the artist's perilous adventure when he undertakes to make permanent the wonder of time as it passes, light as it changes, beauty as it flies. Marjorie's picture of the mountain coast was a study of what I hope will be a large important canvas. Whether she paints it on a bigger scale or not, this little panel will be a further record of a perfect day at Ravello — a place to be especially enshrined in one's most precious memories.

On our return to Washington, Duncan would attend to the gallery in the morning and then in the afternoon continue his writing on Giorgione.

These passages, as modified in 1947 from the original Giorgione monograph of 1937, show how deeply Duncan appreciated the independence, the originality and great influence of this rare artist — rare in his special genius, as well as in the small number of works painted solely by his own hand existing today:

Giorgione forged the link between his teacher Giovanni Bellini and his illustrious pupil Titian. More significant however than his acknowledged historical achievement in connecting two epochs of professional painting in Venice is the truth that he remained independent of both. His was the prophetic kind of leadership which dares to stand alone. . . . It was Giorgione's destiny to make the art of painting more self-sufficient, fanciful and free. It was his unique aesthetic contribution to invent the easel picture for the home and to conceive and formulate the painted lyric. As in the more abstract art of music, the meaning reaches us subtly through the senses and the subject is almost inseparable from the picture form. Such pure art, in the sense of expression by means only of what is inherent in the technical qualities of the instrument, knows no date. Its ecstasies are for the kindred spirits of artists, amateurs and connoisseurs, of every race and of any time.

Although such a conception of art was far from general acceptance in Venice even in the enlightened period which thrilled to Giorgione's whimsical leadership, a period of unabashed intellectual curiosity and of rebellion against the imposed patterns of stereotyped Byzantine tradition, nevertheless Giovanni Bellini, the old master who was born and trained in that tradition and the head of its Academy, was himself actually the source of Giorgione's haunting lyricism and light enchanted landscape. . . . Bellini contributed to the new century a fused and emotional color-atmosphere for the envelopment of his madonnas, saints and sacred stories. But that glowing space of his was the only unifying element. The figures were neither affected by nor integrated with his interesting and already more important landscape backgrounds of mountain, sky and valley. Other inhibitions persisted. New leadership was needed and wanted. A new age was about to be born. In the words of Berenson "Giorgione, stirred with the enthusiasm of his own generation, painted pictures perfectly in touch with the ripened spirit of the Renaissance so that they succeeded as only those things succeed which simultaneously create a need and satisfy it." His age was ready and waiting for his change of pace and for his epicurean philosophy. It was his good fortune to be born at precisely the right time and place. In a Venice where perpetual activity and costly material detail must have been overwhelming to sensitive self-withdrawing individuals, and when art was cluttered with objective and imitative illusions and descriptive narratives, while religion was dressed in sumptuous vestments and given over to ritual in gilded temples, it is little wonder that there was a thrill in Giorgione's evocations of "the golden age" and of nature as larger and more enduring than man but of man as giving meaning to and drawing elements from nature. His courageous challenge to church and state that art and the human fancy could no longer be bound soon found a sympathetic response. Finally he struck a popular note with his celebration of a profitable leisure, a contemplative idleness in which the inner life was active and the mind mysteriously aware of itself.

When we were in Florence Duncan had planned to look up Bernard Berenson, the great scholar and authority on Italian art of the Renaissance, but he unfortunately developed such a toothache from an impacted wisdom tooth that much of his allotted time in Florence was taken up with the treatment and alleviation of pain. He wanted to be at his best when meeting Berenson for the first time, so instead Duncan wrote Berenson a little later, told him how sorry he was to miss him, and asked if he could send him the Giorgione monograph which he was planning, so that he could have the interest and pleasure of comparing views and attributions. There is no copy of Duncan's letter, but here is Berenson's friendly answer:

> Hotel de Ville
> Rome
> June 1932

Dear Mr. Phillips:

Your letter makes me regret that I missed making your acquaintance. Sizer had prepared me to expect a person whose acquaintance would please me. Your letter convinces me that I have missed an opportunity. Can we find compensation in correspondence? Yes, if you will do the lion's share. I am 67 and sickly, and incapable of much effort and my time is severely curtailed by requiring so many long rests in the course of the waking hours. But I should be refreshed and stimulated to hear from you, and I should answer if briefly.

143

We left Florence May 15th and have been here ever since. After an absence of eight years Rome is to me what the whole of Italy seems to have been to you on this visit.

By all means send me your book — your books and all that you print. Perhaps you do not know that until the war I remained a zestful student of contemporary art in all its phases. Nor is my interest now quite extinguished. Indeed it would flame up if ever I could find fuel to *feed* it.

You ask about Lord Conway's little illustrations (painted). Of course they are echoes of something Giorgionesque. Perhaps themes composed in the Giorgionesque mode. They seem intrinsically valueless.

Your suggestion about "The Three Ages" is valuable. The ever advancing Giambellini probably rolled on toward immortality not influenced greatly by contributing streams. And when he reached his goal, he paralleled any of his juniors, perhaps even Giorgione. It is however possible that he was touched by the latter and deflected toward him.

"The Concert" may possibly have been started by Giorgione and that although the player and the priest are clearly Titian's the youth is too badly preserved to offer material for a conclusion.

A few years ago I was allowed in the Louvre to take down the *Fête Champêtre* and study it in the full sense. It was a revelation. Its superiority to anything Titian was doing at the time became almost distressingly manifest. There is a touch of heavy rusticity in almost all that Titian did before 1530, except portraits and a rare sacred subject.

The Temple Newhaus portrait is by Titian and you will find it on page 571 of my Italian Pictures of the Renaissance, under Lord Irwin, London. — I wish you had seen I Tatti because we are leaving it to Harvard to be an Academy for study and research in the history of art, — of art as distinct from craft and curiosity. I want the moral support of all who care that America should have a saving remnant of scholars and thinkers in the field of art. We have too few in fact in the whole Anglo-Saxon world.

Looking forward to hearing from you and to meeting you both

Sincerely yours,

B. Berenson

Mr. Bernard Berenson,
I Tatti
Settignano
Florence, Italy

Dear Mr. Berenson:

I am thoroughly ashamed that I have never written to you since receiving your kind and stimulating letter of last summer. Shortly after my return from Italy I was stricken with a serious case of influenza and I was more or less of an invalid for two months. After that I set to work on an essay entitled "The Leadership of Giorgione," which I wished to complete before I wrote to you so that I could send it and ask for your criticism. It has been such an absorbing study that I am still at it, and very happy in the task. The essay has become a monograph and I am now sending for photographs. My thesis is contained in the last sentence, the conclusion and summary of the whole, which is as follows:

The practice of collaboration on easel paintings has been completely abandoned in our times and is almost inconceivable to us. I have felt that visitors to museums and occasional students of painting who trustingly consult their catalogues and believe implicitly the attributions there given, are entitled to know what the scholars and specialists have long realized. Why is the information withheld that collaboration was taken for granted in Venetian studios at the beginning of the 16th Century? Personality was almost worshipped in the golden age of art and the greater artists were so richly endowed with it that they did not seem to fear for their own eclipse if the finishing touches were added to their work by their well trained assistants and followers. This was especially true of the studio of Giorgione. He was a leader of a "new movement," to use a modern phrase, a moulder of taste and of opinion but an indifferent executant of his own abundant conceptions. Fortunate was he in the exceptional talent of his friend Titian who seems to have been not only his pupil and assistant but his partner and successor.

When you look over the text you will see my debt to you acknowledged again and again and although I have dared to differ with you on several minor questions yet I have a profound faith in your insight as well as in your long training and experience and I lean heavily on your decisions. One of the cases where I cannot agree is the little portrait of a lady which Duveen now has in New York from the Lord Melchett Collection. If it is by Titian then it must be one of his earliest portraits for it has traces of the Quattrocento. The cool tonality and the choice of clear light colors suggests Titian of course but the Madonna of Castelfranco is no less luminous and bright. The young Titian's so-called Ariosto and his stout woman once called Caterina Cornaro are realistic and forthright statements of objective observation. This lady of the striped scarf is the symbol of a subjective poetic conception — of the siren, the enchantress of men. In that sense it is an Ideal Head rather than a portrait —. Am I right in feeling that the Knight of Malta is an Ideal Head and by that very quality of lyric suggestion and subjective generalization it is *different* from Titian's portraits? The red bearded man of the Altman Collection has the same quality but I miss it in Duveen's sombre portrait of a man in black, fine as it is. I wish I could see the full face portrait of a man with apparently very Giorgionesque handling of the hair and skin in a subtle chiaroscuro which H. Koetser now holds in London. And in the Marquis of Northampton's Collection I am anxious to know what you think of that variant on the pyramidal pattern and the domestic theme with landscape at the apex. Is not that Soldier and Young Mother a first idea for the position and conception which was later to find more satisfactory achievement in the Stormy Landscape with soldier and gypsy, now in the Venice Academia? Since you gave the picture to Titian my guess from this distance would be that Titian carried on an unfinished start of Giorgione's. In your Lists I fail to find any mention of the unfinished Judgment of Solomon of Mrs. Bankes (Kingston Lacy) which with its pillars and pretentious, pictorial shallowness seems to be a probable Sebastiano del Piombo. But I would like to have it properly placed. It may be too clumsy for that usually skillful eclectic. I am so glad to have your confident faith in the authenticity of the glowing Pastoral of the Louvre and your high estimate of its beauty. It has always been for me one of the world's greatest pictures. Lionello Venturi's depreciation and his attribution to Sebastiano has shaken my faith in that expert even if he has now changed his mind as Duveen seems to think. I no longer feel the last period of Bellini in The Three Ages of the Pitti and can only cling to my confident belief that Giorgione painted the boy and perhaps even the Catena-like middle aged man. Is this not a variant of the picture which Vasari says he saw in Florence — the "portrait of Giovanni Borgherini when he was a boy at Venice with his tutor in the same picture"? The old man may have been outlined and laid in by Giorgione, in this version with the three figures, but he certainly did not paint the head we now see, with its meticulous details as to the skin and its wrinkles. Lotto may have been the maker of that head but a modern restorer must have over-cleaned even that realist's second intention. In spite of two or three executants at different periods the picture is still beautiful and preserves a semblance at least of unity, especially in its rich autumnal colors.

We are persistently grieving over our misfortune, my wife's and mine, in not seeing you when we were in Florence. My intimate friend and Associate Director of this Gallery, C. Law Watkins, is to be in Florence this winter and I have given him a letter to you. You were so kind and generous in your letter to me that I feel you are a friend even though I must have disappointed you by my apparent rudeness in not writing when you asked me to do so. It was a great compliment and one of the nicest things that has happened to me in a long time. Please forgive me because of the extenuating circumstances of my long illness and the work on the Venetian painters which I have been wanting to send you. I will send it soon and meanwhile I am sending you an autographed copy of my latest book in two volumes, *The Artist Sees Differently*. I may give my Giorgione paper to the Yale University Press and if you like the work and think it worth printing, I would appreciate a word from you to the publisher. In fact I would like to dedicate the book to you because twenty years ago you formed my taste for Italian painting and have always been my most trusted guide even though I have never met you. Besides I admire your keen and open mind and your lucid and admirable style in criticism.

Sincerely yours,

Duncan Phillips

P.S. The two portraits by Cossa at Duveen's are enchanting! I fell in love with this artist because of his zest for life and light and line when I saw his frescoes in the Schifanoia Palace at Ferrara — especially the white horses and the glimpses of luminous landscape.

Do you still feel that Piero Pollaiuolo painted the profile portrait of a lovely blond girl at the Poldi Pezzoli in Milan? There is much similarity to Domenico Veneziano but it seems to be of a later date and finer than that Primitive. Pollaiuolo and Piero della Francesca were not so susceptible to feminine charm and more interested respectively in living line and in mass and space than in sensuous surface quality. I wonder.

December 16, 1932

Mr. Bernard Berenson
I Tatti
Settignano,
Florence, Italy.

Dear Mr. Berenson:

At last I am getting off to you the monograph of Giorgione. I realize that I have been very rash in assuming that anyone would be interested in my opinion about attributions. You would be entirely justified in reminding me that anyone who ventures into this field should have had years of experience and a seasoned scholarship. When you read my paper however you will see how much I have relied upon your judgments and how my very impulse to express my own opinions, however unimportant, grew out of your encouragement. In fact, the first paragraph of my essay quoting from the Preface to the New Lists citing your views is the specific sanction for what I have done. The manuscript will be supplemented with photographs of all the paintings referred to in the text and most of those entered in the Lists. There is no new research for the scholar. And such theories as I have put forward may seem unsound to you and more fanciful than reliable. For instance my conjecture about the Three Ages of the Pitti sounds more like fiction than fact. There are other pictures which seem to me to bear out my idea, beyond the question of a doubt, that such collaborations were practical. I am thinking of the curious group with two women and a man, now in the Detroit Museum. Titian is only one of several painters who had a hand in that picture. If, as I think, not only Giorgione and Bellini but, much later, Catena and Lotto, are to be found in The Three Ages then my thesis on Giorgione's Leadership and his capacity to fuse the personalities of his followers needs to be published and is, in fact, a curiously belated contribution to what is generally known about the Venetians of the first decade of the 16th Century.

Hoping that by the time you receive this letter you will have my books and that Mr. Watkins, our Associate Director, will have presented his letter of introduction,

Sincerely yours,
Duncan Phillips

Soon afterwards, Duncan decided to develop "The Leadership of Giorgione" into a book with the same title. So in 1935 and again in 1936 we went to Europe with the special idea that he might check and enjoy again the Giorgiones and other Venetian paintings of the fifteenth and sixteenth centuries. These travels were great adventures for us both and we naturally referred to them as "the Giorgione trips." Laughlin, aged ten the summer of 1935, went with us both times, as did my mother. Law Watkins, an associate director of the gallery (I being the other), joined us in Europe for part of the 1936 visit. This time we did not only center on Giorgione, but also went to Arezzo and Borgo San Sepulchro to adore the Piero della Francescas, to Padua to see the great Giottos, and to Ravenna to delight in the famous sixth–century mosaics, in the church of San Vitale.

To Duncan the great Giorgione "Pastoral Music" in the Louvre was the culmination of a series of successful efforts to convey personal conceptions through a language of colorful design. In his Giorgione book he wrote:

In this masterpiece better than ever before he attained to a subtly satisfying organization of interlocking parts and crossed diagonals, of verticals and long slow sweeping curves, of ponderable figures artfully persuaded into postures where their contours function in a persistent rhythmical pattern. His ecstasy over this achievement of a musical self-sufficiency intensifies our delights in the intellectual elements involved, in the reconciliation of opposites, of edges fused in softly rounded masses, of solids in space, of golds against blue, of light enchanted scarlets, browns and greens, an excitement of oppositions resolved with vibrant harmonies.

Duncan said many times that the "Pastoral Music" ("Fête Champêtre") remained one of his favorite paintings in the world, and he writes of it again in his book as follows:

Giorgione (1478–1510). *Pastoral Music* (Photo by courtesy of the Musée du Louvre, Paris)

But the last and the greatest of the themes which Giorgione lived long enough to express in one of the world's greatest paintings is the Relation of Art to Nature. The Pastoral Music of the Louvre, which marks an epoch and anticipates linear and color construction in modern painting . . . There is the elemental abundance of nature in the earth women and in the great old oak trees with their late summer splendour, there is the intimate romance of art in the lute player, the passing glory of rich textured color in the light and the relation of art to nature, when each is well disposed to the other in the incident of the lutanist and his friend the shepherd tuning their instruments to their mutual satisfaction. Giorgione's conception was a dream of a blended simplicity and subtlety. We are made aware of lights that fade and waters that fall, of pleasure's overflow, of sweetness run to waste, of life that is too short a dream . . . All his life Giorgione had been painting the emotion which evades expression yet which has to be expressed.

When we visited Dresden and saw the beautiful sleeping Venus, Duncan thought the landscape at the right was painted by Titian in 1512; and we had the interest of inspecting it closer when the museum's director had it brought into the broad daylight of his office where one could see indications of what the x-rays had revealed, that a small cupid also added by Titian had been painted out by a later hand.

In Berlin we delighted in the beautiful portrait of a "Young Man" in the Kaiser Friederich Museum — the most definitely accepted of the portraits attributed to Giorgione. No one who studies Giorgione's work can help but be fascinated by the need to use his detective powers to try to discern the work of the master of "beauty touched with strangeness," even if it is just the first rare conception or some fragment of a painting which has survived the hands of pupils and restorers.

Duncan said in the third chapter of his book:

It is difficult enough to find autograph works by any of the masters of the Italian Renaissance. We have Mr. Berenson's clear statement in the Preface of his lists that "hand and mind were seldom one" in the pictures of that period when collaboration was taken for granted and when "no important work was undertaken without assistants."

Duncan continues:

The difficulty becomes extreme in a case like that of Giorgione, who died at thirty-three and probably signed none of his works. His whole career as an independent creative artist is contained within a span of ten years, from 1500 to 1510, and more than half of his working time must have been spent on frescoes which have vanished and perhaps on supervising the work of his pupils. . . .

We have seen that he worked in the closest partnership with two pupils who were his friends and very able painters they were, one of them a great technician almost from the outset. It was this greatly gifted junior partner, Titian of Cadore, who took to himself after his leader's death some of the unfinished things which interested him, carried them on or repaired them. In at least one instance he completely repainted the sadly damaged surface of one of his leader's madonnas making the picture his own, with his square brush stroke and his sharper outlines. I refer to the gypsy madonna now one of the great treasures of Vienna. Under the canvas the x-ray has discovered the same oval face with pensive eyes, the same generalized Christ child we know so well in the famous Giorgione at Castelfranco. . . .

There remains but one picture which survives the test of being pure, unadulterated Giorgione, the Tempesta of the Accademia in Venice, that "Thunderstorm at Castelfranco" scene of his childhood memories, wherein are to be found the unique fantasy of his whimsical imagination and his rare genius for closely-knit pattern. Fortunately this little landscape with figures can be the firm foundation for our further study of the man, the perfect equivalent of himself which can and should aid us in our search for just such a person in other less autographic works. It meets all the requirements. It is documented as by Giorgione without mention of a studio assistant or a posthumous collaborator. And God be praised, it is in excellent condition! Let us then study the Tempesta as an autograph of the master remembering however, that although it contains the promise of greater things to come it is still an early work.

It was important for Duncan to study many charming Giorgionesque paintings which were in question. We went from London to Compton Wynyates, home of the Duke of Northumberland, where a small Giorgionesque female figure (the brushwork peeling and in bad condition) intrigued him as having the Giorgione spirit, although now given to Titian.

I'll never forget the astonishing gardens at Compton Wynyates — topiary art brought to its full fruition, where all the plants and shrubbery were clipped to produce the varied forms of birds, great and small — what fun! — an Alice in Wonderland spot!

Back in London, the firm of Agnew arranged for us to see Lord Allendale's collection, in which the "Adoration of the Shepherds," attributed to Giorgione, still hung in his dining room. (It is now one of

Giorgione (1477?–1510). *Adoration of the Shepherds*
(Photo by courtesy of the National Gallery, Washington, D.C.)

the treasures of the National Gallery here in Washington.) Lord Allendale was away, but the caretaker let us in, bolted the great front door behind us, and left us to enjoy ourselves. The door had an intricate system of interlocking bolts which seemed to cover half its surface. No safe could have rivaled it!

We spread some gallery catalogues on a chair and took turns standing on them to see more closely the painting Duncan had come to study. It had a peculiar poetic enchantment and overtones of mystery; and Duncan's conclusion was that it was surely by Giorgione. We looked at it to our heart's content and at the other fine paintings there. There was one outstanding little Sassetta, the monk Saint Anthony meeting a

153

centaur halfway to his meeting with Saint Paul. He is shown on a winding, hilly path in three different stages of his journey.

After an hour or so we began thinking we would like to leave and have lunch. But when we pulled one bell pull after another, there was no answer. Duncan shouted for the caretaker, but again to no avail! We even tried to solve the interlocking bolts on the front door, but their secrets were impenetrable. Duncan kept us entertained by pretending that he was going to steal the little Sassetta. (It also is now in Washington's National Gallery, the gift of Samuel H. Kress.) When the caretaker returned after his long lunch hour (and possible siesta), we were finally released, and Duncan and I made plans to go by train the next night to Glasgow to see the wonderful painting in the museum there, "Christ and the Adultress," well worth the trip. Duncan always wished he could get the single figure of a man which had been cut from one end of the picture — and that we saw in the Arthur Sachs collection in Paris on the same voyage.

He wrote in *The Leadership of Giorgione* that the Glasgow painting is one of those pictures which show the hand of more than one artist. Giorgione's hand was evident in the general conception and in the far left of the canvas, where "his own crackle and thin flowing brushwork" revealed two figures unmistakably done by him. And Duncan adds:

All over the length and breadth of the canvas there is abundant evidence of [Giorgione's] originality and of his genius for imagining moments when men and women are not only affected by but revealed in fateful incidents for which he was able to find equivalents of rhythmical arabesque and colorful light. Christ's compassion for the sinner and his scorn for her hypocritical accusers are conveyed in an impulsive gesture in which his restraining hand saves a hunted creature from the pack by an action as impulsive as it is innate.

Duncan went on to make these keen observations:

Giorgione was the first single-minded independent in the history of pictorial art and the first proponent of art for art's sake. Leonardo had been too versatile and too many-minded for supremacy in any one endeavor. Of all his accomplishments, least of all was he the painter. Giorgione as a sheer painter deserves to rank with the greatest, but he was even greater as an artist and as an affirmative nonconformist, as an isolated inventive phenomenon whose genius for emotional suggestion, conveyed through colors and lines prophesied the nineteenth and a vital phase of the twentieth century. He was far closer to the modern painters of abstract lyricism than to the grandiose and prodigiously masterful High Renaissance painters of churchly or worldly preoccupations. . . . In a sense he never grew up to the business of conforming to a professional and conventional world. His art is full of nostalgia for the wooded foot hills of his homeland and the favorite haunts and dreams of his lost boyhood but it is not the expression of a boy but of a lonely poet of painting, clinging to his freshness of vision as a saving grace for his complex subtlety of expression and his intrepid daring of design. . . . I am amazed how well the "Tempesta" keeps pace with our current aesthetic interests, especially in functional and unified structure and in suggestion of "the stream of consciousness."

Of Titian, Duncan had this to say:

I have stressed the point that the young Titian from 1507 to 1512, first as the apprentice on the frescoes in Venice and finally in completing his leader's unfinished works as his executor, was proudly imitative of Giorgione. After 1512 he tried a pastoralism on his own account which is very attractive but very different. The "Allegory" at Bridgewater House, with the rural lovers — what a contrast it is to the "Thunderstorm" and its family group! It is a contrast of the mind of an average man with the mind of an evasive but entrancing poet. One feels the difference again in comparing the lovely profile of Giorgione's earth woman at the well in "Pastoral Music," her deep shadowed eyes, sensitive lips and softly rounded contours, as plastic and generalized as a fine Greek coin, with what Titian derived from it in his own taste for the Venus in the Borghese Palace as she leans toward her blond and bland client with professional advice. The lovely face of the goddess in that masterpiece of symmetrical decoration is that of a gorgeous model showing one side of her classic features.

Unfortunately, when we were in Florence in 1936, we again missed Berenson. He was away on a trip of his own and so we were deeply disappointed once more! The next year Duncan sent him the completed book, *The Leadership of Giorgione*, which was published in 1937, and this is his acknowledgment:

Poggio Allo Spino
Prov. Di Firenze
August 31, 1937

Dear Mr. Phillips,
Many thanks for sending me your "Giorgione." I have received it with much interest and pleasure. I am pleased that on the whole you are in agreement with me.

I have always felt that Giorgione brought a new vitality, a new romance, a new ideal into painting and not only of Italy but of the Western world.

What remains of his handiwork we shall never quite agree upon. For me we have no data for a scholarly conclusion. The important thing therefore is to recognize and distinguish and enjoy "the Giorgionesque" in the most gracious sense of the word.

I am too busy, and too old to touch upon controversial points whether of an impersonal or personal value. Nor do they matter. The important matter is that — you present the public with a Giorgione as satisfactory as any likely to be done with material at hand.

Sincerely,
B. Berenson

After reading it more closely, he wrote another friendly acknowledgment, with an interesting argument:

I Tatti
Settignano
Florence
September 25, 1937

Dear Mr. Phillips:

As you have recently brought out by far the best book about the Giorgionesque and Giorgione himself that has appeared in decades, I venture to write and tell you my own last, and I expect, final conclusion about the Allendale "Adoration of the Magi." I have just had the original picture for two days with me, and studied it with all that fifty years of training and more than forty years of preoccupation over this very picture have enabled me to do.

I cannot begin to tell you what an enchanting, what a glamorous, what a Giorgionesque picture it looked in this Tuscan light, so different from even the best London sunlight. I have seen it a number of times in the course of more than forty years. I have puzzled my head over it time and time again. In recent years the conviction has grown on me that no one but the very young Titian could have painted it.

To give all my reasons would take a book, and yet leave the realist reasons out, because in fact they can't be stated, can't be put into words. I only wish I could discuss it with you. I am confident that I could at least make you see what paths I have taken to reach my conclusion. It would not surprise me if you then walked the same path yourself and for yourself get to the same end — namely Titian.

Giorgione himself seems to me quite excluded from the authorship of this ravishing picture.

The more I use your book on Giorgione, the more I like it.

Do come soon again to Florence, and when I am there

Sincerely yours,

B. Berenson

Hotel Bristol
Vienna
October 30, 1937

Dear Mr. Phillips:

Yours of August 15th finds me here where I spend the entire day taking cures that are expected to fortify me and immunize me, but meanwhile have succeeded only in tiring me out. I fear I shall have to remain here another fortnight after which I hope to return to Settignano.

I need not tell you how interesting I find your letters and how it fills me with regret that we cannot meet at my house, in my library, and discuss the matter before us point by point. I am confident I could persuade you that tho' the Allendale picture is as Giorgionesque as you please, it has no touch of Giorgione's own hand. I should even hope to convince you that in the more intimate sense, it has nothing of Giorgione's individual spirit — that there is no cogent reason why the author of the picture, close follower as he was, could not have composed the entire thing out of his own head without any assistance, probably without the cognizance of Giorgione; that in short, it is an entirely independent creation.

My proofs? They are in my own heart, too many, and the most probing ones, to me, can not easily go into words for they come from the "sixth sense," the result of fifty years of experience, whose promptings are incommunicable, but will however try to give two or three hints that among other things have buttressed up my own conclusions. In the first place the composition as a whole is empirical, almost in impatient rebellion against Giorgione. No painting universally accepted as by that master has such a stretch of landscape unrelated to the action. Even the one here at Vienna which comes closest to it, is justified by the dramatic exigencies of the composition which demands that all the figures shall be looking at or discussing the situ of the future Roma. In the Allendale panel there is no reason whatever, and every reason opposed to having a display of landscape with no relation to the figures.

I can almost hear the young artist saying he had enough of Giorgione and was going to try something else. Remember that in the world of the spirit those youngsters are apt to turn out best who earliest begin, not necessarily conscious but genuinely creative reacting against what they have been taught.

To return to the landscape. The foliage is spiky and almost brittle instead of the lush softness of Giorgione's. The drawing of the slabs on the roof, the base of the tree trunk are bad. Harsh too are the contrast of light and shade. A young Titian might have made these lapses just because, in these parts, he was working against the grain.

You say that we are agreed that the composition as a whole, despite the ultra-Giorgionesque elements of the landscape is essentially Bellinesque.

Coming to the figures, I find something un-Giorgionesque in the way they are placed, interrelated and silhouetted. They lack the unity, the fusion as it were of grouping that Giorgione would have given them, or a docile follower. Here too I find that creative reaction, that urge toward setting up for himself of a young genius.

That this young genius was Titian seems to follow out of general considerations, namely that there was no other follower of Giorgione capable of such successful effort at standing on his own feet, no other who in Giorgione's own earlier years could have produced such a masterpiece so much on his own lines and yet so independent.

Coming down to more specific considerations I find that all the edges, or the lines if you like, are lacking entirely in that smoothness and swiftness as of running water, or cigarette smoke that never fail in Giorgione. For Giorgione was a Quattrocentist to the end for whom edge and line were supreme. To the author of the Allendale picture line is indifferent, for he is a painter in the modern sense for whom edge can not exist with exquisite precision as in Giorgione's contours or draperies, because for the real painter solids merge into the light and atmosphere with a photosphere as it were, with a halo or a vagueness as to where solid precisely meet off into the ambient light and atmosphere.

In the Allendale picture, the draperies of the Blessed Virgin are crinkly so as to give more scope for pictorial effect and the draperies of St. Joseph are brittle, while the long drawn draperies of the shepherds which could offer such opportunities for smooth flowing edges, lack them.

I come now to two most decisive points. 1) The entire figure of Our Lady, but, *and* her head particularly are already definitely Titian's. She is rustic as never in Giorgione or his more slavish pupils, but always tends to be in Titian. The folds over her breast are distinctly Titian's. I feel as if we could visualize her as frontal and enlarged of course, she would already resemble the Cherry Madonna that is here in the Kunst Museum. 2) My second clenching reason is that the crackle all over the Allendale picture is rectangular in the main and with a tendency to parallel lines as *always* in Titian's earlier years, but *never* in Giorgione's, whose crackles are invariably *polygonal*. I conclude therefore that responsible criticism can admit only two alternative attributions of the Allendale Nativity.

1) If we wish to confine ourselves to what will be universally accepted, let it be School of Giorgione.

2) Or, as I hope will in the long run win thro' *Titian* E.

I must stop for I have tired myself and I feel I shall greatly tire you, the more so as I make you decipher a difficult handwriting.

Let me again assure you that it would make me very happy to have you agree.

Very sincerely yours,

B. Berenson

November 18, 1937

Mr. Bernard Berenson
I Tatti, Settignano
Florence, Italy.

Dear Mr. Berenson:

I cannot tell you how grateful I am to you for having written me your long letter from Vienna dated October 30th. I hope it did not tire you too much. I have been quite ill and I am now extremely busy with work that has piled up during my absence from the office. Lacking the leisure necessary to express my thoughts on the various points in your letter I will postpone that until some more favorable time. Meanwhile I am meditating a good deal in odd moments on your very interesting attribution of the Allendale ADORATION to the young Titian. As I said in my last letter, one of my chief difficulties in agreeing with you is my conviction Titian was born about 1489. Since the picture in question seems to belong to a turn of the century, and since it bears the looks of Bellini's studio at that time, I find it impossible to believe its superb execution could have been within the powers of so young a boy. Since writing to you I have seen the picture again and it looks even finer than when I saw it in London, having had a thorough cleansing which brings out its full beauty of color. I am now sure that the picture was done over a period of years by one hand and that hand Giorgione himself. The Madonna, the little rocks of the foreground, the spiky foliage and the sky typify to a date around 1500 with Bellini's influence still predominant. But the rocks, the landscape and the shepherds seem to belong to the approximate period of the Tempesta. I cannot agree with you that the landscape is emotionally independent of the figures and certainly in its design it is more integrated and functional than were the early landscapes of Titian. Many of your points are impressive and I am interested to hear about the crackle being characteristic of Titian and not of Giorgione. The picture is certainly a glorious one and I hope that the Trustees of the National Gallery in Washington will buy it on its merits regardless of the divided opinion as to its authorship.

The sentence from your letter which I used for the circular about my book was not the generous one stating that it was the best in decades on the Giorgionesque for I knew that might embarrass you and I also felt I hardly deserved such praise. I did quote you as follows: ". . . You present the public with a Giorgione as satisfying as any likely to be done with the material in hand. . . . The more I use your book the more I like it." This will overcome the handicap of some very bad publicity and advertising and do a lot to achieve my purpose, namely to get the book into wide circulation. I think it was very magnanimous of you to praise my work in spite of your difference of opinion about Titian's birth date and the Allendale picture and I can only say again that I am deeply indebted to you for your assistance and very happy that you like my interpretation of an artist about whom you have written so beautifully and who is evidently close also to your heart. Hoping that you are now improved in health and looking forward to a possible meeting in the spring,

Sincerely yours,
Duncan Phillips

In Duncan's letter of November 18, 1937 to Berenson he mentions that he has again seen the painting "The Adoration of the Shepherds." This happened in New York, on a visit to Duveen's gallery. The painting looked beautiful, but somewhat different than in London, because it had been newly cleaned. After studying it closely and looking at two other small Giorgionesque paintings, with Lord Duveen at his most gracious and employing his grandest manner, Duncan suddenly got into one of his prankish moods and said: "Lord Duveen, how does it happen that all your great gifts have been to British Museums, never to American ones, although you have an important establishment here in New York and have sold countless treasures to Americans? The Phillips Collection is a public gallery, a poor little struggling museum. Why don't you give us a painting?"

Duveen, through his suavity, was visibly stunned and sputtering. But he rose swiftly to the occasion and called out to Mr. Bogus, an assistant who always stood behind a nearby curtain and served as a walking encyclopedia for supplying swift information, dates, etc. "Bogus, what can we give to Mr. Phillips?" Bogus also rose to the occasion immediately and said: "Your Lordship, how about the Dosso Dossi?" "Why yes," said Duveen, "show it to Mr. Phillips." So the painting, which was standing nearby on an easel was uncovered and we all admired it, but of course Duncan did not accept it, and everyone was able to relax again.

Using material from his book, Duncan developed a distinguished lecture with the same title, "The Leadership of Giorgione." He gave it first at the Pennsylvania Museum in Philadelphia, at the National Gallery in 1942, and at a fascinating symposium on Giorgione at Johns Hopkins University, Department of Fine Arts, also in 1942.

We should have gone to Europe in 1937 or '38, so that Duncan and Berenson could have had the pleasure of meeting each other. For then came the war, with its long interruption of travel for most people, and from 1942 on, when Laughlin went to Yale, we wanted to be here in Washington or in Ebensburg for whatever vacations from college or home leaves from the Army he could take. Also there were our own trips to the university, or to training camps to see him, and our wish to be here after his return from service in the Japanese war in 1946.

Soon after that, Duncan's zest for European travel was much abated because of an unsuccessful hernia operation. Since no doctor would promise that another operation would be more successful, Duncan resigned himself to wearing an uncomfortable harness, and our trips were confined to New York, Ebensburg, and other nearby places.

Duncan's friends who habitually made a pilgrimage to see Berenson on their visits to Europe, told him that B.B. was puzzled as to why we also didn't go. They said he often wondered out loud about this. He wasn't exactly provoked, but it mystified him. He said he would like so much to have Duncan there.

In addition to his growing dislike for travel, Duncan actually was a little shy of Berenson — perhaps partly because of his not knowing the Italian language. However, the two men were greatly interested in each other and Duncan would read much that he wrote and enjoyed thinking about and mulling over his thoughts and opinions.

Much later (1967) in reading *Forty Years with Berenson*, by Nicky Mariano, I came across this reference to the Allendale "Adoration" which brings full circle the argument between my husband and B.B.:

It was in the summer of 1937 that the connection between B.B. and the firm of Duveen Brothers came to an end. The cause was the Nativity, from Lord Allendale's collection, traditionally attributed to Giorgione, which Duveen had bought. B.B. felt, as I mentioned earlier, that it was painted by the young Titian and Duveen would not accept the verdict. Duveen turned out to be right for during his last years while working on the revision of the Venetian lists, B.B. ended by considering the Nativity as painted by Giorgione, with the help of the young Titian.

To some degree my husband came to feel this, too — that there were *traces* of the youthful Titian in the painting. This concept was consistent with his thesis that paintings of the Quattrocento or the early Renaissance were almost never completely by one hand.

Now, in 1969, as I complete this chapter, I feel that to do justice to the Giorgione book might take up this whole volume. I want to quote so many of Duncan's appreciations of the various Giorgione paintings and I have not even mentioned some of the best authenticated ones! His good friend H. G. Dwight, who was with the Frick Collection under Frederick Mortimer Clapp (another very good friend), wrote the distinguished introduction to *The Leadership of Giorgione*. The book was published by the American Federation of Arts, which at that time had its headquarters in Washington and of which Duncan was a trustee. When the first edition was sold out, Duncan took pains to retrieve a dozen or so volumes from booksellers to give to close friends.

Duncan regarded *The Leadership of Giorgione* as his best book and later regretted that he had not found time to bring out a second edition. His time had become increasingly occupied in directing the gallery, with its voluminous mail, in seeing its visitors, getting up loan exhibitions, lending paintings to other museums, painting himself, collecting, and doing other writings! My son Laughlin and I are now exploring ways of publishing a new edition.

Here is a letter I especially like that Duncan wrote in 1961 (in thanks for a fine note of appreciation) to Mrs. Philip Amram of Washington, D.C.:

> 2101 Foxhall Road
> November 17, 1961
>
> Dear Emilie:
>
> Thank you, thank you and thank you!! No matter how undeserving my Giorgione book may be of your generous praise, I am deeply gratified and honored. If a few perceptive people like you read it with pleasure and appreciation of scholarship, taste and creative eloquence, then I am very happy and grateful for the expression of such words. No words could have been chosen that would have pleased me more. I am no longer a scholar and my writing now lacks resonance and rapture. The insights at that period were more "spontaneous and the suggestions more subtle." I wish I had written more books while I was in that state of mind but instead I became a passionate collector and sought more simple interpretations — more of our period. It was so understanding what you wrote.
>
> Marjorie joins me in affectionate greetings to you and Philip.
>
> Duncan

Others he gave it to were dear friends, one of them being Walter Lippmann. Walter wrote, "I sip it like old wine."

Henri Rousseau (1844–1910). *Notre Dame*, 13 x 16

9

MODERNIST ART

D UNCAN was always interested in modern art: he once said that he enjoyed his "experiment station" — his testing of new forms and ideas in art — more than any other aspect of his work. Several galleries of the permanent collection were always reserved for contemporary modern paintings, examples were hung throughout the building. There were, in addition, a series of temporary exhibitions featuring modernist work.

In a chapter entitled "Modern Art, 1930" in his book *The Artist Sees Differently* (1931), Duncan notes that "contemporary art is keeping up with contemporary science in arousing and holding public attention no less than in making brilliant advances into hitherto unexplored regions of the mind." Noting with pride that thirty-five thousand Americans had visited the Museum of Modern Art over a three-week period to see the 1930 loan exhibition "Painting in Paris," he wrote that "New York today is no stranger to the latest of aesthetic idioms." His only concern was that modernism would exert a tyranny of its own and in this new book he reminds

. . . gallery visitors and even our connoisseurs that the acceptance of what is new in art today does not require the rejection of what was new only yesterday. . . . The sudden reversal of taste in our period, the violent change of mode from Sargent to Picasso within fifteen years, is startling until we remember that there has been a steady stream of propaganda and publicity, the effects of which have been watched with keen intelligence until finally our deliciously shocked surmises and our subconscious expectations have been not only anticipated but produced at precisely the moment of our desire. At last we know what it is to be modern and what is to be our style of the first half of the Twentieth Century.

Duncan was deeply appreciative of what was new and experimental if he felt it sincere and not just faddist. He admired, although sometimes with reservations, what he called "the improvising virtuoso, Picasso." "That colossus," he wrote, "bestrides both camps, inspiring imitators either to look up at his pose as a formalist of quite formidable power or to guess at his meaning as a supernaturalist most strangely disturbing. Picasso is making history — breaking precedents every day. There is no doubt at all of his inventive genius. The only doubt is in regard to the results of his influence, his making of art not from life but from other art."

But he felt there was no reason why modernism should usurp the whole stage. "Any painter," he continued, "working in a style which is neither formalist nor supernaturalist nor sensationally new is today as one buried alive. Cézanne was useful for a while. Now he is in the words of Leo Stein 'a squeezed lemon.' What matters it if Bonnard, like Cézanne, belongs to the ages?" He mentions his pleasure at the results of the referendum of critics, connoisseurs, collectors and artists conducted in Paris in 1930 to find out who was considered the greatest living painter. Bonnard received the largest number of votes. The collection had nine Bonnards at that time!

Duncan used the term modernist in a broad sense which included works of the past or present which showed a strong individuality and personality. He looked for quality in art in both form, spirit and color; an inherent life and sense of new adventure; something of the universal that is found in true art no matter what the metamorphosis. This would include painters as far apart as Giotto, Daumier, Ryder, de Staël or Rothko!

In his chapter on definitions of "terms we use in art criticism" he wrote

Modernist is a critical term, the opposite of academic. There have always been modernists to complain because there have always been academicians to lay down the law, to require conformity and to despise innovation. Modernism defines a state of mind in art more than any definite method of procedure. As a matter of fact it can and should be applied to so many different kinds of technique that it loses most of its value as a critical category. Its reference is to one and only one sort of human character. It stands for the progressive and challenging type of person in the arts of *any age* from the prehistoric to the contemporary. . . . It is applicable to as many *different kinds* of experimental methods as have been devised by experimental minds in successive periods.

Paul Cézanne (1839–1906). *Self-Portrait*, 24 x 18½

Modernism means different things at different times. Thus the Romanticists, now so demoded and lonely on their museum walls, were the modernists of their day, as were in turn the Realists and the Impressionists. Once upon a time, when formalism hung heavy on the land, to be a modernist meant to be a faithful [but creative] student of nature like John Constable and much later Claude Monet. But when this nature study had been completed and a slavish or photographic imitation of natural appearance became the academic law, then modernists returned to the formalism their ancestors had despised. Regardless of the "whirligig of taste" and the complete difference of outlook boasted by the modernists of later days, all those who were modernists in the past are entitled to keep that honor always on the pages of history. This does not mean that they will at all times give pleasure and it is only when they stir the mind or heart that they truly live. A style in art is, therefore, apt to hibernate and to blossom again, although not at all with the inevitable regularity of the seasons.

These words with their broad view are consistent with Duncan's belief and practice as a collector, expressed forthrightly in *The Artist Sees Differently:* "I have no other advisors. And I have no agents at all among the dealers. The capacity to decide for oneself is one's only safeguard against the contagions of fashion in art which are peculiarly prevalent today. . . . *My own special function is to find the independent artist and to stand sponsor for him against the herd mind whether it tyrannizes inside or outside of his own profession.*"

The new book provided further evidence of Duncan's gift for "lighting up an artist's genius" when writing about a single canvas — a talent also revealed in the lectures he continued to give and which he always wrote out and read in as lively a manner as if he were talking. Of the many characterizations in the book, I especially like the one on Cézanne's "Self-Portrait," which he was so pleased to be able to purchase in 1928 and which he always considered one of the finest paintings in the collection. He wrote:

Cézanne was fundamentally a searcher. In the course of his research he drew closer and ever closer to a great discovery until finally he came upon it and his triumph was one of the greatest in the history of art. He attained to the knowledge of an all-functioning clarity and simplicity of form construction entirely by means of modulated color, one touch laid across another, even as a builder works. As color is the painter's proper building material the world finally realized many years after the death of the Master that Cézanne was "the Columbus of a new continent of Form in painting." This epoch-making discovery, which grew out of the spectral palette of Monet

Albert Pinkham Ryder (1847–1917). *Homeward Bound,* 9 x 18

and his fellow-luminists, gradually made the old hermit entirely indifferent to fame and popular success. Assured of his own genius and of the new trail of which he was the pioneer, he could afford to do without the success of lesser men.

In his stormy youth he had been a defiant radical who secretly longed for recognition from the very authorities he despised and ridiculed. The pictures he painted at that time were romantic in the sense of the word to which its enemies most justly object. They were excessive in their violent distortions of contour, their violent overloading of pigment and their depiction of violent and elementary struggles and desires. Pissarro was the good angel who helped Cézanne to find himself, who made him realize that Rubens and Delacroix would have been embarrassed by his crude emulation of their baroque rhythms, who taught him the function of juxtaposed color touches used proportionately for the desired effect of near or far, of warm or cool. Gradually he made the science of color-division serve his new purpose of color-construction, color-organization, a color-cosmos.

It was about the time when he was becoming a classicist that he painted our famous Self-Portrait from the Behrens Collection, the frontispiece of Meier-Graefe's book and declared by that writer to be one of the two best Cézanne portraits in the world. Here he looks every inch the builder interrupted at his work by cynical questions as to what he is doing and resenting the interruption but only as a lion would object to the yelping of a little dog. In a proud consciousness of genius and pent-up power he regards the hostile world with scorn. There is only one other portrait which can be compared to it and that is Rembrandt's Self-Portrait of the Frick Collection, the one in which he is seated as on a throne, old, thwarted, neglected, reviled of men, yet prouder and more serene in conquest of the world than any tyrant. He is master of fate and unbroken by its trials. The future is his. And it is with the same expression that Cézanne looks up from his palette. For ultimate consummation, for working within self-imposed bounds to the end that there shall be no touch of color which is not functional and structural, for restrained, self-contained mastery of material, nothing in the museums can surpass the subtle, solid modelling of that head of an old lion of a man, the pride and loneliness of him so directly conveyed by purely plastic means. In our Collection, notable especially for its colorists, that sombre, swarthy, tawny portrait says the last quiet word about color. Cézanne was a true and a great classicist but only after a successful struggle with himself.

Although most of the Phillips Collection's Albert P. Ryders were purchased in the early twenties, Duncan wrote about several of them for the first time in *The Artist Sees Differently*. He had this to say about Ryder's "Homeward Bound":

All of Ryder is in the small marine entitled "Homeward Bound." Bred of seafaring folk, he knew the sea with intimate knowledge and in this picture he gave us the eternal spirit of its infinite space and silence and its deep, incessant, inner movement. It became for him the symbol of life itself. That little boat at the center of the composition, as each of us is at the center of his particular universe, symbolized the soul's adventure as it traverses the vast uncharted solitude, travelling toward the unknown in the beckoning of the light which breaks for moments through rifts in the clouds.

And of Ryder's famous little "Dead Bird" (which was invited for the 1970 centennial exhibition at the Metropolitan Museum):

No lyric ever written on the death of a song bird or for that matter on the mystery of the last sleep as it comes to all, has ever surpassed Ryder's tiny picture of a dead canary lovingly laid in a tomb of rock.

Reviews of *The Artist Sees Differently*, especially the one by an old friend, Frank Jewett Mather, were warmly favorable: Another which pleased us very much was by Elizabeth Luther Carey, of the *New York Times*, who recognized those special qualities of Duncan's, his exuberance and his independence, and wrote:

Duncan Phillips brings together pictures as far apart as the North and South and shows how kind they can be to each other. The result to the thoughtful observer, seems nothing short of a miracle. . . .

The latest publication by Mr. Phillips, *The Artist Sees Differently*, approaches art, artists and their work from different angles, taking its stand in each case at a point where the author can connect his ideas with his practice as a collector. Whatever this critic writes is written with an opulence of curve, a richness of quotation supporting his statements and above all with an exuberance of appreciation that carry the reader into a state of mind to think for himself. Looking over the illustrations we see the new American spirit of fusion in active functioning.

To give a sense of changing life to the museum while at the same time keeping a large part of the permanent collection always on view, Duncan arranged for a steady flow of temporary exhibitions, large or small, borrowed from other museums, artists, or dealers. During the thirties he exhibited and bought the work of Bonnard, Vuillard, Rouault, Kokoschka, Munch, Soutine, Picasso, Braque, Dufy, Marin, Dove, Knaths, Burchfield, Graves and many others. In the catalogue of *American and European Abstractions* in the spring of 1932, he com-

Albert Pinkham Ryder (1847–1917). *Dead Bird*, 4¼ x 9⅞

Édouard Vuillard (1868–1950). *The Newspaper*, 13½ x 21½

Pablo Picasso (1881–1973). *Studio Corner*, 8 x 10¼

pares two American artists, Dove and Karl Knaths, with European artists in the same show.

In contrast to the pure artistry of the Braques in this exhibition and to the sophistication of the two little Picassos and the Juan Gris, we can see in the abstractions of our Americans, Dove and Knaths, a greater reluctance to separate art from life. Dove is familiar with earth and water, sensitive to textures rough and smooth, to old weathered wood and rusty iron, to gritty sand, damp soil and ore from the mines, to waterfalls and rapids over rocks, to light absorbed and light refracted. Post Impressionism may have started his experiments, but he is wholly independent of the School of Paris. There is a rugged and robust quality about him, an exhilaration about his lights, his dominant tones of silver and bronze, his varied, richly painted surfaces, his often unconsciously Indian patterns. . . . There is no progressive *system* in his work which can be followed, like the various stages of Cubism. His abstractions, therefore, escape the standardization which is the fate of more easily demonstrable design. His abstractions are made from homely objects, not from theories and dogmas which have issued from other theories and dogmas of the year before.

Karl Knaths has a sense of humor and a zest for life and nature. Although he is going in for abstraction, because his approach to line and color is musical, nevertheless his titles . . . give an idea of the salty tang of his inspiration down on Cape Cod and of the essentially whimsical, lyrical turn of his mind. His painting seems more facile and spontaneous than it really is. For underneath the clever calligraphy and the apparently sensuous improvisation is a keen intelligence which simplifies and selects for the creation of a subtle harmony of rare colors and for a reference to experience no more inconsequential in its nonsense than the fancy of Lewis Carroll. America *can* have an abstract art of its own, as well as an art which reflects Main Street.

For some years, beginning in the middle twenties, Homer Saint-Gaudens, director of the Carnegie Institute's Museum of Art, would

Karl Knaths (1891–1971). *Frightened Deer in Moonlight*, 36 x 48

Louis Marcoussis (1883–1941). *Abstraction, Brown and Black*, 13 x 16¼

visit the Phillips Gallery each season, and Duncan was always pleased to see him. He was the son of the sculptor, Augustus Saint-Gaudens, and had given up a career in the theater (where among other things, he was the producer of Maude Adams' plays) to enter the museum world. From time to time we went to the annual International Exhibitions held at the Carnegie, and Saint-Gaudens, who liked to take his foreign jurors on sight-seeing trips to New York and Washington, would regularly bring them to the Phillips Gallery. On one of these visits he brought Raoul Dufy to lunch with us at our home on Foxhall Road. The living room at that time was hung with Bonnards, and when Dufy stepped into the room he exclaimed, "Ah, Temple de Bonnard!"

We liked him immediately. He was humorous and charming, and looked more like an Irishman than a Frenchman in his rough tweed

Juan Gris (1887–1927). *Abstraction*, 11¼ x 7⅝

Arthur G. Dove (1880–1946). *Waterfall*, 10 x 8

suit. Over the years Duncan had purchased several of Dufy's always gay and seemingly spontaneous paintings. One reason they hold their own so well artistically is probably the fact that Dufy made thousands of drawings in preparation for his "spontaneity." Although, like Renoir, he later got terrible arthritis in his hands, he maintained his gaiety and courage, and painted doggedly to the end.

176   In 1930 the great French painter Henri Matisse visited the gallery.

Henri Matisse (1869–1954). *Interior with Egyptian Curtain*, 45½ x 35

Arthur G. Dove (1880–1946). *Golden Storm*, 18½ x 20½

He was more urbane than Pierre Bonnard and perhaps because he had taught painting himself, whereas Bonnard had not, he was more appreciative and generous about many different types of painting. He was especially interested in seeing American paintings and he reacted with enthusiasm to a great many of them. Among these was one of my landscapes, the "Open Road," which made me very glad; but another of mine he did not like.

Arthur G. Dove (1880–1946). *Snow Thaw*, 18 x 24

In the American old masters room we were amused and rather shocked to have him say of our great Eakins portrait, "Miss Van Buren . . . funny old thing!" He also noticed that we had hanging at that time about five Bonnards (of the nine the gallery then owned), and only two of his. When Duncan said we were planning to add to his unit, he made an astonishing remark to the effect that we were right to have more of Bonnard's work than his; adding, "He is the best of us all." Actually, we always had a tremendous admiration for Matisse's art and later, after trading lesser examples of his work in 1942 and 1947, the gallery acquired two of its greatest highlights, Matisse's "Studio, Quai St. Michel" and "Interior with Egyptian Curtain." The year of the Matisse centennial at the Louvre (in 1970) these two paintings were considered indispensable for a complete showing of the master at his best.

Charles Sheeler (1883–1965). *Offices*, 20 x 13

Studio in the Phillips Gallery Art School

In 1933 the federal government recognized the desperate financial straits of American artists resulting from the long depression and came to their relief by setting up the Public Works of Art Project (PWAP). Under the able and sympathetic leadership of Edward Bruce, a lawyer turned artist, the PWAP granted innumerable commissions, such as murals for post offices and other public buildings, landscape backgrounds for animal cages in zoos, and paintings of all kinds relating to "The American Scene" — the theme given to all artists participating. Duncan was appointed chairman of the committee for the Washington region (the District of Columbia, Maryland and Virginia) and he soon found himself working almost around the clock at this new job, in addition to his regular museum work. The members of Duncan's committee were Olin Dows, Commander Charles Bittinger, Powell Minnegerode, Grant Code, and Law Watkins. Each was allotted a group of artists whose studios they visited or whose work was brought to them as it progressed.

There were colorful characters among the artists whose work Duncan and his committee commissioned. Julien Lee "Judy" Raford (one of those for whom Duncan was responsible) had exciting proposals for representations of figures from American folklore. For instance, he

Max Weber (1881–1961). *Draped Head*, 21 x 13

used colored plaster-relief plaques to depict the extraordinary doings of Paul Bunyan, the mythical hero of the northwest lumber camps. Another of his projects was a fascinating low-relief wood carving of figures on a bicycle built for two, with mammoth wheels. Raford also hoped to do murals for the Department of Agriculture building, and I remember when Duncan showed some of the designs to Secretary of Agriculture Henry Wallace, he reported that Mr. Wallace was pleased with them and thought the plaques could be used on the outside of the building in the back. Wallace's only stipulation was that there should be plenty of corn incorporated in the designs.

Édouard Vuillard (1868–1950). *Woman Sweeping*, 18 x 19

Raoul Dufy (1878–1953). *Château and Horses*, 23¾ x 28¾

About sixty-six artists of the Washington region were given employment decorating school libraries, hospitals, cafeterias in public buildings; drawing anatomical subjects for the Army Medical Museum; and in other types of work. One of the most ambitious of the mural designs (submitted but not used) was the whole story of creation, with thousands of human figures! Other interesting commissions I remember were a mural panel representing the destructive effect of war, by Auriel Bessemer; "Euclid," a mathematical abstraction by Zerega; and David Barger's portraits of the unemployed. A great many of these paintings or designs were included in the large PWAP Exhibition held in our gallery in 1935.

Privately, Duncan was of two minds about the PWAP. He felt that although some good talents were turned up, there was a good deal of

Paul Klee (1879–1940). *Arrival of the Circus*, 6¾ x 10⅞

mediocrity, too, and when artists were assigned to murals with little experience in that field their murals often remained easel paintings. On the whole, however, he believed that government aid at that particular time did much more good than harm.

In any case, one benefit to the gallery's educational department was that when the PWAP came to an end, three of the artists whom Law Watkins had come to know joined him as assistants in the Phillips Gallery Art School. They were Robert and Margaret Gates, and Val Clear.

In 1934, when Gertrude Stein came to this country on a lecture tour, we heard through Duncan's cousin, James Laughlin, founder and editor of the New Directions publishing firm, that she was to be in Washington. Jay, who had known her in France, was interested in her experimental writing and knew that with her brother Leo, she was also a well-known collector of contemporary French paintings, especially of Picasso. So when we heard that she was planning to stay with our friend Mrs. Ann Archbold, who owned a nearby property, we invited her to bring Miss Stein to see the collection and to lunch afterwards, and Duncan arranged for her to give a talk at the gallery.

Gertrude Stein took a walk every day on Reservoir Road between the two houses, and when Duncan drove home from the gallery for lunch, he had frequently seen her striding along. She was short and stout, with rather a handsome head in profile, somewhat like an Indian chief's; but her overly mannish aggressive mien irritated him before he knew her. It was a very rare thing for him to form such an antipathy, because of his naturally hospitable, generous nature.

When she arrived at the collection, she seemed already hostile. Duncan started to accompany her around the galleries, thinking they might at least enjoy his beloved paintings together. But she said loftily, "Oh, I've seen all these artists before!" She asked, "Don't you have some works by *your own* countrymen, such as cigar store Indians, weathervanes, portraits by itinerant artists?" (One would hardly have thought that she came from Sewickley, Pennsylvania, herself.)

Duncan answered, holding his temper: no, he had not included those in our collecting, but one of the guests, Mrs. McCook Knox, who was coming to our lunch for Miss Stein that day, would he felt sure, be glad to bring some fine photographs she had gathered for the library of the Frick collection, in New York. She was one of Helen Frick's "lieutenants" in this area and was responsible for having photographed

Georgia O'Keeffe (1887–   ). *Ranchos Church*, 24 x 36

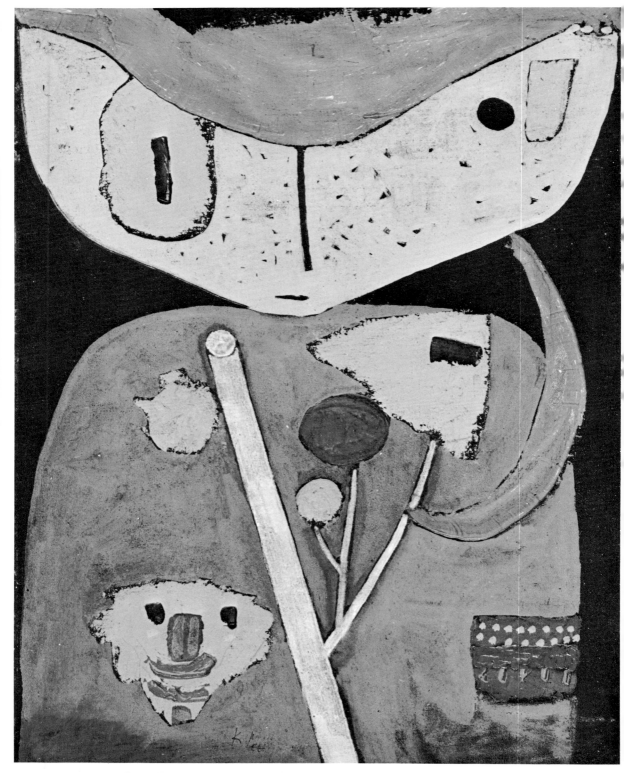

Paul Klee (1879–1940). *Figure of the Oriental Theatre*, 20½ x 15½

for the famous library a good deal of early American art here and in Maryland and Virginia.

Well, we got out to the house and having telephoned Katherine Knox, she kindly brought over several huge portfolios to appease Gertrude Stein. The latter looked at them and snorted, "I can't tell anything from photographs. I would have to *see* the things myself." "Well," said Katherine, "you will have to hire a car or go miles on end by bus or train. This is the work of several years!"

So that was the vein in which our luncheon of about twelve people started. Duncan sat at one end of the long table with Gertrude Stein on his left and Mrs. Eugene Meyer on his right. I was at the other end with Alice B. Toklas at my left. I must say I rather liked this faded, wispy-long-haired woman. She seemed to have a few thoughts of her own, apart from Gertrude Stein's, and was more kindly. I soon saw that there was a verbal battle royal going on at the other end of the table and that Gertrude Stein took exception to everything Duncan said. When he quoted a passage from an art book he was currently reading, she shouted that was crazy and stupid, literally stamping her foot on every idea. Leo Stein, her brother, is said to have been of the two the real connoisseur of painting, from whom she learned everything she talked about — except that she put it over with more color!

As for the lecture, Miss Stein opened with her usual remark, "When I am at a picture gallery my one idea is to look out a window." And further along, after a few rambling words, "When in a picture gallery what I look for is a bench, is a bench, is a bench." These odd repetitions were apt to stick in one's mind more than anything else she said.

During the thirties Duncan continued to lecture at various museums, including the Pennsylvania Museum of Art and the Art Institute of Chicago. In the spring of 1931, he was invited by his classmate, then president of Yale, Charles Seymour, to deliver one of the Trowbridge Lectures. I remember how pleased Theodore Sizer, director of the Yale Museum of Fine Arts, was with Duncan's suggestion that he send ahead a number of his favorite paintings from the collection to be hung in the gallery where he was to speak, so that he could talk with the students informally about them afterwards. We were guests of the Seymours; the audience — half faculty and half students — were very appreciative; and Duncan rediscovered his second cousin, John Allison, one of the most popular Yale professors and a friend of Chauncy Tink-

Edgar Degas (1834–1917). *Women Combing Their Hair*, 12¼ x 17¾

er's. This was the first of several occasions when Duncan spoke at the university, and it pleased him to be made an honorary Fellow of Berkeley College, where John Allison was a Fellow, and at the commencement that June to receive from President Seymour's hands the honorary degree of Master of Arts.

All this time Duncan was keeping up his strong interest in sports, not only in his own golf and tennis, but as a great baseball fan, especially when it came to the Washington team, the Senators. He and our son Laughlin shared much baseball talk following the games, discussing box scores and the records of individual players with devout interest. Laughlin and I enjoyed going with Duncan to many games at the colorful old Griffith Stadium.

Once in the early thirties a very amusing incident took place because of Duncan's special brand of humor. It happened at the time a group of men connected with the Washington Senators suddenly appeared one morning at his office in the gallery. Their spokesman said, "We see you in the same box regularly at the ball games and wonder because of your great interest if you would like to take over a part ownership or some shares in the team."

Duncan toyed with his paperweight, seemed to give the proposal great thought, and then announced, "I will do it on one condition, in fact I will even sell the Collection and buy the team if you meet my requirement." Of course, they were all ears to know what that would be, and Duncan continued, ". . . that is if you will make me your playing manager, at my old position, second base!" So they filed out and Duncan was left with the collection.

When I went to the baseball games, I had additional pleasure in sketching the players in action, singly and in groups, including even the structure of the grandstands. These little pencil drawings eventually became paintings, the best of which was "Night Baseball," which I gave to Duncan and which he often hung in my unit in the collection. The color reproduction of it is one of the best sellers in our postcard room since every family has its baseball fan.

When Marianne Moore, the distinguished poet in love with baseball, came to the gallery, she proved to be as much of a baseball addict as Duncan and she took such delight in my picture, identifying immediately the little figure of Joe DiMaggio at bat that I was tempted to give it to her, but remembered just in time that it belonged to Duncan. Some years later, when I included it in an exhibition of my work at the Palace of the Legion of Honor in San Francisco, a representative of

Wildenstein's wanted to buy it for the Baseball Hall of Fame at Cooperstown, New York.

The thirties were an exciting time for us both and also for the gallery. Toward the end of that period Paul Sachs, director of the Fogg Art Museum at Harvard, and his associate, Professor Jakob Rosenberg, the great Rembrandt scholar, brought a group of their graduate students to Washington in the Easter vacation and asked Duncan if we would talk with them about the pictures. This visit was repeated and became a tradition continued by John Coolidge after Paul Sachs had retired.

Another colleague whom Duncan particularly enjoyed was Daniel Catton Rich, for some years director of the Art Institute of Chicago. They first met when Dan was assistant curator and came in 1933 with Mr. Robert Harshe, then director, to borrow our Renoir for the Century of Progress Exposition. In 1936 Dan persuaded Duncan to lecture on "Personality and Design" at the Art Institute. Later Dan was to remark that Duncan had influenced him more than anyone else in this country — a touching tribute from a much younger man.

Of the gallery's acquisitions in this decade Duncan was especially pleased with the great Goya, "The Repentant Peter," acquired in 1936. Other important additions included several Braques, Bonnard's "Open Window" and "Terrace," nine more John Marins, six Klees, Picasso's bronze "The Jester," a fine small abstraction and "Studio Corner" also by Picasso, and in 1939 de la Fresnaye's "Emblems" ("Mappemonde")! Two wonderful Degas were bought the following years 1940 and '41, "Women Combing Their Hair" and the lovely small canvas, "Reflection."

10

THE BRAQUE AND PICASSO UNITS

WHENEVER possible Duncan collected "units" of favorite artists' work; building up the number of paintings in each group over the years. By a unit he usually meant enough paintings by a given artist to hang together in one gallery large or small. Of course many painters are represented by a single distinguished work; for example, de la Fresnaye, Constable, Eakins and Homer.

Among the most important of the larger units in the Phillips Collection are those of Honoré Daumier, seven oils and two drawings and a group of lithographs; sixteen oils and four brush drawings by Pierre Bonnard; fifty Arthur Doves, twenty-one John Marins, over forty Karl Knaths, twelve Paul Klees, six Oskar Kokoschkas, and twelve paintings by Georges Braque.

Outstanding smaller units, sometimes enough for a single wall, include four Edgar Degas, four Corots, three small Delacroix, three Van Goghs, three Courbets, eight Albert Ryders, four Twachtmans, and six outstanding Cézannes. There are also many units of the work of contemporary painters, including a special room of Mark Rothkos.

We have six Picassos, among them the beautiful blue and rose "Still Life with Portrait" (1905), "The Blue Room" ("La Toilette") (1901), as well as the "Bull Fight" (1934); and the bronze "The Jester" (1905). Duncan's admiration for Picasso became somewhat qualified in the middle period when he felt that Picasso was painting with tongue in cheek, and after that Picasso's prices were higher than Duncan was willing to pay, even though he recognized his special genius.

One of the most important of the large units is that of Georges Braque — the last acquired in 1966, the first in 1927. To us Braque

Winslow Homer (1836–1910). *To the Rescue*, 24 x 30

and Bonnard were the two best French artists of their period, and in the museum world of the twenties it was fashionable to speak of them as the two greatest colorists. Although Braque's color is more aristocratic, we never doubted that Bonnard was the "finest most original and inventive colorist living." Between 1927 and 1929, Duncan bought two Braques of identical size, "Plums, Pears, Nuts and Knife" and "Lemons, Peaches and Compotier." They were our first and we reveled in them; we used to borrow them from the gallery for periods to hang in the dining room at home, and at such times Duncan and our guests, especially Henri Focillon, the eminent French critic, always ended up comparing the two. He and Duncan felt that the "Lemons, Peaches and Compotier" was more freely painted with more impasto, and Focillon said of "Plums, Pears, Nuts and Knife" that it was "trop cartesian!" But they agreed that both were little beauties and foils for each other as the artist intended.

In 1930 Duncan bought "Still Life with Grapes," and from then on it was his favorite. The picture deeply satisfied him and I can see him now talking about it with infinite delight as he stood before the canvas. When it was reproduced in color for the handsome *Twin Editions* (large prints), he wrote the following brief essay to be included with each print in leaflet form:

Georges Braque was born at Argenteuil near Paris in 1882. His boyhood was spent at Le Havre. There he found an art school which however had less influence on his career than the proximity of the sea and his memory of his first aesthetic experience in sharing the preoccupation of his parents and their environment while at work. They had a shop for art materials. His father was a house painter skilled in decorative lettering and in the imitation for commercial uses of the grain of wood and the vein of marble. This youthful interest had a formative influence upon the discovery and

Paul Cézanne (1839–1906). *Still Life with Pomegranate and Pears*, 18¼ x 21⅞ (*Gift of Gifford Phillips, 1939*)

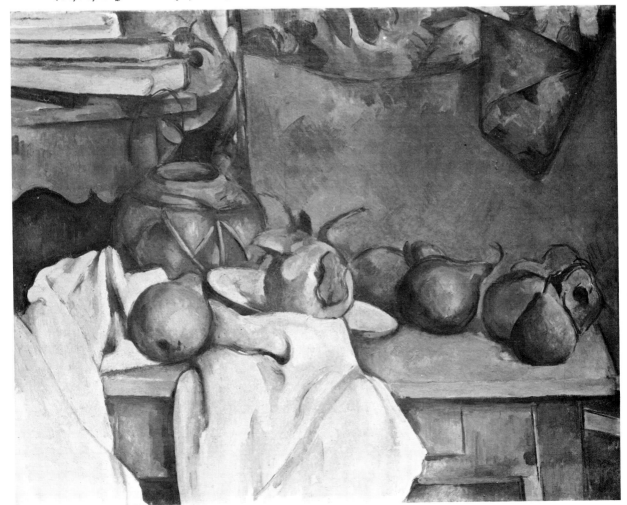

Georges Braque (1882–1963). *Plums, Pears, Nuts and Knife*, 9 x 28¾

Georges Braque (1882–1963). *Lemons, Peaches and Compotier*, 9 x 29

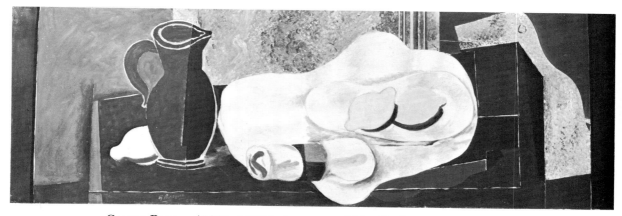

George Braque (1882–1963). *Lemons and Napkin Ring*, 15 ⁵⁄₁₆ x 47½

Georges Braque (1882–1963). *Still Life with Grapes*, 21 x 29

development of Braque's mature style similar to Renoir's early apprenticeship to porcelain and Rouault's to stained glass.

In the first years of the new century Braque was an impressionist and a pointillist. In 1906 he had joined Matisse, Derain, Dufy, and the other Fauves. This association, although for him a step in the wrong direction, linked him with pictorial innovators who were determined to stress functional uses of the elements of design. By 1909 Braque had tried his hand at seascapes, landscapes and figures, which revealed the study of Cézanne's mutually related planes and his famous sayings about the geometry in nature. Matisse noted at an exhibition that Braque's trees and ground forms were stated in cubes, a remark which led to the consciousness of a new ism, cubism. Braque and Picasso then proceeded to a disciplinary practice in diagraming planes. They dreamed of new symbols for the pictures of the new age. First there was the idea of extending Cézanne's "little sensation" into an abstract conception. Then came the rough-hewn many-faceted block, to mark on the picture plane all the dimensions of space — next the almost colorless edifice of modulated and rectilinear planes with a curve or two, or a letter or two, as foils — next an arrangement of cards tiptilted and over lapping on a background no deeper than the surface of the canvas. Texture contrasts were gradually permitted as an enrichment of surface and a new innovation. Real fragments, actual odds and ends were inserted. Ultimately all this "collage" would lead to a variety of painted surface effects, spotted.

In 1914 Braque was interrupted by the outbreak of the First World War just as he was arriving at the real starting point of his personal style. After being severely wounded [in the head] and restored by surgery he returned to his easel and revealed at once the same creative purpose as before the war, but now clarified and with craftsmanship almost instantly at concert pitch. From 1918 to 1930 Braque painted the outstanding decorations of his age. His influence on applied design spread from France around the world. He had evolved a curvilinear rhythm sometimes simple, more often complex. No longer restrained from rich sensuous painting he stylized bowls, and goblets, mandolins and guitars, fruits and flowers, and a few monumental nudes, and "decors de ballet." It was the best style in Europe during that interval between the wars when epicureanism flourished for a little while and when cubism finally justified itself by producing works of art at once architectural and lyrical. There has seldom been more subtle color in painting and certainly never logic more charming.

The adjective lyrical is always needed to describe the artfully balanced and unquestionable relations of color and form in the best paintings of Georges Braque. There is poetry in their painterly appeal both to the senses and to the mind. By the time he had found his true course he had resolved to be content with limited means, believing as he did that "the limitation of a method secures its style while extension of methods in art leads to decadence." He trained himself for a life work as an artisan, a master craftsman in the great classic tradition of "nothing in excess." He would be both a builder and a stylist. He would make so sensitized and subtle a use of technical means that his art would be pure self-sufficient creation, a proof of which he called "the pictorial fact." It cannot be denied that, no matter how acceptable his aesthetic, the secret of the unique pleasure he was able to give was due less to doctrine and certainly less to formula than to his own distinguished sensibility. He belongs to the family of great French painters who mastered their instruments because they were born for them.

In the twelve years of his finest and most personal achievements almost every picture Braque painted was a masterpiece of geometrical arabesque. Generally the angles of his earlier cubism had been subordinated to rhythmical curves and the severe limitations formerly imposed on his palette had been modified, not so much by addition of many new colors as by enrichment of the same ones with sanded, color saturated surfaces and with luminous pigments of the most surprising subtlety and harmony. There were canvases in which luxuriant shapes and tones gleamed in dappled light and shade. Yet even in this curvilinear period which was really a new Baroque, some of the finest works were consummations of the austere experimental diagrams of about 1912–14.

Still Life with Grapes, 1927

In the "Still Life with Grapes" of 1927, here reproduced for the first time in color, the vignette of color shapes is a mass of rounded heavy contours, flat, straight-edged rectangles and inverted diagonals. Around this exciting center are quiet areas of opaque tones on unobtrusively tilted horizontals. The pattern can be analyzed as revealing a logical progression from the circles of the black spots on white cards and the green grapes in clusters to the ovals of the fruit bowls and the goblet and thence to the objects which curve only at the corners. The movement is vertical and circuitous, in and around the overlapping, radiating planes. They slip back in all but parallel recessions to a shallow space which is indicated by contours and directions, no longer by modulation of the planes. Each flat sheet seeks its place within the containing frame for the whole composition. Does this sound like a complicated organization? The reply from the eye is no. The effect is of life, crackling with expanding energy through a persuasive reason. The colors sing in vibrant chorus their unusual song of coal black and oyster white, of aristocratic intermediate tones, of pale blue, gunmetal gray, "café au lait," terra cotta, sand yellow and grape green.

He wrote of a Picasso in the Phillips Gallery purchased in 1929:

Our Picasso Abstraction in oil is a small but excellent creation of his period of flat cubism. It is dated 1918. By that time he had moderated his bleak austerity and was balancing restrained colors and varied textures to an abstract design in overlapping planes, edged and angular. There is an inevitableness and strange distinction about the colors. The robins-egg blue of a singular intensity is made more sonorous by an accompaniment of oyster-gray, ivory white and tobacco-brown. The pure abstraction without a trace of representation, with only vague hints of objective forms, can perhaps be compared to a bit of difficult modern music which vaguely stirs the senses and the mind with its unfamiliar scale, its strange intervals, its Orientalism. . . . One is never certain about this artist. If he made himself more clear or if he were more consistent he would not be Picasso, the most generating force for better or worse in the realms of art today.

Pablo Picasso (1881–   ). *Still Life, 1905,* 32¼ x 39½
(*Owned by Marjorie Phillips*)

Of the collection's earliest Picasso, Duncan wrote:

The interior, entitled "The Blue Room" wistfully and poignantly blue, with a blue unlike any other in painting, with accents of clouded white, green-gold, wine-red, dates from the year after his arrival in Paris from Barcelona. Already he was celebrated as a prodigy of dazzling skill and arresting intellect. Ours is a succulent, sumptuous little picture. Enjoying its strange, heady color we cannot resist a sharp regret that he could not have worked for at least ten years in so rich a vein. The design is rhythmical and in spite of the realism of the bed and the early morning light the distortion and unreality of the figure are appropriate to a scene which is already more of a Hispano-Moresque pattern than a picture.

In 1944 Paul Rosenberg loaned us for temporary exhibition a room of stunning Picasso still lifes from his family collection; very colorful,

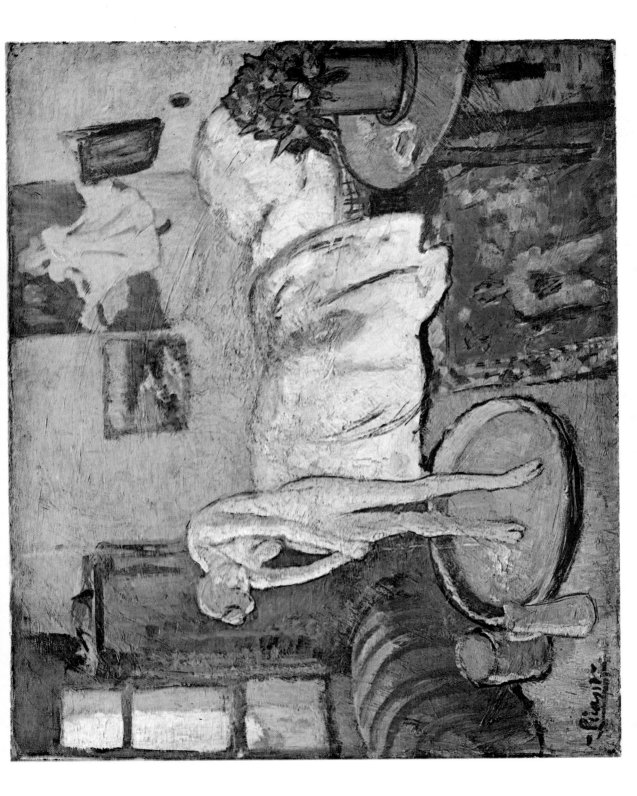

Pablo Picasso (1881–1973). *The Blue Room*, 20 x 24½

Pablo Picasso (1881–1973). *Abstraction Biarritz*, 14 x 10¾

Pablo Picasso (1881–1973). *The Jester*, bronze, 16″ high

great designs. We always hoped to have them on loan again; unfortunately none were for sale.

In 1938 Duncan got up a Picasso and Marin exhibition for the gallery: twenty-five Picassos and twenty-one Marins. Eight of the Marins were loaned by Stieglitz; the rest came from the Phillips Collection.

Pablo Picasso (1881–1973). *Bull Fight*, 20 x 26

The Picasso group included our gallery's "Blue Room" ("La Toilette"), 1901; the "Bull Fight," painted and purchased in 1934, and the sculpture "The Jester" which Duncan described in a few lines: "The equivalent in nervous modeling with lively contours for the paintings of adolescent acrobats and comedians, the hollows of the eye sockets and the cheeks accentuate the pathos and poetry Picasso was seeking to express." Of the collection's small painting called "Abstraction" in the show, he said: "Though subjectless the design maintains a magnetic life and vitality because of sensitiveness and the perfection of these relations."

There were several paintings loaned by the Marie Harriman Gallery; one personally by Mrs. Harriman, which Duncan would have given

John Marin (1870–1953). *Back of Bear Mountain*, 17 x 20

anything to have in the collection. It was "Lady with Fan," 1905. He wrote of it: "Painted in praise of the profile and curves of Picasso's own Fernande, the oracular pose and even its romantic symbolism are only important in providing the excuse for a Greco-Egyptian silhouette which fills a space with linear rhythm and a satisfying plastic harmony in key of blue." As a painting it had a bewitching fascination for him. Others were borrowed from the collections of Miss Etta Cone, Stephen Clark, the Valentine Gallery, and the Pennsylvania Museum.

Another Picasso which Duncan admired tremendously and would

Georges Braque (1882–1963). *The Round Table*, 58 x 45

have loved to acquire was the Museum of Modern Art's "Three Musicians," 1921. He had great respect for and delight in the strong light and dark pattern as well as its resonant color scheme. He wrote of our collection's "Bull Fight":

This abstraction is vividly expressive of the light and excitement of a bull fight in the Spanish sun. It is a composite of Picasso's life extending from his racial background to his latest emotions in the bull pen of Europe today. Symbolical clashes of color and a swirl of ferocious lines mark this new Baroque with the special significance of an aesthetic dictator's impetuous and ruthless calligraphy.

The Braque unit continued to grow. In 1934 Duncan purchased "The Round Table," a choice that seems to have been admired around the world for it has been wanted for every Braque retrospective held in the past decade. Duncan acquired it from Paul Rosenberg, with whom he always had a good time looking at paintings. They shared a mutual zest even if they now and then differed. For instance, Duncan never shared Rosenberg's enthusiasm for Picasso's period in the twenties when he painted very large seated women with one foot on a square block.

Duncan considered Braque's "Round Table" one of his greatest and most exciting works — "a consummation of the artist's best powers." It sums up, he wrote,

all that was hoped for in founding a school on Cézanne's cubes and cones. In this large decoration the familiar and intimately characterized objects such as the red apple, the clay pipe, and the short thick kitchen knife are "the visible medium of exchange" between Braque and his public. The rest is architecture — and music. It is functional and majestic in its forms and in its chromatic range it is exultant. It seems to open and to absorb the light over its rough surfaces with an organic life of its own. The contrasted colors, planes and lines are arranged so that they will serve as the instruments for an orchestral symphony. In his life Braque is essentially the craftsman and the robust man of his hands. He is also a philosopher and an epigrammist of design. He is both an aesthete and intellectual, both craftsman and poet, in such a picture as the "Round Table." It is not esoteric enjoyment which art thus provides but pleasure in the daily exercise of our human sensibilities and perceptions.

Of course Picasso and Braque had invented cubism together before the First World War; each had come to it at the same time. After the

Georges Braque (1882–1963).
The Wash Stand, 63⅞ x 25¼

Georges Braque (1882–1963).
Music, 36⅛ x 23½
(Bequest of Miss Katherine S. Dreier, 1953)

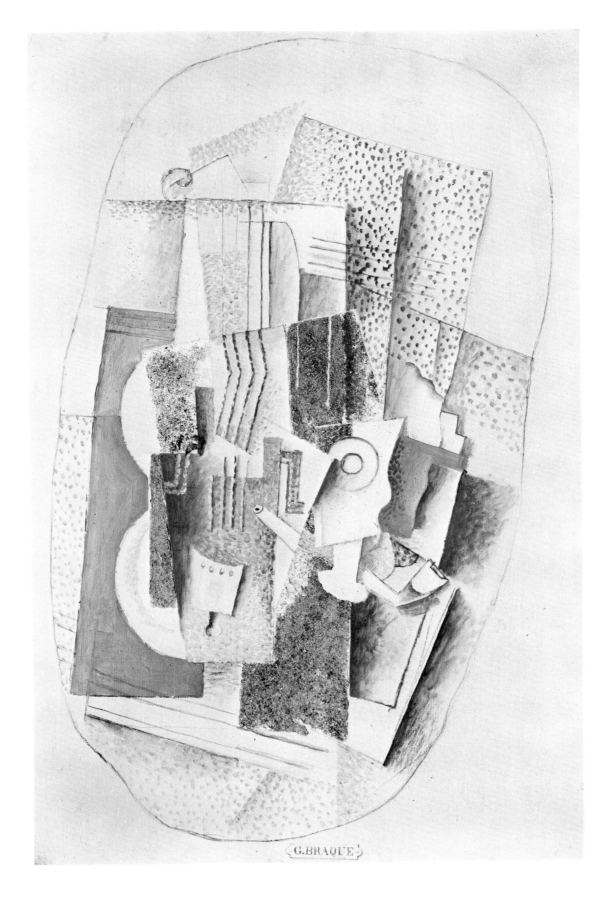

G.BRAQUE

war they each went through many phases. Duncan felt that in everything he did Braque showed a wonderful balance and classic manner of seeing — qualities which he especially admired. When we had a retrospective exhibition of fifty-five Braque canvases in 1939–40 Duncan wrote:

In the literature of cubism the adjective "lyrical" is often used to describe the artful, disciplined arrangements of Georges Braque. There is indeed poetry in their thrilling and personal appeal both to the senses and to the intellect. And there is a poetry in their varied patterns, their contrasted textures [often sanded] and their selective, subtle, autographic color schemes. The art of Braque is a lyricism of pure aesthetic relations in which the complexities of our age are fused in a serene balance and harmony. Irrefutable logic and perfect taste, an emphatic contrast of straight and curved lines, and the organization of tilted planes across shallow space characterize the stylism of this culmination of 20th century Baroque. It renounces the all-over pattern of curvilinear design with three dimensional forms in depth, in order to merely suggest and to symbolize spacial relations while decorating a wall with Gallic grace and architectonic grandeur. All the experiments of cubism are justified by the emergence of this great master of design who now takes his place in history among the French masters of the classic tradition.

A retrospective exhibition necessarily reveals the formative and transitional stages of an evolution of style. On his way to his present unique eminence Braque experimented rather laboriously with materials, and disciplined himself with an austere suppression of his charm, first in the analysis and later in the synthesis of almost completely abstract lines and shapes. While in the cubist period he worked in close association with Pablo Picasso and his paintings often lost their individuality because of the concentration which he practiced and the discipline which he shared with his more dynamic friend. However the assembled products of thirty years of his striving compared with the retrospective show of Picasso that is now in New York reveals Braque's consistent intention to work out a new classic balance and a kind of modern chamber music while Picasso was constantly being swayed by a variety of insistent creative impulses and of more or less personal discoveries. It is my belief that although Picasso's range has been far wider and his influence far greater and although he is perhaps the more indisputable genius, time may rank the mellowed craftsmanship and enchanting artistries of the reserved Frenchman higher than the restless virtuosities and eccentric innovations of the Spectacular Spaniard.

11

THE WAR YEARS

D UNCAN was always intensely interested in politics and world affairs. In fact, I believe he was as absorbed by developments in
these fields as he was by developments in the art world. He read vora-
ciously — newspapers, magazines, and books. His interest in public affairs must have started through growing up in the Capitol and became
stronger when his brother Jim entered politics.

One of his main concerns was the danger of overstressed nationalism; he consistently thought in terms of some kind of super-sovereign
body with its own police force and of a stronger codification of world
law. Over the years Duncan became more and more liberal in thought.
From the New Deal on he described himself as an "Independent," although we both leaned more to the Democratic party. In 1952 we
voted, in the District of Columbia's first presidential election, for
Adlai Stevenson.

Much earlier Duncan had thought with favor of Clarence Streit's
Union Now, but he eventually concluded that it was probably "not
feasible in these times." Although his good friend Walter Lippmann
argued strongly against the movement, saying that his own stress was
always on "the science of the possible," Duncan kept on giving it token
contributions. He also supported the organization Federal Union, because he liked "to help keep these ideas alive and in the air."

He later became impressed with the development of Atlantic Union;
and the one time that he met Churchill and had a chat with him (while
Churchill was sitting drinking red wine instead of cocktails) at a reception at the British Embassy, Sir Winston agreed that it was a *very*
good thing. In fact we heard the prime minister talk in its favor the
next day in New York at an Atlantic Union luncheon.

At the bottom of all this was Duncan's passionate concern to find avenues to peace. Both before and after World War II it occupied his mind continuously and his conversation on the subject was fervent. But when the war in Europe reached the stage of utterly imperiling our friends and allies, he felt strongly this country must join the fight against Hitler's Germany and — after Pearl Harbor — the Japanese.

In 1941, when the magnificent new National Gallery was completed and accepted at a vast opening reception by Franklin D. Roosevelt "on behalf of the people of the United States of America," Duncan and I were proud and pleased that this splendid building, with its many treasures, should be in Washington.

Andrew W. Mellon had bequeathed to it his own great collection of old masters; and other outstanding collections were to follow. David Finley, its first director, had been an indispensable right-hand man to Mr. Mellon when he was Secretary of the Treasury, and he knew everything that Mellon had in mind for the gallery's development. David was indefatigable. With his extraordinary diplomacy and drive he quickly obtained new gifts for the gallery, including a great many important individual paintings, as well as whole collections. As I mentioned earlier, David Finley and Duncan had served together during the early twenties on a planning committee for a larger national gallery and had become good friends. In 1941 David made him a charter trustee and member of the acquisitions committee — positions Duncan held for twenty-three years before he resigned.

David humanized the National Gallery for his trustees by telephoning them frequently between meetings to tell them about all sorts of interesting details and consult them on problems. They could not help but feel close to it all. He said to me later with a nostalgic chuckle, "Duncan certainly said what he thought!"

When it came time for David Finley's retirement, Duncan was strong in his conviction that John Walker, then chief curator of painting, should follow him as director. Duncan was devoted to John and considered him exceptionally well qualified in the field of old masters as well as a good administrator. Both he and David gave the vast building a definite warmth and liveliness which would not have been there under the detached scholar-director of old. And within twenty-five years, they had helped Washington develop one of the greatest national galleries of the world.

As a trustee, Duncan wanted to give the National Gallery something especially distinguished which would speak for him personally as well

Alice Marie Nelson gives one of the gallery's regular concerts; Linda Hall at the piano.

as fill a definite need. Since it had no example of Daumier's painting, he purchased for it the marvelous "Advice to a Young Artist." This painting, which has perhaps as fine a provenance as any Daumier, was a gift from the artist to his friend Corot. Duncan also presented several other paintings to the National, one an intriguing Hogarth called "The Concert."

In 1940 Duncan participated in a symposium held at the Phillips Gallery and spoke of "The Place of the Arts in the World Today" — a moving plea for the continuance of art for as long as possible in a world at war. He returned to this theme in an address written soon after America entered the war and delivered before the American Association of Museums at Williamsburg, Virginia. Here are a few excerpts from it:

Art can serve the cause of victory. It can do a very considerable part in total mobilization. Those of us who create works of art and those of us who, in Galleries, protect, exhibit and interpret them in their significant relations,

Chaim Soutine (1894–1943). *Windy Day, Auxerre*, 19¼ x 25⅝

can dedicate ourselves and our special knowledge and skills to the morale both of the fighting forces and of the home front. After we have done all we can in our Museums to safeguard our treasures from fires and explosions, there should remain on view a succession of instructive, inspiring, timely and pleasurable exhibitions with special welcome for soldiers, sailors and tired war workers from the offices.

. . . .

The artists of America are enlisting for the Army and Navy, some are in training for camouflage, contributing their paintings for camp chapels and recréation rooms, for war relief or to aid in Civilian Defense. In camps they are being encouraged and provided with materials to carry on their crafts. Many of them have been reporting factually and with authority, on our war industries, on the tremendous task of converting our country into Democracy's mightiest arsenal.

. . . .

The pictured thrills of the new ships, tanks, planes and armies are no more important for us to see than graphic warnings against complacency

Honoré Daumier (1808–1879). *The Uprising* (*L'Émeute*), 34½ x 44½

and overconfidence and what might well be a fatal dependence upon our expected might in 1944 while Hitler is staking everything to win in 1942.

. . . .

Of course Daumiers only occur once in a thousand years. But he should be the inspiration to the artists of our democracy. His masterpiece depicts the volcanic explosion of all enslaved people everywhere. The Paris of its background might be the tragic Europe of today. The magnetic agitator of its focus is the rallying point for the Uprisings of tomorrow, pent up now and ready to burst. I shall never forget an evening when Henri Focillon, a passionate lover of democracy whose wit, wisdom, generosity and idealism make him the perfect commentator on Daumier the artist and the man, held an audience spellbound as he spoke of "L'Emeute." The picture was for him one of the kindred creations, (they seek and find each other down the ages) in which the humanitarians of art pay their quick tributes of understanding to all the nobler passions of revolt. The praise is for the visionaries of the apparently "lost causes," who fight on and on and win out in the end. The leader of Daumier's picture is the eternal nomad of the questing spirit. Blind to the immediate perils of his positions, haunted by his dream of the future, he is the anonymous standard bearer of innumerable battles without name. He is pure flame. Such fire will liberate and cleanse the world.

So, in wartime Washington, the responsibilities of the Phillips Collection were greater than ever. The most difficult problem to be solved was how to continue its activities and keep it a live and beneficent force in spite of the imperative need to protect its treasures. The danger of air raids was considered to be very real. As Duncan wrote to one of our lecturers at that time:

We have consigned our greatest paintings to the William Rockhill Nelson Gallery in Kansas City and to the Colorado Springs Art Center for the duration of the war. However, we carry on as best we can with a few enchanting pictures to make each room a joy to our visitors. In spite of the war, Washington gratefully seeks what art has to give and we continue our work with sincere conviction of its importance to public morale.

All during the war years Duncan stepped up the number of lectures, concerts, loan exhibitions, and rehangings of the collection. Among the many distinguished people who lectured were Martha Graham "On the Dance"; Helen Appleton Read, art critic of the *New York Times;* Archibald MacLeish reading his poetry; and Charles Sterling, curator of the Louvre, who spoke on "The French Primitives."

In a good, typical letter received at this time a stranger writes

February 3rd 1943

Dear Mr. Phillips:

. . . What especially impresses me about the Phillips Gallery is that you keep it open to the public and make every visitor feel welcome. In this way you help to spread the love of pictures and music into circles that otherwise might not go to galleries and concerts. I realized this strongly in hearing John Dewey lecture at the Phillips Gallery and have thought of the same many times since. To me this is cultural democracy and I like it.

Yours appreciatively,

Jolan Loewe

After the war Duncan received many letters from museum and university people who had been stationed in Washington for war work or special training. They told how much the gallery and its homelike friendly atmosphere had meant to them during that trying and super-worrisome period. When Duncan was given an honorary degree at Kenyon College years later, we were told that the idea of giving it started with the appreciation of several Kenyon professors who had spent off-duty hours in the gallery during the war and found it an alleviating and refreshing experience. We heard variations of this feeling on all sides.

During the troubled period leading up to the war Duncan had keenly and sympathetically responded to the painting of Georges Rouault, with its penetrating comment of protest and pity. He had purchased a number of Rouault's moving canvases for the collection, perhaps the gems being "Christ and the High Priest" and "Circus Trio." In 1940–41 our gallery participated in a circulating retrospective exhibition of Rouault's painting; and in his January bulletin Duncan wrote an appreciation of the artist entitled "Rouault in America." He said in part

It is interesting that the first comprehensive exhibition of the art of Georges Rouault should take place during the terrible autumn and winter of 1940–41. Seen against the fiery background of the Second World War, we can read in the paintings and prints of Rouault a sorrowful exposure of human cruelty and a penitential meditation upon the agonizing repetitions of Calvary.

212

Georges Rouault (1871–1958). *Christ and the High Priest*, 19½ x 13½

Wassily Kandinsky (1866–1944). *Autumn*, 23¾ x 32½

When Rouault said to a friend that he was not so much a Modern as a man from the Age of the Cathedrals he meant that he still believed in Demons and that the shame of Christ's crucifixion remains a continuous torment to his soul. Driven by an insistent inner need to invent graphic and chromatic symbols for the soul's struggle against the human beast, Rouault unconsciously resorts to the grotesque imageries of Gothic gargoyles as foils to the multicolored and dynamic incandescence which is his equivalent for the Divine light, in men and in the creative universe. Beauty and horror, glamour and shame, have always been poignantly combined in his inner vision and subconscious life. There are masterpieces of Rouault, like the famous Mr. X, in which the dominant quality is not spiritual fervour but profound insight into human character in the tradition of Daumier. Then too there are philosophical and imaginative soul-portraits like that of the melancholy "Old King" weighed down by his own splendour.

Georges Rouault (1871–1958). *Circus Trio*, 30 x 42

Gothic stained glass recollections from his early apprenticeship to a "verrier" have no doubt formed to a large extent the pattern and palette of Rouault and have also been ever present in our responses to his mysticism and to his translucent pigments. Yet, strictly speaking, the heavy black lines in Rouault's mature style are totally different from the leading in cathedral glass which was functional, to hold the glass together, and which played no part in the pictorial unity. In Rouault the lines are a structural part of the design and of the emotional and symbolical color.

Too much credit cannot be given to James S. Plaut, Director of the Institute of Contemporary Art, for initiating and assembling this timely exhibition of works by the prophetic Rouault.

. . . .

. . . Mr. and Mrs. Maurice Sterne permitted us to show for the first time a unique and important example of Rouault's consciously disciplined and academically cultivated beginnings. "The Ordeal of Samson" was painted in unsuccessful competition for the Prix de Rome in 1893, while the young genius was still under the guidance of his beloved teacher Gustave Moreau at the Ecole des Beaux Arts. The large ambitious canvas reveals how much the boy Rouault admired the last period of Titian and the mysterious penumbra and golden reds of Rembrandt. It is well that cynics should note the accurate drawing and true anatomy of the tortured head and body of Samson. Yet the expressionism is already in evidence even in the realism; the skin taut over the muscles and the eyeless sockets a foretelling of the cavernous holes in the blanched skulls of his piteous death-head clowns of later years. Although the inventive, more or less instinctive stylizations of Rouault's mature art are not even suggested, the theme of his Samson is already the one which was to dominate his entire career and to fill with blazing anger and soul-shaking pity almost every picture he was to create. That theme of course may be summed up as "man's inhumanity to man."

One of Duncan's most satisfying friendships began during the war with Professor Henri Focillon, art historian and exchange professor at Yale from the Collège de France. They saw most of each other when Focillon was professor in residence at Dumbarton Oaks in Washington. He first came to our home with Charles Seymour, son of the former president of Yale. Charles, a dear friend of Duncan's, was at that time curator of sculpture at the National Gallery. He had been a favorite pupil of Focillon's and they had continued as close friends.

Professor Focillon was stockily built and very stooped at the shoulders. At times he walked with his eyes glued to the ground, giving the impression of extreme nearsightedness. But his spirit soared and he saw with his mind and heart. As Charles Seymour once said, "If there is a piece of true art at the height of a cathedral ceiling he will see it." His vast knowledge and enthusiasm made him a great leader in the field of teaching.

At the Phillips Collection Focillon understood exactly what Duncan was trying to do, admired the way he hung the collection — as in a home, without long explanatory labels. He felt and loved the independence and authority he found in the Phillips selections and was especially fond of the Daumiers and the great little Delacroix "Paganini." Duncan was greatly touched and warmed by the discerning, penetrating appreciations from one he admired so much. He revered Focillon's book, *Vie des Formes*, a classic in the literature of art. Duncan delighted in the professor's profound admiration of one of his own special favorites in the collection — Daumier's large "L'Émeute" (The Uprising) and I remember his pleasure when Focillon bowed down before it in admiration. (When André Malraux visited the gallery in 1961 he said to us, "This is the greatest of all Daumiers.")

In 1940 Focillon was sent by his government to make a study of the art departments of universities across the United States. While he was on this trip Duncan sent him a telegram

March 8, 1940

DELIGHTED TO HEAR FROM CHARLES SEYMOUR THAT YOU CAN LECTURE AT OUR GALLERY IN APRIL. HOPE THURSDAY NIGHT APRIL EIGHTEENTH WILL BE CONVENIENT DATE. WOULD LIKE TO HAVE YOU LECTURE ON DAUMIER AND DELACROIX — CONTRASTING POINTS OF VIEW WITH OTHER ARTISTS — HOPE YOU AND YOUR WIFE WILL STAY WITH US. CORDIAL GREETINGS AND BEST WISHES.

Duncan followed up his telegram with a letter, and this was Focillon's reply:

Saint Louis, April 6, 1940

Park Plaza
Saint Louis

Dear Sir,

As I read your beautiful letter,* full of thought, full of friendship, I pondered upon the surprising affinities which bring minds together and which led us to see the Goya-Delacroix-Daumier

---

* In November 1967 Mr. Gerald de la Villebrunne, counselor of the French Embassy, very kindly translated these Focillon letters for me, and he said when he finished, "Focillon must have been a wonderful man and your husband must have been too"!

Eugéne Delacroix (1799–1863). *Paganini*, 17¼ x 11½

problem in the same manner and almost in the same words. But further, I see in your remarks bright points, lights which, up to now, I had perceived but imperfectly. I am also delighted to hear that my dear Charles Seymour is a third party in our plot of friendship. There is no young man more worthy of nearing the big works and better able to penetrate them. My lecture will be a conversation between three people. Although I shall be the only one to speak, I shall try not to betray you.

Your letter shows an intellectual trust that I shall endeavor to deserve. In the little respite I find during my long voyage, I am beginning to weave in my mind the web of correspondences, to search for the key to agreements and disagreements. As for the article, I shall do my best, if it is possible to write it or at least to give the gist of it in well prepared notes, and I would be sorry, should you have to go to the trouble of searching the French documents. As for the slides, I rely absolutely on your good care. It seems to me that we would have the main landmarks with two Dos de Mayo, a few moving crowds such as the funeral of the Sardine, a few massacres of the Miseries of War; so much for Goya; the liberty on the barricades (which you characterize so well and which I also see as a sublime piece of panorama), the assassination of the Bishop of Liège, the Boissy d'Anglas; this for Delacroix; finally, for our Honoré, everything that is violent, even gay, with a few scenes of theatre or of popular circus (the leader of the rising being at the same time Robespierre and a romantic actor without knowing it). And if we do not have them, I shall try to represent them with words, and if need be, with my hands which is forbidden by American custom but allowed in the interpreters of the Gods.

Dear sir, I thank you for the check enclosed in your letter. I appreciate very much your friendly thoughtfulness but you did not have to do that. May I also suggest that you are much too liberal for a few moments of conversation which, in themselves are already to my eyes, a great and priceless reward? Please allow me to say it to you in Washington with all affection.

We are looking forward to the hours ahead of us. The landscape which I have seen, the people whom I have met allowed me to better understand certain aspects of America. I am amazed at its natural and human dimensions, its diversities, the different ages of civilization which are juxtaposed here at the same time. What lessons for an historian. History is not a river of the Hegelian evolution but a superimposition of geological strata which always remain there. What a fine theme for our lectures, at least if our mutual passion for painting permits it.

I shall see you soon, dear sir, please convey to Mrs. Duncan Phillips my respects and my wife's compliments. To you, I send my feelings of deep and cordial friendship.

Henri Focillon

LIST OF SLIDES FOR LECTURE BY PROFESSOR FOCILLON

April 18, 1940

These slides give the feeling and nature of the lecture which was never printed.

GOYA

Dos de Mayo (oil)	Prado
Executions after the Dos de Mayo	Prado
Two men fighting as they sink in quick sand	Prado
Saturn Devouring His Children	
Pilgrimage of San Isidro	
Fête of San Isidro	
Spiral Horned Goat wearing cassock and preaching to women	Prado
Narrow panel of two old men	Prado
Carnival scene: *The Burial of the Sardine*	
Mad House	Academy of S. Fernando
Tribunal of the Inquisition	Academy of S. Fernando
Girls tossing mannequin in blanket	Prado
The Phantom of Fear (etching)	from the Disparates series
No se Puede Mirar (etching)	from Disasters of War

DELACROIX

Liberty Guarding the People	

DAUMIER

Types de L'Ancienne Comédie (oil)	Esnault Pelterie
Le Malade Imaginaire (aqua)	formerly Bureau Collection
Crispin and Scapin (oil)	Lenore

DAUMIER (*Continued*)

Don Quixote and Sancho (wringing his hands) in big landscape	Mrs. Payson Collection
Après L'Audience (aquarelle)	Esnault Pelterie
La Pladouie (aqua)	Esnault Pelterie
Les Emigrants (oil)	Palais des Beaux Arts (Petit Palais)
Les Voleurs et L'âne (oil)	Louvre
Chanson à Boire (aqua)	Esnault Pelterie
Le Soupe (dessin)	Louvre
Chasseurs se Chauffant (aqua)	Esnault Pelterie
La Parade Foraine (dessin)	Louvre
Le Drame	Munich Staatsgalerie
Le Badigeonneur	

April 22, 1940

Professor Henri Focillon,
Hotel Taft,
New Haven, Connecticut.

Dear Professor Focillon:

Your visit was a delight to my wife and myself and your lecture was a triumphant success. I can say with strict sincerity that I never heard a more brilliant and beautiful one. No one who heard it could ever forget it. I was glad to hear from Charles Seymour that you would write an article on the same subject for publication on your voyage to South America. Although the article will of course be different from the lecture, nevertheless I do hope that you will remember some of the inspired thoughts which you gave us that evening since otherwise there would be no record of them.

I am sending you a copy of the Giorgione book but since you are to be travelling I will not send the big two-volume edition of *The Artist Sees Differently*. We will soon be getting out a revised edition with the illustrations of the Collection brought up to date and I will publish some of my earlier essays in a more convenient format. I did not know until after you had gone that you had presented us with your book *Vie des Formes*. I thank you for this with all my heart and also for the inscription which we deeply appreciate. Your friendship means a great deal to us both. To you and to dear Mme. Focillon we send our most affectionate greetings and best wishes,

Sincerely yours,
Duncan Phillips

New Haven, April 28, 1940

Dear Sir,

What a glorious book and how friendly the lines written on the first page by the hand of a Friend. I am taking *Giorgione* with me so that I can read during the hours of perfect rest at sea, the only ones (together with those spent in the noble mansion on Foxhall road) apt to carry elevated thoughts. Thus, from afar, we shall be able to carry on the conversations we had in Washington. They started with many masters, they continued in the sombre and violent universe which is that of Goya and Daumier (and perhaps did I somewhat darken the shadows?) and now they are going to converge on Giorgione, this golden fruit, this apple from Hesperides. I already feel in anticipation a great happiness of the mind about it and for this I want to convey to you my most friendly thanks. And I also hope to be able to tidy up and to adjust my notes of the lecture which I was so pleased to give at your fine Institute under the auspices and close to your thinking. These memories accompany me in my travels as the nostalgia of a mutual fatherland of the mind.

To you, dear Sir, to Mrs. Duncan Phillips and to your dear son many friendly regards from your faithful

Henri and Marguerite Focillon

Focillon's superb lecture "Les Visionnaires," prepared under difficult circumstances, while traveling in a strange country, had been given at the Phillips Collection to a packed audience in April 1940. He spoke in French, in such a moving outpouring of words, so spontaneous and so electric, that at the close he was given a standing ovation many minutes long. When he bowed deeply in acknowledgment, he said, "I take this to be a tribute to my country."

The Focillons stayed with us a few times and while in Washington frequently came from Dumbarton Oaks for meals; which was a delight as he was full of fun and wit as well as wisdom. Madame Focillon (an American), immensely warm and friendly, helped tremen-

Paul Cézanne (1839–1906). *Seated Woman in Blue*, 26 x 19⅝

dously because she instantly translated every idiom or unusual turn of thought. At lunch one day Focillon said partly in earnest, partly mischievously, "In government I believe in democracy, *doo-ble democracy;* in the museum — absolute *autocracy.*" He had been for a while the head of the Gustave-Moreau Museum in France. Duncan of course enjoyed this remark, since he dwelt so much on the thought "Art is the last stand of the *individual.*"

Focillon's vast knowledge and vast enthusiasm made him a great and revered teacher and when he stayed with us, former pupils would appear out of the blue to pay homage to their master. He was a passionate de Gaullist and later suffered agonies of spirit — not only when his beloved France fell, but all through the occupation period. His heart condition worsened, and although he returned to Yale to teach, his health gradually failed him.

In 1947 Duncan among others wrote a glowing tribute to Focillon in the memorial number of the *Gazette des Beaux Arts:*

If it is true, as I believe, that there never was, and that there might never again be a greater historian of art than Henri Focillon, then it is due at least in part to the truth, so well known to those who were privileged to share his vivid impressions and his illuminating conceptions, that he was himself a great creative artist. He had a genius for words and for imaginative intuitions, and with these artistries he combined the logic and the constructive criticism so characteristic of the French intellect at its best. Fortunate were his pupils who could stake a claim to his mind of global, world-uniting erudition and partake of his liberal, noble mind and heart. He could lecture gloriously. He could hold his classes and his audiences enthralled and profoundly inspired with the miracles of art and the cycles of civilization.

The thrilling voice is now still. We shall not see again the massive head, the heavy shoulders and stooped back, the indomitable eyes behind the thick lenses which, through the inner vision of his matchless mind, could penetrate far beyond the boundaries of what he once called his "habitual obscurity." With those eyes of the imagination Focillon could, from his first peering glimpse at any part, comprehend the style of a whole painting or building.

His greatest work *The Life of Forms in Art* takes its place on the shelf of indispensable books. It is so full of dynamic substance that one can draw from any page the motive power for creative thinking, according to one's special aim or need.

Duncan at Ebensburg, 1947

In our intimate gallery of paintings in Washington, Focillon recognized that I was bringing together kindred spirits and contrasting them with other kinships which appealed for different qualities. He approved the mobility of the collection, its creative, plastic change, its sense of being lived with and worked with and loved. We can never forget the great man's pleasure in our pictures, his generosity of encouragement and guidance. My wife and I admired him so much and became so fond of him that I cannot write of him with impersonal detachment. Best known perhaps as a supremely great authority on Byzantine, Romanesque and Gothic architecture and sculpture, Focillon was for me the best of all critics of XIX Century painting and drawing, and especially of Daumier; one who truly loved the artist's point of view and the many varied felicities of his touch; one who could interpret all the great modern artists with spontaneous inspiration.

The United States borrowed Focillon again and again. It was in our midst, during the dark days of the German occupation of his beloved France, that he spent for the cause of freedom all that remained of him of his ardor, his eloquence and his very life. America can be proud that our scholars appreciated him; that his American pupils will translate him into

English and carry on in his techniques of teaching; that he will always be remembered as one of the best loved and most reverently followed of our college professors. Words were his medium and the clarity and grandeur of the French language his natural element. Yet he was one of us — a universal artist. His kind and soaring spirit was at home wherever men are free or aspire to be free.

April 28, 1947

To name a few more outstanding exhibitions held at the Phillips Gallery during the war period: there was a group of Charles Demuth's very personal watercolors; a retrospective loan exhibition of John Marin paintings, and others of Marsden Hartley, Marc Chagall, Morris Graves. Probably the most important was an exhibition of Roger de la Fresnaye, that brilliant artist who died soon after the First World War as a result of having been gassed. Duncan wrote for the catalogue introduction:

Roger de la Fresnaye, destined to be a legendary knight in the annals of art, died in 1925 after a long illness from the effect of wounds received in the First World War. As far back as 1910 he seemed to have had a premonition that, for the great paintings he owed to posterity, he had very little time. In the years preceding the cataclysm he was drawing inspiration both from the classic and the romantic traditions, from Uccello, from Gericault and from Cézanne. He took, with no less hesitation as he approached his consummation, from the latest art movements in Europe, which were still in their formative and tentative stage. What he wanted was a modernized and yet stately decoration in the grand manner. Of the followers of Cézanne he was, I believe, the first to see that a sound geometrical structure of functional clarity could be added to athleticism of design and to mobilities of color in order to convey a quickened sense of the adventures of mind and body in the twentieth century. While Picasso and Braque were still in the laboratory charting their challenging course and diagramming various problems of assorted shapes and textures related, with analysis or with synthesis, to a field of shallow space, la Fresnaye was already free for his own personal expression, free to show how the new language of color modulations and of Cézanne's cubes, cones and cylinders, could sum up for him the chivalry of his dreams, the pageantry of a swiftly changing world which he cherished in his mind's eye. Before he had reached his thirtieth year he was mature enough in his understanding of himself and of what he wished to do to paint a few clearly individualized and superbly organized masterpieces.

Unlike Braque, whose disciplined distinction for logic, rhythm and bal-

225

ance is in his own vein of plastic chamber music and the finest French taste, de la Fresnaye was not content to limit himself to art for art's sake. For him the Cuirassiers, the Artillery and the Conquerors of the Air were symbols of glorious youth-defying death. In the [Phillips Collection's] over-mantel "Mappemonde," which is more of a mural than an easel picture, emblems of scholarship and the arts are vignetted upon shifting planes of buoyant clouds and of celestial blue which suggest space without breaking through the wall and which symbolize a world in perpetual change and hope. The expressive instruments of man and his mind are placed as they should be at the center of all the spherical and the cosmic mystery and movement. This is very far from literary painting. It is more truly the painter's tribute to the philosopher and the lyric poet. Even in his semi-abstract still life, as in the beautiful Diabolo, with its lush, sensitive colors and its thrilling rectangle of pure white, might he not have been conveying to us a painter's appreciation of life's challenging contrasts?

Roger de la Fresnaye was an aristocrat of an ancient Norman lineage. His noble art is as aristocratic as his name. Now that, once again, artists of the free nations fight as once he fought to keep civilization alive, we do well to remember with honor this gallant Frenchman.*

In 1942 we had an enthralling retrospective of the work of Paul Klee, one of Duncan's favorite artists. From then on Duncan devoted a small gallery of the collection to his Klee purchases — a group considered to be outstanding by connoisseurs everywhere. It has always been hard to keep the group together; with individual paintings invited so often to other museum exhibitions through the year. Duncan, entranced with "Arab Song," one of the rarest of the group, would say, "It is a poem of witty contrivance. Burlap stained, a few lines sketched in it and there is evoked hot sand and sun, desert dust, faded clothes, veiled women, exotic eyes, strange plants — North Africa."

In part of his preface to the catalogue he wrote of Klee:

. . . in Switzerland . . . he joined a group of searchers in the arts who called themselves the Blue Riders. They sought "to externalize the inner life." In 1920 the architect Walter Gropius called Klee to his famous and advanced art school, the Bauhaus, to teach design.

· · · · ·

From childhood he was a dreamer, a poet and a brooding rebel, who refused the compulsion of the imposed pattern, the cultivation of intolerance and the worship of brutality. Always an alien in a nation poisoned [at that time] by inhuman ideology, he was exiled by Hitler and died in Italy after

226

* The collection had acquired this painting, a masterpiece (now called "Emblems"), in 1939.

Roger de la Fresnaye (1885–1925). *Emblems (Mappemonde)*, 35 x 78¾

Paul Klee (1879–1940). *Arab Song*, 36 x 25¼

Jean Auguste Dominique Ingres (1780–1867). *Bather* (*La Petite Baigneuse*), 12¾ x 9¾. Duncan added to the collection at this period (1948) one of its highlights, or "sources," of modern art. This is a small edition of the great Baigneuse in the Louvre. He found it at Rosenberg's.

taking what comfort he could from the inexhaustible resources of his own creative imagination.

. . . .

His virtuosity in craftsmanship was Klee's instrument for conveying suggestions of the stream of consciousness and for expressing a poignant awareness of the strangeness and sadness of life. Whimsy and a fine sense of nonsense relieved the all-persuasive melancholy of his mind and the irony of his comments on modern man's confusions and pretensions.

Of course our son Laughlin was always close to us. But during the war period he occupied our minds and hearts constantly as he was overseas in the Pacific area of the war in Army intelligence. He had enlisted during his sophomore year at Yale. Duncan wrote him frequently, taking turns with me so as not to inundate him, and luckily for us Laughlin kept up his end well. How we pounced on those letters! Duncan could not help admonishing Laughlin about health; and tried to interpret the larger problems and decisions across the world, as well as pass on our own and our gallery news. He was always proud of Laughlin in the best sense; and they were basically congenial in many ways. In one letter he writes:

> The men of my generation failed to do what had to be done and passed it on to you — both the fight to the finish — we never finished before — and world collaboration. The International police will have to use both courage and vigilance but also wisdom, tolerance, social psychology, and just plain neighborliness, being well informed and helpful and mindful of the fact that the world is just one big distracted community — which needs law and order but above all justice and kindness. How I go on! . . . The Washington ball team is making a nose dive — down, down, down.

At last came the day when Laughlin wrote from the Philippines the letter all of us had longed for — August 24, 1945!

> The first time I meant to write was on the eleventh, the morning after we first heard about Japan's willingness to accept the Potsdam Declaration. It was the gala opening of a large new movie theatre, complete with news photographers, a G.I. band, a U.S.O. troupe, and "The Big Sleep." Toward the end of the pro-

gram, in the midst of the movie (just about the time when people were discovering they couldn't possibly keep up with the plot), there came a pause and an announcement: "This is your Public Relations Officer. Word has just been received that Japan has accepted the terms of the Potsdam Conference." There was a moment of stunned silence, then the roar of a multitude. Wild shouting, thrashing, jumping, slapping, clapping. It had come totally unexpected, like a sudden powerful electric shock. Instantly the pent-up emotions of men held as if in confinement for several years were vented. No one wanted to stop shouting; it went on for ten or fifteen minutes. One of the members of the U.S.O. troupe managed to lead a chorus of "God Bless America" through her tears. Finally an attempt was made to resume the movie. Continued uproar from the audience. The lights went on again. An exodus of all men who had vowed to get good and drunk was successfully accomplished, after which the movie was allowed to grind through its not very exciting intricacies. Later of course came news that this might not be the finality: perhaps we would not accept the offer. But no one cared particularly. This was just about the end; it had come as a surprise, and with an unforgettable impact.

This is from a letter which Duncan wrote to Laughlin in November 1945, when Laughlin was still in Japan:

I am all worked up about our need for an enlightened and consistent foreign policy, especially in regard to the atomic bomb and its control by a world federation. If I could get time I would edit a little booklet of what is being thought and said and written and I would be the discussion leader making my quotations from Einstein — Compton — Swing — Lippmann and others sound as if they were answering my questions or debating with each other and the whole imaginary conversation would be the most contemporaneous and thrilling reality — the finest minds quickened by the challenge of a terrible crisis.

Duncan had been pleased when in the late thirties Walter Lippmann, whose widely read newspaper columns he had always deeply admired, came to live in Washington and particularly so when on meeting him he found Walter's *talk* to be as *forthright* as his writing — like Duncan's own! They became great friends, enjoying each other's con-

Oskar Kokoschka (1886–1980). *Courmayeur*, 35½ x 52

versation and corresponding from time to time. Duncan always enjoyed
the Lippmanns' parties and the people they gathered together, particularly those of the press; Duncan considered them "the most interesting
men in Washington." There would be James ("Scotty") Reston, Herbert Elliston (for years editor of the *Washington Post*), Marquis
Childs, Howard K. Smith, Chalmers Roberts, and many others, as
well as diplomats, government officials, and old friends. The setting itself was beautiful — the high-ceilinged living room, with its black car-
pet and robin's-egg walls, the dark pictures, lovely furniture and tall
French windows. Everyone seemed to look and be at his best. Helen
and Walter were *both* so good as host and hostess that they gave a special sparkle and glow to those evenings — like the salons of earlier
times.

230   At our own dinners Duncan enjoyed nothing more than the talk

Oskar Kokoschka (1886–1980). *Lyon*, 38 x 51

with the men afterwards. He relished the role of being a sort of intermediary drawing them out on art, politics, and world affairs.

Duncan first wrote Oskar Kokoschka in 1945 in connection with a loan exhibition of his paintings he was planning for the gallery. By that time we already had four of his works, "View of Prague from the River," the great "Courmayeur," the exquisite and original "Portrait of Mme. Franzos," and "Lac d'Annecy."

Dear Mr. Kokoschka,

I am writing to ask you if you would use your influence with owners of your work in European collections to lend their paintings for a large exhibition. I would especially like that early Portrait of Forel and the landscape of Amsterdam and earlier paintings of Vienna and Prague which I have seen or admired in color prints. We think you are one of the *great landscape painters of all times* and also one of the best painters of *psychological portraits.* . . .

Of one of our own paintings, "Mme. Franzos," Duncan writes:

This is a portrait from Kokoschka's youth in Vienna, when he had a precocious talent for psychological insights in painting his friends. This young woman was understood in her wistful inner life — and the artist painted her face with deep affection and her nervous hands with compassion. The placement of the delicately drawn subject in an encirclement of warm blue against a tonality of opalescence like what time does to an old picture on faded paper or on parchment, is poignantly nostalgic. Far from being sentimental however, the artist is frank to a fault and the delicately colored drawing stands out of its aura with clarity and power.

By 1948 we had the wonderful loan exhibition of Kokoschka's work which covered the whole second floor of our old building. Kokoschka was there and it was a great experience to have him preside in person the opening day. He talked to hundreds of people in relays in the large upper gallery, standing informally among them. Everyone was captivated by his warm heart, his wit, his winning manner, vitality and awareness. He talked about his art, politics, and philosophy of life.

The collection has received hundreds of heartwarming fan letters through the years from strangers and friends. Duncan and I felt this

one to be unusually fine in its charming, articulate gratitude for the Kokoschka show:

12 January 1949

Dear Mr. and Mrs. Phillips,

This is a letter of appreciation to tell you how much I have loved the Kokoschka exhibition at the Phillips Gallery. Since it arrived in December, I feel that his pictures have been my second home! I have been to see them three or four times every week, often taking my friends, and I can hardly bear to think of them leaving Washington in a few days. On Tuesday I battled my way into the gallery to hear Kokoschka speak, and was charmed by his warm, welcoming manner. I was thrilled to observe in Kokoschka the same wonderful excitement, color, and large vision that I have so long admired in his work. . . . But I never expected to see five rooms full of Kokoschka, or to see the man himself as I did this week. I have had more real pleasure from the Kokoschka Retrospective than from any other exhibition I have ever seen. I'm sure that many other Washingtonians feel as I do, because in the gallery on Tuesday I heard many people saying that they had been five or six times.

I hope that you and Mrs. Phillips realize, as I'm sure you must, what endless inspiration is provided by your collection of modern art. If I ever have to leave Washington, the place I should miss most would be the Phillips Gallery. It always seems such a friendly place to me, as informal and comfortable as though the pictures had been hung in my own home for me to enjoy. I have been there so often that I have even become attached to the brass door-handle and certain favorite chairs — as well as the paintings themselves. One of my happiest memories was one rainy winter afternoon when I went to the gallery to see the lovely colors in Kokoschka's "Prague." It was not hanging that week because a special show was in progress, but one of your curators brought it out for me, stood it against the wall and let me look at it as long as I wanted to! . . .

Sincerely,
Diana Merritt

At the time of his opening Kokoschka stayed with us for a few days, and we enjoyed watching him carry on his lifelong habit of fill-

Oskar Kokoschka (1886–1980). *Portrait of Mme. Franzos,* 45 x 32½

ing notebooks with drawings, using mostly Crayolas (for travel). He drew everything that interested him — the philodendron plant, flowers, and whatever took his eye around the house or terrace.

One day Duncan and I went with him to the National Gallery and found great pleasure in his keen remarks. He delighted in pointing out passages of favorite paintings that gave special pleasure to him and he was talking of how important and beautiful the floor plane in certain paintings can be. When he passed his hand caressingly over a lovely section of one picture with the ardour of a true artist, a guard rushed forward and pulled him back by his elbow, telling him that it was forbidden to touch the paintings. He looked startled, but much to the surprise of the guard threw his arm around him and said warmly, "Now don't you worry, I am an artist and you understand how used an artist is to touching paintings. I've been close to them all my life." The guard grinned all over and did comprehend perfectly that this was a special case — perhaps feeling Kokoschka's great distinction.

12

THE 1950's

DURING the relatively calm period of the fifties with Dwight D. Eisenhower as President for eight years, this country was outwardly thriving and the Marshall Plan had restored a good economic balance in Europe. We were terribly worried, however, by the apparent success of Senator Joe McCarthy in spreading blighting suspicions that many liberals were Communists, and greatly relieved when his prolonged exposure on national television showed him up to the public as the warped, unstable figure that he was. Duncan passionately denounced his approach and followed the political overtones with intense interest.

In the political campaign of 1952 Duncan and I were strong supporters of Adlai Stevenson, and after he lost that campaign, Duncan, along with a group which included Lewis Mumford, John Steinbeck, and Mark Van Doren, was asked to write a tribute to him for a special number of the *New Republic*. Duncan wrote in part:

Any other year against any other candidate Stevenson might have won. He showed us what a splendid day it will be when a candidate does win with a majority of the people's votes by talking to them as he did, trusting their intelligence, their sense of relative values, their innate idealism, talking with conscientious restraint and scrupulous honesty, frankly, fearlessly, brilliantly, always the gentleman, the scholar and the artist. Even if he never occupies the White House, his countrymen for five months have taken to their minds and hearts a truly great *Presidential personality*. It was a great experience for him and for us. His charming humor and keen wit, his suddenly flashing smile, his apt quotations, his poetic feeling for our country and its varied landscape, his definition of patriotism — "not as frenzied outbursts of emotion but as the tranquil and steady devotion of a life time" — all that and more can never be forgotten.

Public enthusiasm for the arts in America of the nineteen fifties was increasing by leaps and bounds. It was a wonderful period for our museum.

One of the milestones in the history of the Phillips Gallery was the publication at last (in 1952) of a handsome, complete catalogue of the collection illustrated with both color and black and white reproductions of many of the outstanding paintings. The listings were divided into two parts, the permanent collection and the experimental or encouragement collection. Many of the paintings in the latter group were done by students or relative beginners. Duncan's consistent support of their work at crucial times helped many to go forward.

The catalogue contained an introduction by Duncan, but there were so many artists listed that he did not attempt to comment on the work

Naum Gabo (1890–1977). *Linear Construction, Variation*

236

Pierre Soulages (1919–   ). *July 10, 1950*, 51¼ x 63¾

of individuals as he had in previous volumes. It was an attractive, unusual book published by the Thames Hudson Press in London, and there has been a steady demand for it for many years. In the sixties Duncan began planning for a new catalogue which would include the many subsequent additions to the collection.

To name a few of the most exciting additions: perhaps Matisse's late painting "Interior with Egyptian Curtain" would come first; Corot's "View of Genzano," not as provocative but of first importance and very beautiful; and in the same year (1955) Cézanne's great unfinished "Jardin des Lauves." Duncan delighted in studying the Cézanne because its half-finished state revealed so clearly the method of the artist's late period. It proved a great favorite also among artists, especially with abstract painters.

In 1957 we had a fine exhibition of collages by Kurt Schwitters, one

Richard Diebenkorn (1922–   ). *Interior with View of the Ocean,*
49⅝ x 57¾

of Duncan's favorite artists. The two outstanding works which he
bought from the show reminded him from a distance of Persian minia-
tures in their fineness of color and disposition of shapes. We also acquired a large Bradley Walker Tomlin masterpiece, which gave Duncan very great pleasure and satisfaction.

Other exciting purchases during this period included our first two
Mark Rothkos, which inspired our 1960 exhibition of his work; two
Richard Diebenkorns and a Sam Francis (from San Francisco); works
by Morris Louis, Willem de Kooning, Philip Guston, Morris Graves,

238

and Kenneth Noland; a group of fine Knaths to add to our unit of his work; and an Adolph Gottlieb.

The discovery of Nicolas de Staël's painting was a great event. One day Duncan came home to lunch and said, "I have just purchased a remarkably fascinating little canvas from a young man, Theodore Schempp, who drove up with half a dozen paintings in his car, for sale; all of them had quality but I especially liked this little abstraction by de Staël, whose work I have not seen before."

From then on through the first half of the nineteen fifties Duncan built up a unit of Nicolas de Staël's paintings, and by 1954 the collection had six splendid examples. Duncan was genuinely thrilled by the new star on the horizon. I believe the one he purchased from Schempp, the roving dealer and artist, was the first to be acquired in this country by any museum or collector. De Staël later had a large exhibition

Willem de Kooning (1904–   ). *Ashville*, 1949, 25⅝ x 31⅞. Another 1952 purchase which the collection is constantly asked to lend.

Nicolas de Staël (1914–1955). *Parc de Sceaux*, 63¾ x 44⅞

Nicolas de Staël (1914–1955). *Musicians*, 63⅞ x 45

Francis Bacon (1909–   ). *Study of a Figure in a Landscape*, 78 x 54

Nicolas de Staël (1914–1955). *Fugue*, 31¾ x 39½

at Knoedler's, and then Paul Rosenberg added him to his stable of artists. Duncan derived untold pleasure from those he collected, especially "The Fugue." He wrote

"The Fugue" in 1952 represents for me one of the peaks of de Staël's achievement. It is evidence of a time when he was a poet-painter and a protégé of Braque. This is a masterpiece of pondered construction and original craftsmanship, of balanced shapes and elusive modulations within a restricted tonal scale. The brush strokes are heavily troweled irregular rectangles, large and small. They seem to build a desert city of sun-baked walls, row upon row, in an iridescent sky-blue Morocco, a memory of de Staël's years in the Foreign Legion. This is like lyric poetry and like measured ancient music and like architecture when the planes are many-faceted in a serenity of space. The greatness of composition and conception in a painting like "The Fugue" grew in the very act of spreading the thick pigment and balancing the scale of the strokes. They are vertical and horizontal in direction instead of curved and overlapping as in the Cézanne "Jardin des Lauves." Yet de Staël's improvising with his masonry of color-shapes is more like the old Cézanne searching in his latest beginnings for both structure and rhythm than like the uncontrolled subconscious automatism which is so much more in fashion today.

The shock of de Staël's sudden death was unbelievable to all. Duncan wrote:

When, on March 17, 1955, a tragic death by suicide ended abruptly the meteoric career of Nicolas de Staël at the age of forty-one, he was considered by many to be the most gifted, the most influential and the most painterly of the younger painters in Europe. It must be noted, however, that the brilliant promise of his art had been dimmed by a diminishing power revealed in his latest period. The promise had been threatened a few years earlier by a dazzling display of colors, too unadulterated and too delectable, which perhaps had become too popular and too successful for his own peace of mind. It is to the earlier work, more roughhewn, more subtle and more abstract, that the artists and the critics were attracted. In some of the earliest works the sombre tones and crossed diagonals conveyed a sense of inner struggle. During the years 1950–52, however, there was a monumental architectonic grandeur.

In May 1956 we got up a small loan exhibition of Nicolas de Staël's work. And in June of the same year we exhibited a large memorial show circulated by the American Federation of Arts. After that Duncan kept all of our de Staëls hanging in one room or another of the gallery.

Georges Braque (1882–1963). *The Shower*, 14 x 21⅝

In 1953 Theodore Schempp presented in his New York house a remarkable exhibition of the latest paintings by Georges Braque. Many were very large canvases — the beginning of the pool table and studio interior series — and they were high in price, in accord with the increased values in France for that master's work. We purchased the not very large but exciting and colorful "Philodendron" (1952) and I will never forget our ecstasy over it — that we had acquired it for the gallery and therefore could always see it. During this period we bought another 1952 Braque entitled "The Shower" — a fine example of his experiments with an almost expressionistic realism. Duncan was fascinated by this little landscape with its moody, rather lowering sky and tawny stretch of sandy ground inspired by his regular bicycle trips between Paris and Dieppe.

A few years later, just before Braque's death in 1963, Schempp wrote to Duncan telling of a recent visit with Braque:

The day before yesterday will remain in my memory as one of those never-to-be-forgotten days — a day spent with Braque at Varengeville. One of his remarks which most impressed me was his belief that the most im-

Georges Braque (1882–1963). *The Philodendron*, 51¼ x 29⅛

portant thing for an artist is that the artist express *his* personality and most *profound* feeling about the *subject* or the *object* which he *paints*, not only visually but *inwardly* and spiritually, and that he *search* always to approach the subject more closely and to *understand* it better.

Back in 1941 we had made the acquaintance of Miss Katherine Dreier — artist, collector, and founder of the famous Société Anonyme, which opened in New York City as a small museum of modern art at about the same time that the Phillips Collection opened its doors to the public in Washington. Both had only a few rooms at first and alternated groups from their basic collections, as well as lending pictures and holding invited exhibitions. Miss Dreier and the artist Marcel Duchamp, who was secretary and trustee, confined their exhibits to contemporary and experimental works. Duncan on the other hand, always had the idea of showing contemporary (and experimental) art along with paintings from the past in which he saw qualities of form and vitality that were to him forever modern and therefore important sources as well as great company when shown with the new.

One day we received unexpectedly the following invitation:

> Hotel Great Northern
> 118 West 57th St.
> New York City
> March 24th 1941

My dear Mrs. Phillips:

It would give me great pleasure to give you a little informal tea at the Colony Club the week of March 31st and since my days are all free at tea time that week I am going to ask you to choose which date will fall in best with your plans. It gave me so much pleasure to meet you and feel the artist in you — that I would love to gather a few friends with whom to share our interest in art.

Hoping very much that you and your husband can be my guests, believe me

> Faithfully,
> Katherine S. Dreier

The place we had met Miss Dreier was at the opening of an exhibition of my paintings at the Bignou Gallery in New York. She came in quite unexpectedly and to our great pleasure wanted to buy a little painting entitled "The Pink Cup." Unfortunately I could not let her

Henri Matisse (1869–1954). *Studio, Quai St. Michel*, 57½ x 45¾

have it as it was already promised. But Duncan and I did go to tea at the Colony Club and enjoyed it very much. Miss Dreier at that period was rather stout, white-haired, and motherly-looking. Except for her keen intelligent eyes one would never suspect she was the creator of such an original, modern collection. Other guests that day were the painters Tchelitchew and Matta.

Sometime later Duncan wrote Miss Dreier:

March 7, 1945

. . . I have read [your book on Burliuk] from cover to cover and enjoyed it immensely. . . . The part on Russia especially interested me profoundly for I have often wondered about that period of his life. His personality has been made very clear and fascinating. My congratulations.

Sincerely yours,
Duncan Phillips

Like most true collectors Miss Dreier bought so much (and also was so public spirited) that at times her means were overstrained. Quite a few paintings in her collection were contributed by the artists

Duncan in 1956

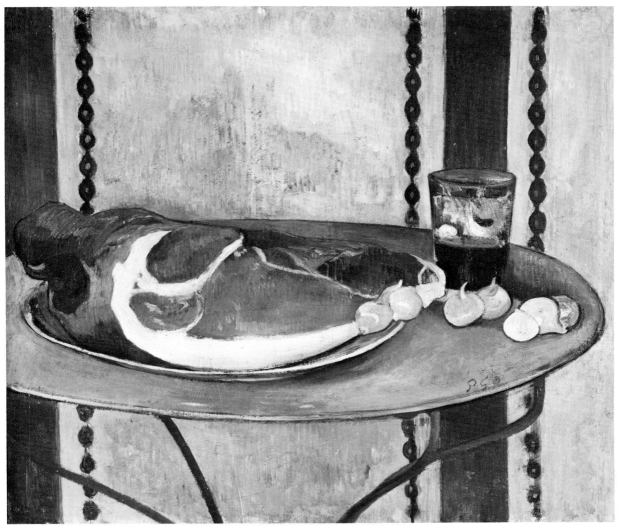

Paul Gauguin (1848–1903). *Still Life with Ham*, 19¾ x 22¾

themselves or collector friends. Knowing how many works by Dove were in our collection, she asked if we would give one to the Société Anonyme. Duncan was happy to do this and wrote her as follows in early 1949:

> I will be very glad to show Mr. Duchamp the paintings by Dove and I hope that we can agree on a picture which would be a fine addition to the Collection of the Société Anonyme . . .
> There is nothing new about the Phillips Gallery as a permanent museum. It has been a *public gallery* since its incorporation in 1918 and we have done active institutional work ever since, with

Duncan, as trustee, meeting Queen Elizabeth II on her tour of the National Gallery, Washington, D.C. Others are Mrs. Ailsa Mellon Bruce and Chief Justice Warren.

many educational exhibitions and publications, many lectures and concerts. The domestic atmosphere is misleading, also the lack of trustees. With warm greetings in which my wife joins me as always

Sincerely yours,
Duncan Phillips

After Duchamp's visit, Duncan wrote again:

April 4, 1949

Dear Miss Dreier:

I think "Barnyard Fantasy" will fit into the Collection better than any other Dove I can think of because of what Marcel Duchamp called "the quality beyond painting." Sometimes Dove is just a great painter or craftsman, then again he is a modern poet.

. . . .

I have been in New York to see the opening of the Braque show and to hear Churchill speak at a luncheon for United Europe. Incidentally I saw some fine work by Jacques Villon* at the Louis Carré gallery. This will interest Mr. Duchamp, who was eager to have me see his brother's new work. We are to exhibit the group next year. This trip to New York and an accumulation of mail which I find on my return has delayed me in writing those paragraphs on Marin and Dove for your catalogue. I will write them during the next few days within the deadline which you gave me. With our warmest regards,

Sincerely yours,
Duncan Phillips

And on April 8, 1949:

Dear Miss Dreier:

I am sending you the paragraphs herewith on Marin and Dove. Next week we hope to send to New Haven† not only the Dove which you selected, the "Barnyard Fantasy" but also a painting by Marjorie Phillips which you requested and we are glad to

---

* The Phillips Collection has three paintings by Jacques Villon.
† Miss Dreier had given most of the Société Anonyme Collection to Yale University in 1941.

Giorgio Morandi (1890–1964). *Still Life*, 8 x 15⅝

Juan Gris (1887–1927). *Still Life with Newspaper*, 28¾ x 23⅝. This
painting was purchased from Miss Katherine Dreier.

Wassily Kandinsky (1866–1944). *Composition — Storm*, 39¼ x 31
(Bequest of Miss Katherine S. Dreier, 1953)

254   Raymond Duchamp-Villon (1876–1918). *Gallic Cock* (*Le Coq*), relief sculpture, 17⅝ x 14⅝ *(Bequest of Miss Katherine S. Dreier, 1953)*

Antoine Pevsner (1886–1962). *Plastic Relief Construction,* 35⅝ x 23½
(Bequest of Miss Katherine S. Dreier, 1953)

Paul Klee (1879–1940). *Small Regatta*, 5¾ x 9
(Bequest of Miss Katherine S. Dreier, 1953)

present to the Société Anonyme of Yale University. It is one of her most distinguished recent canvases entitled "Landscape with Buzzard," a picture which I had intended to keep for our own Gallery. The presentation therefore is from us both.

In 1950, when the Société Anonyme needed to raise extra funds to help pay for its fine catalogue, Marcel Duchamp offered Duncan first chance to purchase Juan Gris' "Still Life with Newspaper." Duncan took him up on the offer, welcoming an opportunity to acquire an important example of early cubism for the collection.

After the death of Miss Katherine Dreier in 1952, Duncan was astonished to receive a letter from Marcel Duchamp saying that Miss Dreier had left a part of her private collection to the Phillips Gallery and asking if he wished to accept the bequest. Duncan was thrilled but at the same time torn — wondering if he should add *en bloc* so much of another collection since his own was thus far so personal. His solution was to ask if he could choose just the things that he would have bought himself — by artists whose work he loved, such as Klee, and also to fill certain gaps in the collection. Fortunately Marcel Duchamp was perfectly happy with this plan. From the sculpture Duncan chose a distinguished Pevsner, a small Calder stabile, and a Duchamp-Villon relief. Of the paintings offered he chose a delectable watercolor "Small Regatta," by Paul Klee, to add to our unit of twelve; an important Kandinsky; a painting by one of his favorite artists, Kurt Schwitters; a fine Mondrian to balance the one he had bought in 1946; and a painting by Franz Marc entitled "Deer in the Forest I."

One morning when Duncan and I were in the gallery we ran into the famous French photographer Henri Cartier-Bresson, who was wandering around studying the paintings. We told him how artistically distinguished we found his work and then I suddenly thought how wonderful it would be if he could do a portrait study of Duncan. I had long regretted that there was no satisfactory portrait of him and that he was very elusive when it came to posing.

Cartier-Bresson said he would love to do it and we asked him to come out to the house for lunch the next day where he could take the photographs. Duncan had agreed, liking him enormously, but stipulating that the whole family should pose — both of us together with Laughlin and his wife Betty. The pictures turned out to be characterful and charming, with fine composition and light and dark patterns.

Family Group by Henri Cartier-Bresson
Marjorie, Betty, Laughlin and Duncan

Piet Mondrian (1872–1944). *Square Composition*, 19¼ x 19¼

Cartier-Bresson insisted on giving us the photographs, explaining that he was terribly fond of the gallery after spending so many hours there over the years enjoying the paintings and the whole place. He said that in his youth he had studied art with André Lhote.

We later had several exhibitions of his photographs, from which we purchased several for the collection, and he gave us some more! —

among them the wonderful portrait in profile of Bonnard in his old age standing in his studio; and a moving scene in Ireland with an old horse grazing.

As I mentioned above, one of the brightest highlights of the period for Duncan was the acquisition in 1955 of the great little Corot, "View of Genzano." He never tired of looking at it and enjoying it with others, pointing out its "breadth of handling, simplification, distinguished color; eye travel through well placed accents." For him "the great Corot was at his best in his early sunny studies of landscape in and around Rome."

Duncan wrote of this picture:

His personal aim was to capture on his canvas his first delight at the sight of a particular place. The spirit of the place called for a particularly felicitous time of day. That required a faithful observation of the light and dark pattern. This famous picture of Genzano, painted in 1843 on his third visit to Italy, shows a broader, more painterly touch than the exquisite little studies of the first visit in 1825 when in crystal clear light he built structures as firm as the architecture he depicted. It still reveals Corot's preoccupation of the early years with a harmony of atmospheric colors and a well ordered composition of selected shapes. Now there is added a sensitive suggestion of tactile values and a maturing mastery of the brush.

I remember how pleased Duncan was when M. Cazoo, a director of the Louvre, said, "This is a painting I would have loved to see in the Louvre."

Along with the many continuing activities of this period — exhibitions, concerts, lectures — the Phillips Collection published a book on Karl Knaths, by Paul Mocsanyi, for which Duncan wrote the introduction. In a passage of his introduction Duncan wrote:

When I first saw the paintings of Karl Knaths over thirty years ago what impressed and charmed me were the integrated qualities of fresh vision and self-reliant invention. Then too I was fascinated by the unusual combination of angular calligraphy with subtle color and sensitive brushwork. I seemed to understand the artist's urgent need for a 20th century economy of means to convey his sense of the simple seafaring life he had found in his Cape Cod environment. The fishermen and their gear, the docks and the shacks, the moors and the dunes, the glimpses of the sea in every light of every season became his intimate experience. And the familiar objects of his house, the lilac at his door, the rooster strutting in

Jean Baptiste Camille Corot (1796–1875). *View of Genzano*, 14½ x 22⅝

his yard, the deer in the pine woods were the lyrical subjects of his brush destined to be his descriptive and decorative symbols of line and plane and color. To find the equivalent for these personal impressions in a pictorial language as painterly and as structural as the years' study and the moment's instinct could discover was already his purpose in such an early masterpiece as "Frightened Deer in Moonlight" with its zigzag of agitated lines and its magic of nocturnal tones. In the electric canvas entitled "Harvest," the turkey, apples and pumpkins were a planned progression of shapes and linear contacts. The logic of abstract design, and the poetry inherent in such structure was to become more and more the passion of Knaths as the years went by. The early works were exciting in their promise, that promise has been magnificently fufilled.

EDWARD HOPPER

One day about 1952 we were at the Whitney Museum's biennial of American Painting. We were pleased that a painting of mine had been invited and we found it hanging next to a canvas by Edward Hopper. Also we encountered the artist standing nearby himself. We all got talking and he turned to me and said, "You know I like your painting don't you?" We were very pleased and thanked him (though we hadn't known). We wandered through the large exhibition with him and in so doing came upon another of his paintings hanging in a room with many more abstract things. His was a group of New York buildings in handsome light and shade against the sky. The remark he made sticks in my mind, and we both felt it exceedingly true. It was to this effect: "Do you know why they keep on inviting — including my work in these increasingly avant-garde abstract shows? It's because in my paintings I take great pains with the underlying design or substructure and therefore in abstract form they are as modern as anything here." His work almost always has a strong interesting pattern of light and dark. The Phillips Collection has three fine examples of Hopper's painting — "Approaching a City," acquired in 1947, is one of his masterpieces.

Throughout this part of his life (the forties and fifties) one of Duncan's main recreations as well as mine was walking with our poodles both in Washington and in the woods and open roads of Ebensburg. They afforded us endless entertainment, affection and worry. They were so human that we were often reminded of the James Thurber story about his own family which did not dare to let their poodle look

Edward Hopper (1882–1967). *Approaching a City*, 27 x 36

in a mirror for fear of the shock it would give her at finding she was not a human being. Our three standard poodles expected to be and were treated as members of the family.

Duncan often spoke of the terrible day when he had two necessary and immediate decisions pending. One was whether to have the great Renoir "Luncheon of the Boating Party" relined and the other was whether to operate on the poodle "C'est Tout," who had swallowed part of a rubber elephant and become critically ill when it swelled up inside of him. What a day! But when the "go aheads" were given, Dr. Curry, a wonderful veterinary surgeon, operated on the dog successfully, and the Sheldon Kecks, outstanding restorers, "operated on" the Renoir successfully!

In 1957 our son Laughlin and Elizabeth Hood were married; she was a very congenial, vivacious girl. We missed them so much that in 1958 we went to Paris to join them when they were on vacation from his Foreign Service assignment in Teheran. We crossed on the *Queen Mary* and landed at Le Havre, May twelfth. En route by rail to Paris we were served the usual four-course, almost gourmet *table d'hôte* lunch. At the Hotel Plaza Athénée all was calm and pleasant, the chestnut trees a joy to behold in their full bloom under our windows. The following morning we went to a Modigliani retrospective exhibition which took up the whole Charpentier Gallery; and in the afternoon we drove together through the lovely Bois de Boulogne and had tea at an attractive restaurant there.

But the very next day France was plunged into turmoil when Charles de Gaulle came into power through a sudden coup. We were fascinated by the newspapers that day with their giant headlines — De Gaulle's "Je vien" — and their smaller print texts of his clear and classic pronouncements. Faced with the threat of a counter coup staged by army extremists, De Gaulle ordered all landing fields covered with barbed wire, and long lines of police lorries filled with uniformed men, civil and federal police, were to be seen for days guarding every important street. There was terrific excitement and even danger in the air.

In this situation it was a great satisfaction and pleasure to Duncan to find that his very good friend Marquis Childs, political columnist of the *Washington Post* and *St. Louis Post Dispatch*, was in Paris. We had many fascinating discussions with Mark and his wife Biddy, of whom we were all so fond, about the prospects for stability in France. Janet Flanner, who writes the Paris letter for the *New Yorker* magazine, joined us for one especially interesting evening of talk and surmise.

Actually the crisis did not prevent us from having many good times driving into the country and visiting Paris's wonderful museums and galleries. One day at the Maeght Gallery, where one of the rooms was given over to several large late Braques of the studio interior series, Duncan was almost knocked flat by one of them. He loved the browns, grays, whites, and blue-green-blacks, with a white bird somewhere in the shallow space. The painting also depicted the bust which Braque often painted, his spectacles, easel, and palette — all with great depth of color and feeling. Duncan felt it was a masterpiece. I never saw him show such sudden dramatic, and sustained enthusiasm for any painting. All of us, including Duncan himself, were somewhat taken aback by his powerful reaction. We had been thinking in terms of the expense of a new wing about to be built for our gallery; and when we found the price of the Braque was $95,000, we simply did not say anything nor did Duncan push it. But to this day I wish we had encouraged its purchase, gone in debt for it, just because Duncan loved it so!

On our return to this country we made a number of trips, as this was a period of Duncan's life for special honors. Yale granted him a second honorary degree: the first in the thirties had been an honorary Master of Arts degree; this time in 1959 it was an honorary Doctor of Humanities.

In the same year Duncan received a citation from the American Federation of Arts, and he and I together received the Award of Merit from the Pennsylvania Museum School of Art. Earlier in the nineteen fifties Duncan had become an honorary fellow of Yale's Berkeley College, received an honorary degree of Doctor of Humanities from Kenyon College, and an honorary Doctor of Laws degree from American University in Washington.

As noted above, Duncan had become increasingly concerned with the need for an extension or annex to the museum, so that more of the permanent collection could be kept hanging while at the same time keeping up our program of loan exhibitions. In choosing an architect he felt that his old friend Frederick Rhinelander King, of the firm of Wyeth and King in New York City, would be the ideal man as he would plan a building that was not too extreme in design to harmonize with the old brick residential gallery. When Freddie King accepted this challenge and submitted several plans, Duncan chose the one that seemed most functional, simplified, and contemporary. The next step was to tear down two houses which we owned on adjacent property and get the grand project underway.

But other important events that took place at this time were more personal — the birth in Washington of our first grandchild, Duncan Vance Phillips, in 1959, followed one year later by our second, Eliza Laughlin Phillips. We were happy that we were able to see them regularly because Laughlin and his wife Betty had settled in a neighboring house on Foxhall Road.

13

FRIENDS AND ASSOCIATES

DUNCAN had an extraordinary capacity for warm and faithful friendship. Even if he did not see a particular friend very often, he would take up exactly where he had left off. If a friend disappointed him in some way he would not hold grudges but see that person whole and soon forget there had been any difficulties or differences. He was not a perfectionist and was sure enough of himself not to be easily hurt, loving to appreciate and talk about the best qualities in those he knew.

To write about Duncan's friends and associates is difficult because in addition to those I can include in this chapter, there were many, many others he especially liked. I name these primarily to show the scope of his friendships. Many extended back to his school days in Washington, to Yale, and to his early days in New York. Duncan's appreciation of these friends remained constant, even though his contacts with them might not be frequent or his viewpoints on art or politics quite different.

Duncan treasured his oldest friendship of all in Washington — the one with Arthur Hellen, who had been a classmate in his first school and who later became a distinguished Washington lawyer. Another friendship that went back to early youth was with Charles Carroll Glover Jr., who was with him at Yale.

A really delightful friendship that started during the tense period of World War II and which Duncan and I both enjoyed was with General and Mrs. Frederick Osborn. They came to Washington from New York when General Marshall appointed him head of Information and Education. Both were interested in art, and Fred Osborn was a trustee of the Frick Collection; his father gave a great Manet — "The Guitar-

Henry Moore (1894–   ). *Family Group*, 17½" high

ist" — to the Metropolitan Museum. Their own pictures range from Frederick Church to Monet.

The warm and enduring friendship between Duncan and Law Watkins began at Yale where they were classmates and fellow members of the board of the "Lit." During Law's fifteen years as associate director for education of the gallery and head of its art school, his enthusiasm, tolerance of many points of view and capacity to encourage touched many students and gallery visitors. One year Law put on an important and interesting educational exhibition entitled "Emotional Design in Painting." This grew into his book *The Language of Design*, which was published by the gallery in 1946. Another high point of Law's career at the gallery was the preparation of an original exhibition, for which Duncan and Law together wrote a catalogue entitled "The Functions of Color in Painting." The exhibition, which included loans from other museums, occupied the entire gallery.

A friendship that went back to Duncan and Jim's early days in New York was that with Elizabeth Hudson. We enjoyed her wit and intense interest in art, and thought of her to some extent as a colleague in that she was a born collector and great appreciator of paintings, drawings, and rare books. In the forties we purchased from her one of the gallery's masterpieces, Van Gogh's "The Road Menders," and another very live and delightful landscape by Van Gogh, "House at Auvers."

Then there were the artists: Duncan always had a special feeling for the true ones. It seemed he was born with a sense of mission to try to help at least a few of them realize their full potential. Any effort to give artists constructive criticism as well as encouragement, is a delicate and subtle matter; for some natures always resent the slightest advice, even though given through sheer appreciation. But Duncan somehow conveyed his friendship as well as his own need for their work. For those few artists to whom he became a sort of patron, I know that his frequent purchases, accompanied by genuinely expressed delight, far outweighed any feeling of being overly influenced.

I have written already of some of the artists whose work Duncan especially loved and with whom he felt especially congenial — for example, Dove, Marin, Bonnard and Knaths. Many others could be added, including Morris Graves, Lee Gatch, Harold Weston, and numerous young painters in Washington and elsewhere. I remember once when I asked Laughlin what came to his mind first when he thought of his father's work, he immediately mentioned the help and encouragement that Duncan gave to young artists he believed in. And of course this was true of older artists, too. The painter Harold Weston said of him, "I am thankful that such a man lived."

Duncan's friendship with Augustus Vincent Tack went back to his early days at the Century Club in New York. Augustus, who was some

Karl Knaths (1891–1971). *Harvest*, 40 x 48

years older than Duncan, was a great favorite in the club with his kindly, outgoing manner. He was a portrait and landscape painter, who had at one time studied with John Twachtman. But during the nineteen twenties, in painting a series of religious subjects (he was an ardent Catholic), he began to experiment with a rough technique, applying the paint in thick, short, mosaic-like strokes, and went on to become a pure abstract painter — one of the very first in this country. Whereas most American abstractionists beginning to work in abstract forms at that time were influenced by the school of Paris, Tack was primarily influenced by great Chinese landscapes.

Duncan applauded Tack's flair for experiment and continued to buy his work throughout his life, particularly enjoying the late abstractions. When Tack and his wife (who was a daughter of the artist George Fuller) would visit us or we would see them in New York, we enjoyed their good-natured story-telling humor and bubbling optimism. One of the collection's largest units is of Tack's work. Aside from this group and those bought by a few other patrons, his abstract work was in comparative obscurity for a period after his death in 1949, but now is beginning to be invited for exhibitions and purchased by other museums.

Duncan thoroughly enjoyed the work of Karl Knaths and the friendship which he developed with the artist. In 1938, after Law Watkins had well established the Phillips Gallery Art School, he and Duncan invited Karl to come to Washington as a guest teacher for about six weeks each season, an arrangement which continued until 1950. Karl taught a strong modern idiom of his own — organic, never merely decorative. Most of the art school students took his course together with many outsiders, and Karl developed an ardent and loyal following.

Everyone associated with the gallery was pleased each year when it came time for Karl to come to Washington from his home at Provincetown, Massachusetts. I can see him now, wearing his artist's beret and navy pullover shirt, which contributed to his rather nautical look. He used to spend the hours between classes sitting in the main hallway looking at the paintings and talking with friends in his warm, direct, and decisive fashion. His mind roved over many subjects — folklore, history, metaphysics, etc. — which he connected directly with his art.

The gallery staff has always been made up of congenial persons (including a number of artists), whose friendship Duncan and I often enjoyed at home as well as in the gallery. All have participated in the museum's development, some having served for over forty years with wholehearted loyalty and enthusiasm. An outstanding example was Elmira Bier, who, as assistant to the director, was in complete charge of a very active and successful program of gallery concerts — planned so as to hear from newly discovered talents as well as musicians who are well known. The standards are high and the large audiences enthusiastic. Both performers and audience enjoy the intriguing combination of music and paintings hanging throughout the concert gallery. Miss Bier said to me once, "I am so glad to have been part of it all!" *

The three men on the staff (as I write there are twenty) who have been with us longest — since the middle thirties — are James Mc-

* Since Miss Bier's death in 1976, the music program has continued under the able direction of Charles Crowder.

Adolphe Monticelli (1824–1886). *Bouquet*, 27¼ x 19½

Thomas Eakins (1844–1916). *Miss Van Buren*, 45 x 32

Laughlin, John Gernand, and Harold Giese.* All are highly versatile; but Jim McLaughlin, it seems, can do anything! On his days off he is artist, architect, or potter. In the gallery, he and John Gernand — also an artist — help conduct the innumerable busloads of people who come daily from clubs, schools, university groups, etc. Many people have spoken of the courteous, kindly, informal atmosphere that these knowledgeable men help provide.

I like Jim McLaughlin's tale of an encounter with Duncan years ago at Dupont Circle, since it brings out Duncan's special feeling for certain flowers. Jim recalls that "Duncan was carrying a bunch of lilacs . . . which he had bought from a flower cart. His delight in the color and odor and the total enjoyment . . . showed in his countenance as he thrust the bouquet into my face to share the experience. Lilacs have had a special meaning to me ever since that day and I think of it every time I experience them. It always reminds me of his magnificent spirit."

Duncan had a series of able assistants looking after the business. Dwight Clark, appointed in 1920 its first treasurer, caught Duncan's spirit for the institution to a remarkable degree, and there was nothing he would not do to help! When he died in the middle thirties, Duncan named Mr. Clark's assistant, Miss Minnie H. Byers, as his successor, to take care of both our own and the gallery's affairs. Miss Byers was a gifted businesswoman and very warm and human besides. The gallery staff as well as the household staff often called on her to help with their own investments and business problems. Although Duncan was acquiring pictures for the collection at a rate which aroused her concern, especially during the depression, she appreciated his vision and enjoyed helping make it a reality. When Miss Byers retired in the early sixties, Duncan chose a bank, the American Security and Trust Company, as treasurer. It was represented very ably and sympathetically by Edward A. Dent.

Duncan enjoyed the stimulation of discussing art with his colleagues, other collectors, critics, and teachers. I have already written about his warm relationship with Charles Seymour and Henri Focillon. Here are some others whose friendship meant a lot to him.

John Walker and Duncan knew each other for many years — in Washington when John was serving first as chief curator (1941) and then as director of the National Gallery (1956–60). But John likes to recall his first dealings with Duncan, when, as a Harvard art student he was assigned to assemble loan exhibitions of contemporary paint-

* Retired in 1978.

ings. He says that Duncan would always lend generously. In Washington we enjoyed the friendships of both John and his wife Margaret. I like the warm way in which John said of Duncan, "Apart from my own family, he and B.B. [Bernard Berenson] were the two people who meant most to me. They were very different but I loved them both dearly."

As I wrote earlier, Duncan always had real affection and admiration for David Finley, the National Gallery's first director, from 1941 to 1956. They recognized character in each other, as well as vision and dedication. David was more indefatigable than Duncan in his ability to see and mix constantly with others — an ability which he still has to an amazing degree.

Perry Rathbone was another of Duncan's favorites in the museum world. After first meeting in Washington during World War II, they saw each other quite often. Perry had held many museum positions, and I know that no one was more pleased than Duncan when he was made director of the Museum of Fine Arts in Boston. Perry admired Duncan's "integrity, his sensitivity and his humanity," and once said, "Duncan taught all of us something about beauty and something about feeling. Few men can do that and all our lives we shall be thankful."

Alfred Barr, director of Collections of the Museum of Modern Art, New York City, was another colleague whom Duncan especially liked and enjoyed. They saw most of each other in the twenties and thirties, when Duncan was an active trustee of that museum. Later Alfred lectured twice at the Phillips Collection, and he and his wife Margot would look us up when they were in Washington. There are two paintings that Alfred and Duncan doted on. In their opinion their respective museums had the two finest Matisses in existence. In New York they both would rhapsodize over the Museum of Modern Art's "The Moroccans," and in Washington the Phillips Collection's "Studio, Quai St. Michel"!

Sir Kenneth Clark, formerly director of the National Gallery, London, and a distinguished art historian, connoisseur and critic, spoke several times in our gallery. Because of his breadth of knowledge, superb delivery, and obvious delight in his subject, each was a great lecture, an evening of a lifetime. The first, in 1946, was "Romantic Painting and Contemporary British Art." A few years later he spoke on Delacroix. Then in 1956 he gave a wonderful talk on Rodin stressing his conviction that the sculptor was being neglected in his importance to art and that a renewal of appreciation was long overdue. On the same visit a week later he gave a strong and poetic lecture on Jean

Graham Sutherland (1903–   ). *Dark Entrance*, 52 x 38½

François Millet, again calling for a revival of interest. We had an exhibition of Millet drawings to synchronize with Sir Kenneth's lecture and Duncan purchased an excellent one, "The Shepherd." At the time of the last two lectures, Sir Kenneth and Lady Jane Clark, both charming and attractive, visited us at our home and we all became great friends. Sir Kenneth later told me that Duncan was one of the few persons whom he revered.

Duncan felt a special friendship and admiration for William C. Milliken, for years director of the Cleveland Museum. They greatly appreciated each other and their respective contributions to art in this country. Other favorite museum colleagues included W. G. Constable, for many years chief curator of the Boston Museum of Fine Arts; Herbert Read; Daniel Catton Rich; and Lloyd Goodrich. Sir Herbert Read was a trustee of the Institute of Contemporary Art here and frequently would come to the gallery with Robert Richman, its director, when he attended meetings in Washington.

Sometimes in New York we saw James and Laura Sweeney with the Frederick Mortimer Clapps (he was director of the Frick) — a wonderful combination of people! A 1957 letter which Duncan wrote to Sweeney, who was at that time director of the Solomon R. Guggenheim Museum, shows Duncan's pride as a collector and museum director. He wanted to postpone James' visit so that his friend could see the collection at its best.

My reasons may amuse you but they are very real to me. We see you so seldom in Washington we would be keenly disappointed to have you lecture and visit at a time when the Collection will seem very sadly diminished by its temporary loss of great pictures out on loan. In the spring I reluctantly yielded to a number of fervent appeals. Consequently the Arts Council got two of our Braques for Edinburgh and the Tate, the Musée de l'Art Moderne in Paris got the "Egyptian Curtain" by Matisse, and the exhibition at Aix–en–Provence got our Cézanne "Self-Portrait." I fear that all these masterpieces would not be back. The Arts Council also had the Marin Memorial show with our best examples. Our best Graves and de Staël are traveling in this country. Our Goya may not be back from Brooklyn and our early Corots will be at Rosenberg's. Never before have I allowed so many of our children to be away from home for so long!

Duncan also developed devoted friendships outside of the art world, especially among persons connected with journalism and public affairs.

He loved good conversations with such people about the major issues of national and international policy.

We knew the Walter Lippmanns almost from the time they first came to live in Washington in the late thirties. Duncan relished Walter's independent thinking and the literary quality of his writing, and we were always fascinated to hear at first hand something of the Lippmanns' annual trips abroad. I remember Duncan's pleasure when one year they told of their audience with Pope John XXIII, whom Duncan tremendously admired. Walter said in a modest but quite thrilled way that the Pope had said to him, "You are a man of truth." Duncan often said of Walter, "He is a great, great man, and Helen is wonderful too." As the years went on, Duncan enjoyed them more than any other Washington friends. He would go to their home even when he was quite frail during his last year or two, and they frequently visited us.

Duncan's interest in world affairs was practically equal to his interest in art. I remember Walter saying to me later, "I always wished I could get Duncan to talk more on art." I answered, "It was because he was so eager to get you to talk on your own subject, for clarification and your diagnosis of national and world events."

The Marquis Childs were also among Duncan's favorite friends in the Washington press corps. He found them brilliant, real, and very good company.

Other friends he particularly valued outside of the art world were Senator and Mrs. William Fulbright, for whom he had a great admiration and warmth of feeling; Francis Biddle, attorney general in the days of the New Deal, and his wife Katherine, a delightful person as well as a fine poet; and Mrs. Edmund Purves, sister of the poet Theodore Spenser.

To give a balanced picture of Duncan's nature and his friendships you would have to speak of what a good "family man" he was, and the tremendous support and encouragement he gave to me and to Laughlin. He took an affectionate interest in my mother and my brothers and sisters; and they in turn greatly appreciated him. No fan letters he received for his work in the gallery or his writing pleased him more than the very intelligent appreciation of my sisters and brothers — Eleanor, Alice, Mary Elizabeth, Ernest and William.

Duncan's only nephew, whom he also counted a very good friend, is Gifford Phillips, son of his brother Jim. Although his father died when he was a baby and he moved to Denver when his mother remarried,

Gifford has had the same dominant interests of his father and his uncle — art and politics. He has often visited the family in Washington from the time he was a thoughtful, redhaired child up to the present. He and his attractive wife Joann, who now live in Los Angeles, have built up an important collection of contemporary painting and sculpture, as well as pre-Columbian art. Duncan enjoyed his visits and their talks together, and Gifford always wanted to spend considerable time with Duncan seeing the collection, the latest additions, etc. Giff once said that he thought his uncle's most outstanding trait was the ability to *project* his enthusiasm and thoughts, so that they fired others too. Gifford is a trustee of the Phillips Collection; he is also a member of the board of trustees of the Museum of Modern Art, the Los Angeles County Museum, and the American Federation of Arts.

Another particularly congenial relative of Duncan's was his cousin, James Laughlin, founder of the New Directions publishing house. Although Jay was considerably younger, they always enjoyed each other's company and respected what the other was doing. Each was discovering and working with new talents, as well as established genius — one in literature, the other in painting. In the *New Directions Annual* of 1949 Jay published an article by Duncan on Arthur Dove, with many good illustrations in color and black and white.

No matter how briefly one sees certain people, they become special friends. This was the case with Marianne Moore, whom we met when

The poodles C'est Tout and Ami

she read her poetry at Washington's Institute of Contemporary Art. When she came to lunch with us she brought little paper packages of crumbs to feed squirrels wherever they might be. I remember her as a rather small, slight woman, graying, and quite well along in years, with the liveliest face one could think of! Later we took her to see the collection, and that was a rare treat for all. She enjoyed it as a whole — the color in the rugs or curtains, paintings, whatever happened to appeal to her. As I mentioned elsewhere, when Duncan showed her a picture I painted, "Night Baseball," she looked at it for so long and with such outspoken pleasure that I told her we would send her the color print of the painting. Duncan meanwhile had said he would send her one of the last half dozen copies of his book on Giorgione. She wrote these delightful letters on receiving them.

> 280 Cumberland St.
> Brooklyn 5, New York
> November 1, 1959

It is *here*, dear Mr. and Mrs. Phillips —
The *Leadership of Giorgione* — safe in its notable wrappings, Even the string — the twine — seems precious; and before exploring the pages, I put on a stout, envelopping cover. I did not know I could be so happy — excited — entranced. And to think you would devote to me, one of the few retrieved copies of this luminous book —

Reading every word just as it comes, I admire the paragraphs by your friend H. G. Dwight; but great verbal particularity sets apart — and newly — every thought *you* set down, Mr. Phillips. What could page 30 not teach one? Go to school? One is in despair. One cannot teach *feeling*.

"If we know the young poet-painter who both conceived and executed the autograph *Tempesta* we can hardly fail to find the same man grown older in the pattern of other works and to see traces of the same hand grown bolder in parts, at least, of pictures not completely his."

"at least, of pictures not completely his." That is the way to write if I know anything about it.

Then the glow of the pictures, the maidenhair — fernlike treetops, so tiny yet definite. The resolute mouth and eyes; — and rare poses of feet, and of fingers. I can't gaze enough at the fingers of Titian's central young man — The Concert. The widely separated out, little finger of the left hand makes me think of the standing-apart little finger of the right hand of *Castita* (attributed to Giorgione in my small Italian Rizzoli 1955 Giorgione. page 106), — [pages which had to be numbered by *me!* I never knew attributions so concealed in "Amsterdam": p. 73 and Lanz Collection, on p. 52!]

Well, you do not include her and her unicorn, dear Mr. Phillips, and I now cast doubt upon her.

The binding — the individuality and simplicity! and *Style* (style).

I don't know how I can let you give me so much. Your letter, Mrs. Phillips! making me see my tentative dragon in an entirely different light. And you are *going to give me* a print of *Baseball at Night* in color. Will it not bring to mind your emerald velvet and emerald butterfly! It will.

I don't know how not to be too long in my composite excitement. Excitements, there is no end to it. The paintings! The nasturtium color absolutely identical with the color in the garden — the pallor, the fragility of the poppies mesmerized to stay in place; and the vases themselves! (You will have to stop if I don't!)

What you have done for me can never end, — or my affection.

Marianne Moore

I say not a word about the inscription in the Giorgione. I really don't know how!

260 Cumberland Street
Brooklyn 5, New York
November 10, 1959

Dear Mrs. Phillips and Mr. Phillips,

Am I dreaming? Is it really *true;* every time I stand in the doorway of my room I am looking right at the diamond — your diamond in two senses! Another world, dear friends! Two unbe*liev*able worlds. The world of Giorgione, and the ball-diamond; the runner breathless to get to home plate; the man in the dugout standing on one hip. The umpire so vigilant. The packing is almost as wonderful as the picture — the most wonderful scientific art of protection, the solid pine ends to drive the long screws into without a possibility of splitting the pine. And the printing of the label, a work of art in itself.

I thought you were giving me a *print* — in itself, much. It could not have occurred to me that you were giving me the framed scene — real as life, to hang where it faces me every day of the week. The tones in the color are perfection; and the characterizations. And what a masterpiece of a frame, mouse gray with a subdued variation in the flutes that enhances without the possibility of intruding on "the game".

I have renounced luxury and many unique exhilarations. I think you have counteracted this unwholesome phase of unwise common sense — Backsets and *renouncings* are what should be forsworn! Can I ever say what romance and hope you have brought into my life!

With a most restorative excitement and livened interest in life,

Marianne
Moore

Baseball at Night!

Entrance hall of the new wing, at the time of the special Giacometti exhibition, 1963

14

THE NEW WING, EARLY
1960's

IN many ways this was an incredibly full and rewarding period (of a half dozen years) for Duncan and his collection. He was not as strong physically; but, at his best, his mind and spirit and appreciations remained as vigorous and ardent as ever.

To begin with, the new wing of the museum (rechristened "The Phillips Collection") was completed and opened to the public in the fall of 1960. This building meant a great deal to Duncan and we spent many hours there, not only working, but browsing, enjoying, and studying its treasures. One could enter from the street level, with good elevator service for the three floors. Freddie King, the architect, accomplished what Duncan had wanted. The extension was dignified, intimate, and functional. Its beautiful, tawny travertine marble, with a slight rose tinge, solved the problem of blending with the old red-brick, residential-type building. And its general effect was one of contemporary simplicity.

Over the front door of the new wing Georges Braque permitted us to use a sculptured representation of one of his bird designs. Working from one of Duncan's favorite Braque engravings, Pierre Bourdelle (the son of the sculptor Antoine Bourdelle), created a bas-relief in brown granite of a bird in flight. It adds a piquant yet distinguished element to the building.

About the time it was installed, the French poet St.-John Perse, who knew Braque well, told us about his recent visit to Braque's studio. Noting that all of Braque's canvases had birds in them — some quite stunning and elegant, others looking like dodo birds — St.-John Perse said "Braque, your birds do not fly, they swim." Braque looked delighted and remarked, "I am glad of that. I want them to be at home in any element!"

Since Duncan had planned the hanging of every painting or "unit" in the new wing before it was completed, I was able to choose wall colors, furnishings, carpets and draperies which would harmonize with the paintings in each room. The tall windows throughout the building allow for a perfect combination of daylight and artificial lighting.

The new wing was opened to the public in November 1960 without a grand opening or great publicity, and thus received little newspaper coverage. However, I remember our pleasure when one critic, Florence Berryman of the *Washington Star*, described it as the event of the year and told her readers to run, not walk, to visit the outstanding new addition to Washington's cultural life.

During the first month or two we invited small groups of friends to visit the new gallery with us and see the collection installed to better advantage. One such group included Senator and Mrs. Mike Monroney, Mr. and Mrs. Walter Lippmann, William Walton, Senator and Mrs. William Fulbright, and Henry O. Brandon, Washington editor of the London *Sunday Times*.

While still showing paintings of top quality in the old building,

The new wing becomes part of the old museum

Renoir Room

Gallery with wall of Courbets: *The Mediterranean; Rocks at Mouthiers; Winter Landscape in Jura*

Gustave Courbet (1819–1877). *Winter Landscape in Jura*, 19¾ x 24

Duncan moved many of the greatest ones to the second floor of the new wing. The Renoir "Boating Party" has a room of its own except for a poetic Monet, "On the Cliffs, Dieppe," and a sanguine study by Renoir, "The Judgment of Paris." Most of the Bonnards and several Cézannes and Van Goghs hang together in a lovely daylight gallery with orange curtains, and the third gallery on that floor has a superb wall of three Courbets, the latest of these a snow scene, "Winter Landscape in Jura." When we went through the museum the following year with André Malraux, he and Duncan exclaimed almost simultaneously that it reminded them of Cézanne's stunning "Black Clock."

Malraux and Duncan also agreed that they found increasing enjoyment in sketchy, unfinished painting which kept the artists' first fervor and still left something to one's imagination; and that Cézanne's plaint, "I cannot finish" was probably an indication of his inherent knowledge of when to stop.

Duncan placed several other works of this type in the Courbet room, all painted with breadth and simplification: the great Constable "On the River Stour," Daumier's "The Uprising," and Cézanne's "Self-Portrait." There is also a late Goya, "The Repentant Peter," which is right at home with the Cézanne head and is, in its own way, as live and as modern.

The third floor, originally planned as a large storeroom, became a superb gallery — primarily devoted to contemporaries such as Adolph Gottlieb, Philip Guston, Morris Louis, Kenneth Noland, and Sam Francis, but also available for loan exhibitions.

Duncan hung the collection's Braque unit in the first downstairs gallery, which one enters from the street — a wonderful place to meet visitors or simply to linger and talk. Beyond it is another large gallery, with paintings by Matisse, de Staël, de la Fresnaye, Miró, Pollock, and Picasso. And off to one side is a small but poetic and distinguished Mark Rothko room.

Claude Monet (1840–1926). *On the Cliffs, Dieppe*, 25 x 36. Duncan found the one Monet he most wanted in 1959 and it gave him endless pleasure.

Mark Rothko   Morris Louis   Sam Francis

David Smith's bronze sculptures (loan exhibition)

A gallery in the new wing. Four Bonnards, Degas' *After the Bath*, and Cézanne's *Mont Sainte Victoire* to the right

Corner of the gallery with the Braque Unit

Of the five Rothkos now in the collection, Duncan installed four in this room — large canvases which hang particularly well together. He derived untold pleasure from this room, which came to be for him and for many other people a little chapel for meditation. Mark Rothko always stopped in to see it when he came to visit his brother in Washington. He later said that the Phillips Collection was his favorite of all museums.

I remember when Duncan and I visited Rothko's large loft studio in the Bowery section of New York to choose canvases for an exhibition, Duncan asked him, "Am I right that in your approach to your work, *color* means *more* to you than any other element?" Rothko answered, "No, not color but *measures*." We felt him to have a deeply emotional and intellectual approach, with a strong interest in the metaphysical. In describing our wonderful "Green and Tangerine on Red," Rothko said that the striking tangerine tone of the lower section of the canvas could symbolize the normal, happier side of living; and in proportion the dark, blue-green, rectangular measure above it could stand for the black clouds or worries that always hang over us. His proportions have symbolic meaning. Duncan loved to speak of Rothko's "fields of color painted vigorously in mysterious layers of paint that suggest depth in spite of their flat matte quality; they seem to come forward and envelop you at times." We both regarded Mark Rothko as one of the greatest contemporary American artists. Duncan wrote of his work:

In the two soft-edged and rounded rectangles of Mark Rothko's matured style there is an enveloping magic which conveys to receptive observers a sense of being in the midst of greatness. It is the color of course. These canvases which have been called empty by the resistant skeptics and which certainly depict nothing at all are nevertheless a vibrant life-enhancing experience to those who make themselves ready for them. They cast a spell, lyric or tragic, which fills our existence while the moments linger. They not only pervade our consciousness but inspire contemplation. Our minds are challenged by the relativities; the relative measures of the two horizontal presences, one larger than the other, each acting on the other, and incomplete without the other, each mysteriously compounded of scumbled overtones yet mat, saturated, rich layer soaked into richer depths. Rothko denies a desire to enchant, he only invites reflection. The weather his colors create can be ominous. Frequently it is vaguely troubled. There is never a conflict, not even a dissonance, rather a duality, some evanescent difference, some sudden awareness of the complexity of existence. Color-atmosphere in painting is as old as Giovanni Bellini and his mountain background be-

Mark Rothko (1903–1970). *Green and Maroon*, 90¾ x 54½

Joan Miró (1893–   ). *Red Sun*, 36 x 28

fore sunrise or after sunset. We think also of late Turner and of Bonnard. But in Rothko there is no pictorial reference at all to remembered experience. What we recall are not memories but old emotions disturbed or resolved — some sense of well being suddenly shadowed by a cloud — yellow ochres strangely suffused with a drift of gray prevailing over an ambience of rose or the fire diminishing into a glow of embers, or the light when the night descends.

Duncan welcomed with much pleasure the many letters about the museum and its "annex." I quote one written by David E. Finley (director until 1956 of the National Gallery):

Dear Duncan:

I have wanted for some time to write you and tell you how delighted I am with the new wing which you have added to your Gallery.

It was a difficult problem, which you and your architect — and Marjorie have solved with great success. The wing seems to be part of your house with its carpets and sofas and chairs and at the same time provides an ideal space in which to show your paintings, whether they be El Grecos or Renoirs or Rothkos. And I understand it is fire proof which must give you great comfort.

I have said before but I would like to say again, what a marvelous collection of paintings you have made. It is a great contribution to the art resources of Washington and the country and must give you and Marjorie great pleasure as it does to all of us. . . . Will hope to come for a visit with you soon.

In connection with an exhibition of his paintings which was hung in the old building and held in 1962 Mark Tobey wrote:

I was very delighted that my work was shown in your very attractive Museum which I visited several years ago; also in the painting you have chosen. . . . I grow very tired of the growth of the hard-edge museums which thank God yours is not.

Other especially interesting exhibitions that year were Joseph Albers' paintings and the sculpture of David Smith, a superb show which occupied the whole first floor of the new wing. These shows inaugurated our policy of alternating fine loan exhibitions between the two buildings.

Hundreds of warm and encouraging letters of appreciation came in steadily over the years from gallery visitors. This one, from a complete stranger, expresses a thought which we were also to hear from various artists; for instance, Seymour Lipton and Mark Rothko.

May 25th, 1962

Dear Mr. Phillips:

. . .

Your conception of an art gallery is a most civilized one, it makes it possible for people to see — and enjoy — the works you have selected in a way that makes the viewer feel that this art was made for man; that man comes first, whereas most galleries convey the feeling that man is there at the sufferance of the management and is being permitted to behold something greater than man.

The chamber music, with its variety and its imaginative programming, has likewise been a joy to us. We look forward to next winter and frequent visits to the Phillips Collection.

Sincerely yours,
Burton T. Wilson

With the added space of the new wing we at last had the opportunity to borrow more sculpture for exhibition. At this period as associate director for loan exhibitions I would write the letters arranging for and sometimes initiating shows which lasted about a month or six weeks; Duncan and I would consult on them, plan the installations together and he would make the end decisions as to what to purchase if anything from each show. Sculpture at first was shown indoors; until a few years later when the outdoor court was ready. In 1963 the most important was a large exhibition of Giacometti's sculpture and paintings shown

Duncan and I enjoying the
Giacometti show

Alberto Giacometti (1901–1966). *Monumental Head*, 37″ high

Giacometti's sculpture (temporary loan exhibition)

on the whole first floor of the new building, 1612 21st Street, and also in two rooms of 1600. From it Duncan purchased the "Monumental Head" in bronze. He wrote in our catalogue of Giacometti (born 1901, Italian Swiss):

Starting from archaeological references of his indebtedness to Africa and Egypt he soon emerged and found his own originality across the labyrinth of twentieth century "isms" — Cubism, Sur-realism, Existentialism and lately an Expressionism of astonishing three dimensional power. Out of all this creative exploration there emerges one constant——one single "artistic personality" — Berenson's sine qua non. It is to be found in his every period. It is the image of a human being, miniature or massive, the image of a lonely estranged presence beyond specific description. There was the linear phase of the famous, fragile wooden Construction in the Museum of Modern Art in *The Palace at Four* A.M. and the similar phase of the little men walking their separate ways in some city square. There are the portraits, and even the paintings are more drawn than painted, which are more like ghostly hallucinations than like old memories. There are the delicate figurines and the startling tall effigies of fantastic attenuation. And finally we are confronted by the rugged Heads, somehow universal, with their perhaps unintentional, certainly monumental tributes to the average man.

About this time Charles Seymour, professor and head of the history of art department at Yale, gave a lecture at our gallery that was one in a generation — so full of depth and insight in bringing the artists Van Gogh and Cézanne utterly alive. Charles, the son of Duncan's Yale classmate and former president, was a dear friend. It seemed that age made no difference in their congenial talk, admiration of each other, and attitudes about art. Charles has lectured several times at the Phillips Collection. His latest lecture, in May 1964, was "Landscapes of Provence by Cézanne and Van Gogh," following a tour he and Charlotte his wife (an equally good friend) had made through Provence, the part of France both artists immortalized. It was a splendid lecture with, to us, a moving introduction, which follows:

LANDSCAPES OF PROVENCE BY CÉZANNE AND VAN GOGH

Introduction

My feelings about the Phillips family and the Phillips Collection run very deep. It seems as if there has never been a time in my life when I did not know, or know of, Duncan Phillips who was a college classmate of my father's and a life-long friend and associate of my uncle, Law Watkins, whose spirit is everywhere still in this place. I learned how to look at painting at the Phillips Memorial Gallery when I was still in school. While I was privileged to live in Washington as a member of the staff of the National Gallery of Art, among our closest friends and dear neighbors were Duncan and Marjorie Phillips.

This has been a wonderful experience. And if I seem to be speaking very personally, it is the only way I can speak in the atmosphere of intimacy and hospitality which has been created here. And yet I feel as if I were also speaking not for myself alone but a countless multitude of grateful persons whose eyes have been opened and whose inner lives as individuals have been permanently affected by Duncan and Marjorie Phillips' vision — a vision which has taken enduring form in the works of art and associated activities of the Phillips Collection.

In his book *The Artist Sees Differently* Duncan Phillips has written his credo as a critic, historian, and collector in words of nobility and generosity:

> The true artist needs a friend and the true patron of art has nothing better to give the world than the helping hand he extends to any lofty life made perilous because a free spirit cannot or will not see eye to eye with the crowd. . . . My own special function is to find the independent artist and to stand sponsor for him against the herd mind whether it tyrannizes outside or inside his own profession.

The independent artist has here in truth been sought out and helped not only in the present but in the past, or better, in the time of art which has no boundary between present and past. Among the great forerunners of the present in art there are few painters who are not represented, and in superb examples, in the Phillips Collection. In particular Duncan and Marjorie Phillips very early recognized the towering stature of Van Gogh and Cézanne — free spirits indeed, who could not or would not "see eye to eye with the crowd." They very early saw that these two painters in transforming the vision of the natural world had in fact enhanced the world's appreciation of Nature, that they had in more than theory provided over again examples of the age-old contrast between the classic and the romantic, and that through them preeminently have flowed the currents of tradition which have helped to give form to the exciting innovating forces of the art of our times.

Duncan and Marjorie Phillips have also helped us to understand that landscape in art is not just a genre to be taken up or dropped according to the whims or dictates of esthetic theory. Landscape is symbolic. It is symbolic of the faith that men and women may hold of the continuing potential of goodness of the world we live in and live with.

Seymour Lipton (1903–   ). *Ancestor*, monel metal, 87″ high

And so I have thought that the landscapes painted by Cézanne and Van Gogh in the warm sunlight of Provence, where the modern world mingles with the living memories of the worlds of Greece and Rome, where art in its deepest continuities seems to provide the surest touchstone of values of the topic of this lecture as a tribute to Duncan and Marjorie Phillips, in some suggestion, insofar as words may express it, of a feeling of appreciation for them first of all, for what they have done, for what they are doing, and for what they stand for.

Duncan was not well at the time of the lecture and could not attend; so at his request Charles sent it to him and he was much moved by it. Charles wanted Duncan to know how he felt about him and his great contribution at that period, and not write it years later, perhaps in a memorial essay.

Other brilliant lectures that year were by Professor Albert Elsen of Stanford University on Seymour Lipton's sculpture, and one by the artist himself. When Duncan and the sculptor Seymour Lipton first met it seemed they were drawn to and understood each other immediately. We were planning a large exhibition of Lipton's work for the gallery in 1964, and when we were in New York went to his studio deep in the basement of his house where he created his abstract sculpture; welding it with fiery torch from sharp strips of metal, some still covering the floor; he worked in monel metal, steel, or bronze as the case might be. Duncan felt the depth of overtones beyond his unexpected and fascinating abstract shapes. He spotted one, a large piece, the artist had not yet shown us in a dark mysterious corner and asked to see it better. It was called "Ancestor" and proved to be the one Duncan was most drawn to and which was to join the collection! Later Duncan wrote of Lipton's work for the catalogue:

Seymour Lipton is one of the great innovators of modern art, a pioneer and a great master of direct-metal sculpture. What constitutes his originality in this period of stylization as a self-sufficient end, is that he combines abstract form with intellectual conception in metaphors which reveal the importance of fusion, of integration itself. His inventive craftsmanship is one with his imagination. His new ideographic idioms convey to viewers of his works, those at least who are willing to think as well as to see, images of nature and of man which are not concerned with illusion but with suggestion. If, as he thinks, 20th century revolution in design has made abstraction irreversible, yet as a dedicated philosopher, he is not dismayed in his urgent will to deal with man's condition. Without figures, with his cuttings of steel and his weldings and bronzing of metals, never ceasing

Jacques Lipchitz (1891–1973). *Harlequin with Mandolin*, bronze bas-relief, 50 x 41

to be abstract, he is essentially a humanist and, at times, even as impressionist as Rodin — but in a conceptual and technical sense of course, which is the opposite of optical and incidental. The impressionism of Lipton is a quality of the volumes in light corresponding to a flash of thought.

His symbols of inner force in concave depths move grandly from dark to light and back again in expressive contours and convolutions. . . .

The Phillips Collection is proud to present an abstract sculptor who stresses meaning in all he has to say.

Seymour Lipton said later that he felt that "what made Duncan's collecting so special, so satisfying was that there was always something in his choices beyond just form and bared formal qualities, perhaps the word would be 'mystic.' " "Although I only met Duncan a few times I responded to him in perhaps a strange way — as my spiritual father. He had a toughness that deeply supported his rich sensibilities. He was a genuinely free spirit and uncompromising. Altogether I loved and respected him."

Later that year, 1964, Duncan purchased a superb Jacques Lipchitz cubist period bas-relief from an exciting exhibition we had of the early period of his work. As for painters, there was the exhibition of Robert Motherwell's collages (and we have two from that show — 1965). He and his wife came down from New York at the time and we found them both delightful. Alfred Manessier's work was a challenge to Duncan as to myself in hanging. Some of them were so large (the same was true of Riopelle's work). He purchased in 1964 a small rare Manessier oil entitled "Du Fond des Ténèbres."

Each spring successive directors of Harvard's Fogg Art Museum, carrying on the tradition established by Paul Sachs in the nineteen thirties, brought a group of their museum students to meet Duncan and see the Phillips Collection. His interest in these responsive students never waned and he continued to escort them as late as 1965. That year John Coolidge, the director, wrote this delightful note in appreciation:

May 3rd, 1965

I returned to Cambridge to be laid low by a singularly persistent bug, so please forgive me not writing you more promptly.

All of us greatly appreciated your kindness in talking to us when we were in Washington. It must be a tremendous satisfaction to both of you to see how passionately interested young Americans are in the art whose discovery you pioneered. It would embarrass you to hear the mixture of rapture and admiration with

Karl Knaths (1891–1971). *The Blue Heron at the Tide Wash*, 24 x 30

which they refer to you and your achievement. But what could be more important than the chance to meet individuals who actually did create an institution that is basic to their professional world (and, indeed, to mine). For young people who are going on into museum work, the knowledge of what two people can accomplish in one devoted professional lifetime, through meeting those two people, is an incomparably important experience. I am afraid the afternoon took a great deal out of you both. I can only assure you that you gave far more, and that what you gave was of far greater importance than you can possibly realize. I can struggle to express

Milton Avery (1893–1965). *Girl Writing*, 48 x 32

my own appreciation of your kindness; I cannot possibly convey their gratitude. . . .

John Coolidge

During his last two years Duncan held temporary exhibitions of several old favorites. In 1965 we went to Rosenberg's in New York so that he could choose personally a Karl Knaths show and see Karl again in a happy enjoyable meeting. He purchased from that exhibition a little painting he thought fascinating, "The Blue Heron at the Tide Wash."

After Karl's exhibition he had a retrospective, in the new wing, of my paintings which had just come back from the Edward Root Art Center at Hamilton College in upstate New York. Also we showed there a Milton Avery retrospective of his late work, from which Duncan pur-

Milton Avery (1893–1965). *Black Sea*, 50 x 58

Georges Braque (1882–1963). *Bird*, 18 x 19½

chased the distinguished "Black Sea." I got up an exhibition called
Birds in Contemporary Art, and from that he purchased the gay, play-
ful, masterful Calder, the "Only Only Bird," and Braque's small distinguished painting "Bird," which was the original for the poster for
the great Braque retrospective at the Louvre.

How the circle comes around! Ever since Duncan's discovery of
Arthur Dove's work he had some from the permanent collection on

view as well as circulated retrospective shows; but now the last show he planned was putting up the collection's whole Dove unit of approximately thirty paintings. On May 7, 1966 we met a student there by appointment who was writing a thesis on early Arthur Dove, and with whom he reminisced enthusiastically about what Arthur Dove and his painting had meant to him. We stayed but a few minutes as Duncan felt symptoms of fatigue and high blood pressure more marked than usual.

Two days later he died quietly, painlessly of heart failure just as he was getting to bed. His doctor was here at the time and of course I was at his side. Just the day before he had read his Sunday papers through as well as a book of art criticism. He never was bedridden at all but savoured life to the last.

Naturally Duncan had thought a great deal during his later years about the future of the Phillips Collection, the museum which embodies a lifetime of his work and love. In early 1965 he wrote a statement of his wishes for its future, expressing his deep-lying, tremendous hope that the museum would not change too much from his original

Birds in Contemporary Art (loan exhibition)

conception of it — as a *home* for the arts, installed in a house where people feel close to the paintings and sculpture. Here are the main points of his statement:

To my wife who is to be my successor as Director, to all future Directors, to my son and nephew and all future Trustees and to the Treasurer of The Phillips Collection

A STATEMENT OF MY WISH FOR
THE FUTURE OF THE PHILLIPS COLLECTION

I wish that The Phillips Collection which I founded as an educational institution in 1918 — having in recent years attained to its essential character as a home for a wide diversity of paintings with a unity in all the diversity — and as an intimate personal creation, this creative conception having been achieved it must in the future be maintained and not altered.

Since the new wing has been built and connected with the older residential building — the impression is now right. The setting and the spirit are right. These are fundamental for the future no matter how many lesser changes are later required. Such a creation can no more be changed than any fine work of art can be transformed into something different.

This does not mean that The Collection should be closed. It must be kept vital as it always has been, as a place for enlightenment, for enjoyment, for rediscovery, by frequent rearrangements of the collection and for the enrichments of new acquisitions. There should be two or three important purchases each year of a character and up to the standard of the works now hanging on the second floor of the new wing and the 19th century room of the older building at 1600 21st Street.

The Exhibition Units of favorite painters — such as Marin, Dove, Knaths, Klee, Rothko, should be a continuing characteristic. One of them should appropriately be devoted to Marjorie Phillips exhibited, as now, in one room or another.

Again — as is our present practice — there should be seasons of loan exhibitions to stimulate sustained public interest and attendance, these to be supplemented with selections from our own store rooms. The seasons of chamber music concerts must be carried on. They have been in complete accord with my policy for the paintings, adding the contemporary to the classic, and the regional to what has proved to be universal and for all time.

It is my wish that my partner in forming The Collection, Marjorie Phillips, who is now Associate Director in charge of the Loan Exhibitions — and who has been active director when I have been inactive — shall on my death or voluntary retirement become Director and that she will select a Chief Curator who might become Director in her place when she retires. It should be his function to administer the staff of the Gallery and keep the interest alive in all the Gallery's activities.

We have a staff of devoted, loyal and experienced museum assistants and custodians, both secretarial and curatorial, who have been with The Collection for many years and who will be needed during the transitional period. My assistant in charge of the music should be consulted when it is necessary to appoint her successor.

It has always been the policy of The Collection to stress the continuities of art, the evolution of tradition by experience and the necessity to test the innovations of the present hour by reference to the sources in the past which have stood the test of time and which remind us of Focillon's "the families of artists, for example, the builders, the mystics, the realists, the mannerists, and the decorators." This Collection which my wife and I have made together, respects all these creative varieties and welcomes new directions. We have believed in a separate standard for the best of each kind. We are skeptical about extremist fads, such as so called "pop art" and optical art. In our recent acquisitions since the first catalogue we have been exhilarated by the painterly freshness and the spontaneous invention and freedom from enclosures of the so called abstract expressionists. We have new favorites, de Staël and Rothko to cite but two, who do not conform to any school, old or new, but who are inspired artists in their own right.

The founder's son will have the title of President and his functions will be to preserve the unique character of The Collection and to fill vacancies on the always small Board of Trustees with that purpose in mind. He will make known his wish as to his successor in consultation with his mother even after she has retired as Director.

Duncan Phillips

Our grandchildren, Eliza and Duncan, enjoying the Gallery. (*Photos by René Missel*)

Henry Moore (1894–   ). Loan exhibition in new sculpture court

Alexander Calder (1898–1976). Loan exhibition in new sculpture court

15

THE COLLECTION TODAY

W<small>E</small> have tried to carry out Duncan's wishes and been privileged to do so. I wish he could have seen recent exhibitions in the sculpture court, such as Alicia Penalba, Alexander Calder's stabiles, and Henry Moore, as well as mixed groups including Barbara Hepworth, David Smith, and Pomodoro. There was an important exhibition of

Alicia Penalba (1918–   ). *Annonciatrice*, bronze, 16½" high

Ben Nicholson (1894–1982). *Zennor Quoit II*, 46 x 102¾ (*Gift of Marjorie and Laughlin Phillips in memory of Duncan Phillips, 1967*)

David Hare (1908–   ). *Mountain Night*, 53½ x 69½

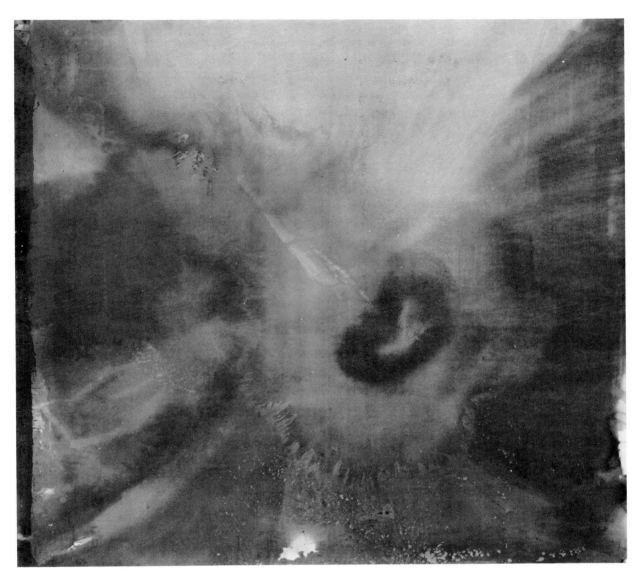

Sam Gilliam (1933–   ). *Petals*, 87¾ x 93

Contemporary Italian Art from the Mattioli Collection, Milan (circulated by the International Exhibitions Foundation). As memorials to him I purchased a Penalba from our show of her work; and Laughlin and I together a Ben Nicholson masterpiece when we were in London in 1967.

Among other acquisitions since 1966, which as director I have

Clyfford Still (1904–1980). *1950B*, 83½ x 67⅜

chosen, are Sam Gilliam's "Petals" (1967) and Jack Youngerman's "Ultramarine Diamond" (1968), both purchased out of one-man shows at the museum. We have also acquired paintings by Howard Mehring ("Interval," 1968); Clyfford Still ("1950B") and David Hare ("Mountain Night") in 1969; and a Picasso, "Head of a Woman," (bronze) in 1972.

The year 1971, which marks the fiftieth anniversary of the Phillips Collection's opening as a public museum, is being celebrated with a fine loan exhibition of paintings by Paul Cézanne. The collection which is now on its own will always be alive with Duncan's spirit.

The Phillips Collection
Principal Acquisitions, 1916-1972

THE following list of most of the principal paintings in the Phillips Collection shows the approximate order in which they were acquired. I have also included groups of paintings which Duncan purchased over the years to encourage talented younger artists.

To quote Hilton Kramer, art critic of the *New York Times*, "For nearly a half century Mr. Phillips collected art — all styles, all periods, all forms. He bought from the struggling as well as the famous, the avant-garde and the traditional. And his aim, always, was the same: To develop a collection that would creatively express his own joy in art."

1915	Decamps, Alexandre	Interior of a Turkish Café
	Maris, Matthijs	A Corner of the Hague
	Maris, Matthijs and Monticelli, Adolphe	The Queen's Entry

1916	Davies, Arthur B.	Visions of Glory
	Lawson, Ernest	Twilight in Spain (*part of a unit of paintings purchased 1914–1939*)
		Under the Bridge (*traded later*)
	Monticelli, Adolphe	As You Like It
	Myers, Jerome	Band Concert Night (*acquired 1910*)
		Little Mother
	Spencer, Robert	End of the Day
	Weir, J. Alden	Pan and the Wolf
	Wilson, Richard	Classic Landscape (*deaccessioned*)

1917	Davies, Arthur B.	Eve's Garden *(traded later)*
	Hassam, Childe	Bailey's Beach *(traded later)*
	Inness, George	Gray Day, Goochland, Virginia
		A Windstorm *(deaccessioned)*
	Lawson, Ernest	Spring Morning, Washington Bridge
		Warmth in Winter *(traded later)*
	Tack, Augustus Vincent	Allegro Giocoso *(part of a large unit of paintings purchased 1914–1948)*
	Weir, J. Alden	Visiting Neighbors

1918   *(Founding of the Phillips Memorial Gallery)*

	Chardin, Jean Baptiste Simeon	Bowl of Plums
	Homer, Winslow	Rowing Home
	Kent, Rockwell	Burial of a Young Man
		The Road Roller
	Lawson, Ernest	Early Morning *(traded later)*
	Luks, George	Blue Devils on Fifth Avenue
		Verdun, France (watercolor)

1919	Davies, Arthur B.	Springtime of Delight
	Lawson, Ernest	May in the Mountains
		New England Birches
	Monet, Claude	The Road to Vétheuil
	Myers, Jerome	Night, Seward Park
	Ryder, Albert Pinkham	A Barnyard *(traded later)*
	Sloan, John	Old Clown Making Up
	Spencer, Robert	Barracks *(traded later)*
	Twachtman, John	Summer

1920   *(Gallery incorporated in the District of Columbia; many paintings were transferred to it which had been acquired earlier)*

	André, Albert	House in the Olive Trees
	Beal, Gifford	The Garden Party
	Daumier, Honoré	The Three Lawyers
	Davies, Arthur B.	Along the Erie Canal
		Children, Dogs and Pony
	Fantin-Latour, Henri	Dawn
		Dusk
		Manet in His Studio
		seven lithographs
	Henri, Robert	Little Dutch Girl
	Inness, George	Lake Albano
		Moonlight, Tarpon Springs *(purchased 1911, but transferred to Collection 1920)*

318

	LaFarge, John	Fijian Chiefs (*purchased 1914, but transferred to Collection 1920*)
	Lawson, Ernest	Spring Night, Harlem River
	Luks, George	The Dominican
		Otis Skinner as Colonel Bridau in *The Honor of the Family*
		Sulking Boy
	Magnasco, Alessandro	A Shipwreck
	Ménard, René	Le Pointe Fauconnier
	Myers, Jerome	Field of Joy (*deaccessioned*)
		Market Arch, Paris
	Picknell, W. L.	Cottage by the Sea
	Prendergast, Maurice	Afternoon, Pincian Hill
		Fantasy
	Puvis de Chavannes, Pierre	The Wine Press
	Robinson, Theodore	Giverny
		Two in a Boat
	Ryder, Albert Pinkham	Macbeth and the Witches (*small version, traded later*)
	Spencer, Robert	The Evangelist
	Tack, Augustus Vincent	Chinoiserie (*deaccessioned*)
	Twachtman, John	My Autumn Studio
		Winter
	Whistler, James McNeill	Miss Lillian Woakes
1921	Beal, Gifford	On the Lawn (*deaccessioned*)
	Boudin, Eugène	On the Beach at Trouville (*deaccessioned*)
	Hassam, Childe	Washington Arch in Spring
	Lawson, Ernest	Harlem Valley, Winter
	Monticelli, Adolphe	Woodland Worship
	Prendergast, Maurice	Picnic Party
		Under the Trees
	Tack, Augustus Vincent	Court of Romance
	Twachtman, John	The Emerald Pool
	Young, Mahonri	The Blacksmith (bronze)
1922	Beal, Gifford	The Terrace (*formerly* The Promenade)
	Corot, Jean Baptiste Camille	Portrait of a Woman
	Daumier, Honoré	On a Bridge at Night
		Le Ventre Legislatif (lithograph)
	Delacroix, Eugène	Paganini
	du Bois, Guy Pène	The Arrivals
	El Greco (Domenikos Theotokopoulos)	The Repentant Peter
	Guys, Constantin	Vanity Fair (pen and wash drawing)
	Homer, Winslow	On the Cliff (watercolor, *traded later*)

	Lachaise, Gaston	Peacocks (bronze)
		Sea Lion (bronze)
	Lawson, Ernest	After Rain
		City Suburbs
	Manet, Édouard	Boy with Fruit (watercolor)
	Monticelli, Adolphe	Fête Champêtre
	Myers, Jerome	Evening on the Pier
		Waiting for the Concert
	Prendergast, Maurice	Near Nahant, Massachusetts
		Ponte della Paglia
	Puvis de Chavannes, Pierre	Sacred Grove (watercolor)
		Seated Figure (pencil drawing)
	Sloan, John	Six O'Clock
		The Wake of the Ferry, II
1923	André, Albert	The Concert
		Renoir in His Studio at Cagnes
	Beal, Gifford	Hauling the Net
	Boudin, Eugène	Beach at Trouville
	Chase, William Merritt	Hide and Seek (1888)
	Davies, Arthur B.	Dewdrops
		The Hesitation of Orestes
		Tissue Parnassian
	Dickinson, Preston	Along the River (pastel)
		Winter Landscape, Harlem River
	Guys, Constantin	Une Elégante (watercolor and pencil drawing)
	Luks, George	Coal Town (watercolor)
	Meryon, Charles	The Morgue (etching)
		Notre Dame (etching)
	Miller, Kenneth Hayes	Apparition
	Puvis de Chavannes, Pierre	Marseilles, Port of the Orient
		Massilia, Greek Colony
	Renoir, Pierre Auguste	The Luncheon of the Boating Party (Le Déjeuner des Canotiers)
	Sisley, Alfred	Snow at Louveciennes (1874)
1924	Bellows, George	Emma in Black
	Courbet, Gustave	The Mediterranean
	Daumier, Honoré	Don Quixote *(traded later)*
	Davies, Arthur B.	The Flood
	Hunt, Diederich	The Spanish Rider (bronze)
	Kent, Rockwell	North Wind
	Myers, Jerome	Old Woman in Doorway
	Renoir, Pierre Auguste	La Dame au Parasol *(deaccessioned)*
	Sloan, John	Fifth Avenue Critics *(one of nine etchings)*
	Tack, Augustus Vincent	Mystical Crucifixion
		Passacaglia
		Voice of Many Waters

1925	Beal, Gifford	Circus Tent
	Beal, Reynolds	Beach Ponies
		Inner Harbor, Rockport *(deaccessioned)*
	Bonnard, Pierre	Woman with Dog
	Bourdelle, Antoine	Virgin of Alsace (marble sculpture)
	Cézanne, Paul	Mont Sainte-Victoire
	Constable, John	On the River Stour
	Corot, Jean Baptiste Camille	Dairy Farm *(deaccessioned)*
	Courbet, Gustave	Rocks at Mouthiers
	Daumier, Honoré	Two Sculptors
		The Uprising (L'Émeute)
	Demuth, Charles	Monument, Bermuda (watercolor)
		Red Chimneys (watercolor)
	Dickinson, Preston	Decanter and Bottle
	Gauguin, Paul	Idyll of Tahiti *(traded later)*
	Karfiol, Bernard	In Our Shack
	Kent, Rockwell	Azapardo River
	Kuhn, Walt	Tulip Buds
	Miller, Kenneth Hayes	Consulting the Cards
	Morisot, Berthe	Two Girls
	Prendergast, Maurice	Inner Harbor, Salem *(traded later)*
	Redon, Odilon	Mystery
	Zorach, William	New York Harbor (watercolor)
		Sailing by Moonlight (watercolor)
1926	Beal, Gifford	Little Circus Ring
	Bonnard, Pierre	Early Spring
	Burchfield, Charles	Cabin in Noon Sunlight
	Dickinson, Preston	Street in Quebec
	Dove, Arthur G.	Golden Storm (metallic paint on wood panel)
		Waterfall
	Hirsch, Stefan	Lower Manhattan
	Homer, Winslow	To the Rescue
	Hopper, Edward	St. Francis Towers, Santa Fe (watercolor)
		Sunday Afternoon
	Knaths, Karl	Geranium in Night Window
	Marin, John	Black River Valley *(first three of a unit)*
		Grey Sea
		Maine Islands
	Miller, Kenneth Hayes	Portrait of Albert Pinkham Ryder
	O'Keeffe, Georgia	My Shanty, Lake George
		Pattern of Leaves
	Prendergast, Maurice	Blue Sea (watercolor)
	Roussel, Ker-Xavier	Faun and Nymph under a Tree

	Sheeler, Charles	Offices
	Speicher, Eugene	Girl's Head
	Sterne, Maurice	Afternoon at Anticoli
		The Reapers
		Still Life
	Weber, Max	Draped Head
1927	artist unknown	Egyptian limestone head from Tel-el-Amarna, Eighteenth Dynasty
	Bonnard, Pierre	Children with Cat
		Grape Harvest
		Interior with Boy
		The Lesson
		Woods in Summer
	Braque, Georges	Plums, Pears, Nuts and Knife
	Derain, André	A Brunette (Tête Brune)
		Landscape of Southern France
	Dickinson, Preston	Old Quarter, Quebec
	Eakins, Thomas	Miss Van Buren
	Elshemius, Louis	Samoa (*first of a unit of twenty-one paintings*)
	Fuller, George	Ideal Head
	Graham, John	Iron Horse
	Knaths, Karl	Studio Table
	Maillol, Aristide	Head of a Woman (bronze)
	Marin, John	Franconia
	Matisse, Henri	Anemones and Mirror (*traded later*)
	Picasso, Pablo	The Blue Room (1901)
	Spencer, Niles	Dormer Window
	Toulouse-Lautrec, Henri de	Miss May Belfort (lithograph, signed in pencil)
1928	Beal, Reynolds	In the Rips off Montauk (etching)
	Bonnard, Pierre	The Palm
		The Riviera
	Braque, Georges	Lemons, Peaches and Compotier
	Carpeaux, Jean Baptiste	Street Scene
	Cézanne, Paul	Self-Portrait
	Daumier, Honoré	The Strong Man
	Davies, Arthur B.	Horses of Attica
	Derain, André	Mano, the Dancer
	Despiau, Charles	Head of Mme. Derain (original plaster)
	Dove, Arthur G.	Huntington Harbor I (collage)
	du Bois, Guy Pène	Soldier and Peasant
	Faggi, Alfeo	Head of Noguchi (bronze)
	Fautrier, Jean	Flowers of Disaster

	Graham, John	Flowers in a Pink Vase
		Harlequin and Heavy Horses
	Manet, Édouard	Ballet Espagnol
	Mangravite, Peppino	Exiles
	Marin, John	Mt. Chocorua
1929	Braque, Georges	Pitcher, Pipe and Pear
	Chirico, Giorgio de	Horses
	Knaths, Karl	Cock and Glove
	Krogh, Per	The Blacksmith
	Kuhn, Walt	Girl and Mirror
		Performer Resting
	Mangravite, Peppino	Ecstatic Colt
	Marin, John	Ship Fantasy
	Picasso, Pablo	Abstraction, Biarritz (1918)
	Vuillard, Édouard	The Newspaper
1930	Bonnard, Pierre	The Open Window
	Braque, Georges	Still Life with Grapes
	Burchfield, Charles	Ohio River Shanty (watercolor)
		Road and Sky (watercolor)
	Dove, Arthur G.	Coal Car
		Snow Thaw
	Dufy, Raoul	Polo
	Gogh, Vincent van	Entrance to the Public Gardens at Arles
	Graham, John	Road by a River (*one of a group of paintings acquired in the thirties*)
	Gris, Juan	Abstraction (1915)
	Guys, Constantin	The Team (sepia wash drawing)
	Hartley, Marsden	After Snow (1908)
		Mountain Lake, Autumn (*two of a unit of eight*)
	Jacob, Max	Christ Stilling the Tempest (watercolor)
	Kantor, Morris	Night, Union Square
	Klee, Paul	Tree Nursery (1929)
	Knaths, Karl	Clam Diggers
		Interior
		Red Table
		Up Along
	Marin, John	Fishing Smacks
	O'Keeffe, Georgia	Ranchos Church
	Picasso, Pablo	Studio Corner (watercolor)
	Rousseau, Henri	Notre Dame
		Pink Candle
	Sickert, Walter	Makings of an Omelette
	Tamayo, Rufino	Mandolins and Pineapples
	Vuillard, Édouard	Across the Fields (lithograph)
		Tuileries Gardens (lithograph)

1931	Beal, Gifford	The Quarryman *(one of a unit of fifteen oils)*
	Berman, Eugène	Daybreak *(one of several works purchased between 1931 and 1933)*
	Bonnard, Pierre	Movement of the Street
	Braque, Georges	Lemons and Napkin Ring
	Burchfield, Charles	Barn (watercolor)
	Davis, Stuart	Corner Café *(first of a unit of five paintings)*
	Delacroix, Eugène	Le Roy René (drawing)
	Dove, Arthur G.	Sand Barge
	Flannery, Vaughn	Ten Broeck
	Kantor, Morris	House by the Sea
	Knaths, Karl	Peaches in a Basket *(deaccessioned)*
	Marcoussis, Louis	Abstraction, Brown and Black
	Marin, John	Street Crossing, New York
	Rouault, Georges	Tragic Landscape
1932	Berman, Eugène	Souvenir of Ischia
	Elshemius, Louis	Madge in the Morning
		The Rejected Suitor
		Verandah in Spring
1933	Berman, Eugène	Courtyard
		Park at St. Cloud
	Burchfield, Charles	Moonlight over the Arbor (watercolor)
		Woman in Doorway (tempera, *part of a unit of nine paintings*)
	Dove, Arthur G.	Red Barge, Reflections
		Sun Drawing Water
	Elshemius, Louis	Bridge for Fishing
		Cabs for Hire
	Rouault, Georges	Circus Trio
1934	Braque, Georges	The Round Table (Le Guéridon)
	Dove, Arthur G.	Life Goes On (Tree Trunks)
1935	Bonnard, Pierre	The Terrace
	Dove, Arthur G.	Electric Peach Orchard
		Morning Sun
		Red Sun
	Gates, Robert F.	Sheridan Circle
	Knaths, Karl	Harvest
	Poe, Elizabeth	Loneliness Unbroken
	Sickert, Walter	Queen Victoria and Melbourne

1936	Beal, Gifford	Scene from *Parnell*
	Biddle, George	Winter Landscape
	Dove, Arthur G.	Cows in Pasture
		Tree Forms II (wax emulsion on canvas)
	Friedman, Arnold	The Brown Derby
	Goya, Francisco	The Repentant Peter
	Knaths, Karl	Bar Room
	Kuhn, Walt	Show Girl with Plumes
	Maril, Herman	Modern Gleaners (*one of a group of paintings purchased 1934–1954*)
	Marin, John	Harbor Scene (ink wash drawing)
	Rosenfeld, Edward	Cabin Interior (*and others*)
1937	Bluemner, Oscar	Oranges (gouache)
		Warehouses (gouache)
	Bonnard, Pierre	Ants, Canaries, Cows under a Tree, Grasshoppers (four ink brush drawings for *Histoires Naturelles* by Jules Renard)
		Narrow Street
	Cross, Bernice	Pansies (*first of a large group*)
	Daumier, Honoré	For the Defense (ink wash drawing)
	Derain, André	Head of a Young Woman
	Dove, Arthur G.	Goin' Fishin' (montage)
		Reminiscence
	Dufy, Raoul	Versailles
	Elshemius, Louis	Approaching Storm
		Balcony
	Grosz, George	Street in Harlem
	Guys, Constantin	Jeune Fille Espagnole (watercolor)
	Knaths, Karl	Frightened Deer in Moonlight
	Marin, John	Fifth Avenue at Forty-second Street
		Quoddy Head
	Picasso, Pablo	Bull Fight (oil, 1934)
1938	Dove, Arthur G.	Flour Mill II
		Shore Front (wax emulsion on canvas)
	Friedman, Arnold	Baseball
	Gernand, John	Memory of Night, St. Thomas (*one of a group of paintings purchased 1936–1956*)
	Klee, Paul	Botanical Laboratory
		Efflorescence
		Garden Still Life
		Land of Lemons (1929)
	Kokoschka, Oskar	View of Prague from the River
	Kollwitz, Käthe	Self-Portrait (lithograph, *one of several, Dwight Clark bequest*)

	Maril, Herman	Farm Woman
	Marin, John	Sketch *(deaccessioned)*
	Picasso, Pablo	The Jester (bronze, 1905)
1939	Burliuk, David	Evening
		On the Road
		Rainbow
	Cézanne, Paul	Still Life with Pomegranate and Pears *(gift of Gifford Phillips)*
	Daumier, Honoré	Le Dimanche au Jardin des Plantes (lithograph, *one of a large group*)
	Davis, Stuart	Boats
		Eggbeater #1
	Dove, Arthur G.	Rise of the Full Moon
	Dufy, Raoul	Château and Horses
		Epsom Downs (watercolor)
		The Opera, Paris (watercolor and gouache on paper)
	Hartley, Marsden	Gardener's Gloves and Shears
		Off to the Banks
		Sea View, New England
	Hicks, Edward	The Peaceable Kingdom (1846)
	Klee, Paul	Arrival of the Circus
	Knaths, Karl	Moonlight, Harbor Town
	Kopman, Benjamin	Tragedies of War *(and other lithographs)*
	La Fresnaye, Roger de	Emblems (Mappemonde)
	Peto, John F.	Old Reminiscences
	Pittman, Hobson	Nine P.M.
	Poe, Elizabeth	Agate Heights
	Rouault, Georges	Afterglow, Galilee
		Bouquet I
		Bouquet II (two decorative panels)
		Cirque de L'Étoile Filante (book)
		Still Waters (Yellow Christ)
	Seurat, Georges	First Study for *La Parade* (drawing)
	Utrillo, Maurice	Place St. Pierre *(deaccessioned)*
	Vuillard, Édouard	Nurse with Child in Sailor Suit
		Woman Sweeping
1940	artist unknown	A twelfth-century limestone head from St. Gilles du Gard, Provence
	Beal, Gifford	Circus Ponies
	Cézanne, Paul	Fields at Bellevue (1892–1895)
	Degas, Edgar	Women Combing Their Hair
	Delacroix, Eugène	Hercules and Alcestis (1862)
	Dufy, Raoul	Hotel Subes
		Joinville

	Gropper, William	The Pretzel Vendor *(traded later)*
		Refugees
	Guardi, Francisco	Piazza San Marco (drawing)
	Klee, Paul	The Way to the Citadel (1937)
	Kuniyoshi, Yasuo	Maine Family
	Marin, John	The Sea, Cape Split
	Matisse, Henri	Studio, Quai St. Michel (1916)
	Maurer, Alfred	The Florentines
		Still Life with Doily
	McLaughlin, James	The Barn *(first of a group of paintings purchased 1940–1969)*
	Renoir, Pierre Auguste	The Judgment of Paris (sanguine)
		Mother and Child (bronze)
	Rouault, Georges	Christ and the High Priest
		Self-Portrait (lithograph)
	Ryder, Albert Pinkham	Macbeth and the Witches
	Seurat, Georges	The Stone Breaker
	Soutine, Chaim	The Return from School after the Storm
	Utrillo, Maurice	Abbey Church of St. Denis
	Watteau, Jean Antoine	Musicians (small sanguine drawing)
1941	Beal, Gifford	Impression from *Life with Father*
	Bishop, Isabel	Lunch Counter
	Braque, Georges	Lemons and Oysters
	Degas, Edgar	Reflection (La Mélancolie)
	Dove, Arthur G.	Gold, Green and Brown (oil and wax emulsion on canvas)
		Pozzuoli Red
	Elshemius, Louis	Street in Lugano
	Feininger, Lyonel	Spook I
	Gatch, Lee	Marching Highlanders *(part of a unit purchased 1941–1956)*
	Goya, Francisco	Evil Counsel (china ink and wash drawing on white paper)
	Klee, Paul	Arab Song
	Kokoschka, Oskar	Courmayeur
		Portrait of Mme. Franzos
	Myers, Jerome	East 22nd Street, New York (drawing)
		Street Singer (drawing)
	O'Keeffe, Georgia	The White Place in Shadow
	Picasso, Pablo	L'Abreuvoir (etching, 1905)
		La Coiffure (lithograph, 1923)
		Les Saltimbanques (etching, 1905)
	Sickert, Walter	Porte St. Denis, Paris
		Portrait of Fred Winter

1942	Avery, Milton	Harbor at Night
	Chagall, Marc	The Dream (gouache and pastel)
	Corot, Jean Baptiste Camille	View from the Farnese Gardens, Rome (1826)
	Davies, Arthur B.	Viola Obligato *(gift of Mrs. Wendell T. Bush)*
	Dove, Arthur G.	1941 (wax emulsion on canvas)
	Graham, John	Blue Abstraction
	Graves, Morris	Chalice
		Eagle
		Surf and Bird
	Hartl, Leon	Dairy Farm (panel)
	Hartley, Marsden	Wood Lot, Maine Woods (oil on panel)
	Karfiol, Bernard	Seated Nude (drawing)
		Wrestlers
	Klee, Paul	The Cathedral (1924)
		Figure of the Oriental Theater
	Knaths, Karl	Orarian
	Lawrence, Jacob	Thirty panels from the *Migration of the Negro* series (masonite panels)
	Marin, John	Bryant Square
		Four-Master Off the Cape
	McLaughlin, James	Glass, Fish and Plate
	Watkins, Franklin	Autumn Recollections
1943	Avery, Milton	Apples, Grapes, Gladioli
		Girl Writing
		Pine Cones
		Shells and Fishermen
		Still Life
	Crawford, Ralston	Boat and Grain Elevators No. 2
	Dove, Arthur G.	Indian One
		Rain or Snow
	Feininger, Lyonel	Village (1927)
		Waterfront (watercolor)
	Gatch, Lee	City at Night
	Gogh, Vincent van	Moulin de la Galette (pencil drawing with ink accents)
	Graves, Morris	In the Night (gouache on rice paper)
		Sanderlings (gouache on rice paper)
		Scoters and Surf *(traded later)*
		Tree Frog (drawing)
	Grosz, George	The Survivor (ink drawing)
	Hartley, Marsden	Off to the Banks at Night
		Wild Roses (oil on masonite, 1942)

	Kainen, Jacob	Hot Dog Stand
	Kuhn, Walt	Fright Wig
	Magnasco, Alessandro	Singing Birds
	Masson, André	Will-o'-the-Wisp
	Myers, Jerome	Tambourine
	O'Keeffe, Georgia	Large Dark Red Leaves on White
	Pippin, Horace	Domino Players
	Rattner, Abraham	The Sun
	Shinn, Everett	Tenements at Hester Street
	Soutine, Chaim	Windy Day, Auxerre
		Woman in Profile
	Tack, Augustus Vincent	The Crowd (Barabbas)
		Night Clouds and Stardust *(given to The Metropolitan Museum of Art, 1964)*
	Toulouse-Lautrec, Henri de	La Loge, *Faust* (lithograph, unsigned, rare proof)
	Weber, Max	After an Ice Storm
1944	Baker, Sarah	Circus Clowns *(one of a group of paintings purchased 1939–1977)*
	Bradley, Mary	Late Summer *(one of a group of paintings purchased 1939–1952)*
	Calfee, William	Digression *(one of a group of four paintings)*
	Cross, Bernice	Hallelujah
	Degas, Edgar	Dancers at the Practice Bar
	Dove, Arthur G.	Primitive Music (tempera on canvas)
		Rose and Locust Stump (wax emulsion on canvas)
	Despiau, Charles	Seated Nude (red conté drawing)
	Dufy, Raoul	The Artist's Studio
	Gates, Margaret	Suburban Morning *(one of a group of paintings purchased 1934–1954)*
	Géricault, Theodore	Two Horses
	Jones, Lois	Place du Tertre, Montmartre
	Kainen, Jacob	Sleep
	Kandinsky, Wassily	Succession
	Kokoschka, Oskar	Lac d'Annecy
	Kuhn, Walt	Bread and Knife
	Laughlin, Clarence	Fourteen photographs, 1944–1956
	McCarter, Henry	Hudson River Mists
	Morris, George L. K.	Heraldic Abstraction
	Rattner, Abraham	Window at Montauk Point
	Tomlin, Bradley Walker	The Goblet
	Watkins, Franklin	Angel Turning a Page in the Book

1945	Bellows, George	Irish Town (lithograph)
		My Family No. 2 (lithograph)
		Murder of Edith Cavell (lithograph)
	Delacroix, Eugène	Horses Coming Out of the Sea
	Dove, Arthur G.	Woodpecker (wax emulsion on canvas)
	Elshemius, Louis	New York Rooftops (*part of a unit purchased 1927–1946*)
		Yuma, Arizona
	Fragonard, Jean Honoré	Two wash drawings for Ariosto's *Orlando Furioso*
	Gatch, Lee	Can-Can
		Fire in the Harbor
	Graves, Morris	Wounded Gull (gouache on rice paper)
	Gris, Juan	Bowl and Package of Cigarettes (*deaccessioned*)
	Kandinsky, Wassily	Autumn
	Knaths, Karl	Cin-Zin (*part of a unit purchased 1926–1965*)
		Cylinders
	Kuniyoshi, Yasuo	Thinking Ahead
	Lurcat, Jean	Le Belvedere
	O'Keeffe, Georgia	Red Hills and the Sun, Lake George (1927)
	Phillips, Duncan	V-Day (1945–1947)
	Prendergast, Maurice	Snow in April
1946	Burchfield, Charles	Sultry Afternoon
	Cézanne, Paul	Seated Woman in Blue (1902–1906)
	Corot, Jean Baptiste Camille	Civita Castellana (oil on paper, mounted on canvas)
	Davis, Stuart	Mandolin and Saw
	Elshemius, Louis	Evening by the Sea
	Gatch, Lee	Cartwheel Inn
	Homer, Winslow	Girl with Pitchfork
	Marin, John	Tunk Mountains, Autumn, Maine
	Mondrian, Piet	Square Composition (1922–1925)
	Moore, Henry	Figures in a Setting (watercolor, ink and crayon, 1942)
	Pippin, Horace	Barracks
	Shahn, Ben	Evening
	Soutine, Chaim	Gorge du Loup (*deaccessioned*)
	Sterne, Maurice	Benares
1947	Bonnard, Pierre	Circus Rider (1894)
	Dove, Arthur G.	Lake Afternoon (wax emulsion on canvas)

	Hopper, Edward	Approaching a City
	Knaths, Karl	Mexican Platter *(gift to the Whitney Museum of American Art, 1958)*
	Moore, Henry	Family Group (bronze, 1946)
	Munch, Edvard	Self-Portrait (lithograph, 1895)
		Woman by the Sea (woodblock, 1896)
	Ozenfant, Amédée	The Grotto
	Phillips, Laughlin	Flare
	Piper, John	Russell Monuments at Strensham
	Rouault, Georges	Verlaine
	Sutherland, Graham	Vine Pergola
	Tobey, Mark	Marriage (tempera on masonite panel)
1948	Braque, Georges	The Wash Stand
	Flannery, Vaughn	The Governor's Cup
	Gabo, Naum	Linear Construction, Variation
	Ingres, Jean Auguste Dominique	The Bather (La Petite Baigneuse)
	Kainen, Jacob	The Old Canal
	Klee, Paul	Picture Album
		Young Moe
	Knaths, Karl	Deer in Sunset (1946)
		Kit and Kin
		The Moors
	Picasso, Pablo	Bull Fight (lithograph, 1946)
	Piper, John	Bolsover Castle (gouache)
		Church (oil)
		Llyn Bochlwyd (gouache)
		Thunderstorm (oil)
	Rosa, Salvator	St. Francis in Ecstasy
	Toulouse-Lautrec, Henri de	Aristide Bruant (lithograph, signed in pencil)
1949	Ben-Zion	Abstract Rooster
	Degas, Edgar	After the Bath (pastel)
	Gatch, Lee	Industrial Night *(part of a unit of paintings)*
		Three Candidates for Election
	Gogh, Vincent van	The Road Menders (Les Paveurs)
	Knaths, Karl	Green Squash
	Kokoschka, Oskar	Cardinal Elia dalla Costa
		Lyon
	Maurer, Leonard	Hunter
	Modigliani, Amedeo	Elena Pavlowski
	Pereira, I. Rice	Transversion
	Shahn, Ben	Still Music
	Solman, Joseph	The Broom
		The Room

	Stamos, Theodoros	Moon Chalice (oil on masonite)
		The Sacrifice of Chronos (oil on masonite)
	Stieglitz, Alfred	Equivalents *(set of nineteen photographs, gift of Georgia O'Keeffe)*
	Villon, Jacques	The Grain Must Not Die (Le Grain Ne Meurt)
1950	Burchfield, Charles	Three Days Rain (watercolor)
	Cross, Bernice	Stone Angel
	Graves, Morris	Young Pine Forest in Bloom
	Gris, Juan	Still Life with Newspaper
	Knaths, Karl	Connecticut Clock
		Lilacs
	Maril, Herman	Construction
	Matisse, Henri	Interior with Egyptian Curtain
	Nicholson, Ben	Composition in Relief *(traded later)*
	Picasso, Pablo	Head of a Young Girl (lithograph)
	Piper, John	Stone Gate, Portland
	Shahn, Ben	Skaters (drawing)
		Whispering Politicians (drawing)
	Staël, Nicolas de	North
	Stamos, Theodoros	Fountain
		The Mosses (gouache)
1951	Bonnard, Pierre	Landscape with Mountain
	Calder, Alexander	Red Flock (mobile)
	Gauguin, Paul	Still Life with Ham (Le Jambon)
	Gromaire, Marcel	The Edge of the Forest
	MacIver, Loren	New York
		The Window Shade
	Miró, Joan	Red Sun
	Munch, Edvard	Ibsen in the Grand Café (lithograph)
	Nicholson, Ben	Still Life, Winter (oil and pencil on masonite panel)
		Tendrine, Cornwall II
	Noland, Kenneth	Inside
	Pereira, I. Rice	Vertical Flow
	Schneider, Gerard	Opus 445, 1950
	Soulages, Pierre	July 10, 1950
	Soutine, Chaim	Dead Pheasant
	Vaughan, Keith	Apple Tree and Farmhouse (gouache)
		Man and Child Walking (gouache)
		Yorkshire Farmhouse
	Villon, Jacques	The Little Machine Shop (1946)

1952	Avery, Milton	Trees
	Bonnard, Pierre	Nude in an Interior
	Congdon, William	Palaces, Venice
	Daumier, Honoré	The Family (wash drawing, 1855)
	De Kooning, Willem	Ashville (1949)
	Gates, Robert F.	Fish
	Gogh, Vincent van	House at Auvers (1890)
	Gottlieb, Adolph	The Seer
	Knaths, Karl	Boats
		Duck Decoy
	Lanskoy, André	Bonne Aventure
	Levine, Jack	Under the El
	Noland, Kenneth	In the Garden
	Phillips, Marjorie	Edge of the Village
		Nasturtiums
		Night Baseball (and others)
	Picasso, Pablo	Still Life with Portrait (1905, owned by Marjorie Phillips)
	Staël, Nicolas de	Fugue
		Nocturne
1953	Bissière, Roger	Yellow and Blue
	Braque, Georges	Music (1914, bequest of Miss Katherine S. Dreier)
		The Philodendron
		The Shower
	Duchamp-Villon, Raymond	Gallic Cock (plaster relief, bequest of Miss Katherine S. Dreier)
	Graves, Morris	August Still Life
	Kandinsky, Wassily	Composition-Storm (1913, bequest of Miss Katherine S. Dreier)
	Knaths, Karl	Green Vista
		Pine Timber
	Léonid (Berman)	Berneval
	Marc, Franz	Deer in the Forest I (bequest of Miss Katherine S. Dreier)
	Marin, John	Spring No. 1, 1953
	McLaughlin, James	Green Pears
		Pennsylvania Landscape (and others)
	Meryon, Charles	Le Stryge (etching)
	Mondrian, Piet	Painting No. 9 (1939–1942, bequest of Miss Katherine S. Dreier)
	Pevsner, Antoine	Plastic Relief Construction (bequest of Miss Katherine S. Dreier)
	Schwitters, Kurt	Merz Collage-Tell (1920, bequest of Miss Katherine S. Dreier)
		Radiating World (1920, bequest of Miss Katherine S. Dreier)

	Staël, Nicolas de	Composition (1948) Musicians Parc de Sceaux
1954	Ben-Zion Gatch, Lee Graves, Morris Morandi, Giorgio Mullican, Lee Picasso, Pablo Solman, Joseph Vuillard, Édouard	Path in the Wheat Field Flyway Young Gander Ready for Flight Still Life (1953) Pendulum Factor Faun and Sleeping Woman (aquatint on paper, 1936) Studio Interior Interior (1892)
1955	Bacon, Francis Cézanne, Paul Congdon, William Corot, Jean Baptiste Camille Okada, Kenzo Tomlin, Bradley Walker	Study of a Figure in a Landscape Jardin des Lauves Venice No. 2 (1954) View of Genzano No. 2, 1954 No. 8, 1952
1956	Avery, Milton Gatch, Lee Gernand, John Giese, Harold Knaths, Karl Lanskoy, André Maurer, Alfred Millet, Jean Francois Nicholson, Ben Okada, Kenzo	Morning Landscape Bird in Hand Night Fishing Coffee Pot, Plums and Pears (and other paintings) Winter Tree (and other paintings) Overhauling the Trawl Poids Spirituels Still Life with Artichoke and Bread The Shepherd (drawing) Talisman Footsteps
1957	Mondrian, Piet Morandi, Giorgio Rothko, Mark Schwitters, Kurt Tomlin, Bradley Walker	Self-Portrait Still Life (1950) Green and Maroon Mauve Intersection (deaccessioned) Milwaukee (collage, 1937) Kurt Schwitters Will Recite (collage) No. 9, 1952
1958	Diebenkorn, Richard Francis, Sam Guston, Philip Knaths, Karl	Interior with View of the Ocean Blue (1958) Native's Return Johnny Appleseed

	Mitchell, Joan	August, Rue Daguerre
	Nicholson, Ben	St. Ives, Version II (oil and pencil on masonite panel)
	Pollock, Jackson	Collage and Oil (1950)
1959	Ferren, John	Summer (*deaccessioned*)
	Monet, Claude	On the Cliffs, Dieppe
	Poliakoff, Serge	Sky and Mountains
	Soyer, Moses	Old Man
	Staël, Nicolas de	Collage in Color
	Vieira da Silva, Maria Elena	Stones
1960	Cross, Bernice	Sunset (*and others*)
	Noland, Kenneth	April (1960)
	Rothko, Mark	Green and Tangerine on Red
		Orange and Red on Red
1961	Diebenkorn, Richard	Girl with Plant
	Monticelli, Adolphe	Bouquet
	Vieira da Silva, Maria Elena	Easels (Les Chevalets)
1962	Albers, Josef	Temprano (Homage to the Square)
	Giacometti, Alberto	Monumental Head (bronze)
	Tobey, Mark	After the Imprint
1963	Gottlieb, Adolph	Equinox
	Louis, Morris	No. 182
	Mathieu, Georges	Simon, Comte de Crépy
1964	Cartier-Bresson, Henri	Unit of five photographs
	Knaths, Karl	Shacks
	Manessier, Alfred	Du Fond des Ténèbres
	Rothko, Mark	Ochre and Red on Red
	Staël, Nicolas de	Birds in Flight (ink drawing)
1965	Avery, Milton	Black Sea
	Knaths, Karl	The Blue Heron at the Tide Wash
		Sculling Boat
	Lipchitz, Jacques	Harlequin with Mandolin (bronze relief)
	Motherwell, Robert	In White and Yellow Ochre
	Solman, Joseph	Portrait of Will Sallar
1966	Braque, Georges	Bird (Oiseau)
	Calder, Alexander	Only Only Bird (tin and wire sculpture)
	MacIver, Loren	Spring (Printemps)
	Tworkov, Jack	Highland

(The works listed below were acquired after Mrs. Phillips became Director.)

1966	Penalba, Alicia	Annonciatrice (bronze)
		Small Dialogue (bronze)
1967	Daumier, Honoré	The Artist at His Easel *(gift of Marjorie Phillips in memory of Duncan Phillips)*
	Gilliam, Sam	Petals
	Nicholson, Ben	Zennor Quoit II *(gift of Marjorie and Laughlin Phillips in memory of Duncan Phillips)*
1968	Mehring, Howard	Interval
	Youngerman, Jack	Ultramarine Diamond
1969	Gray, Cleve	Winter
	Hare, David	Mountain Night
	Still, Clyfford	1950B
1972	Picasso, Pablo	Head of a Woman (bronze, 1950)

INDEX